His £5.50

Dcr 19/23

Ronald Williams was born in Rawalpindi, P
Rossall School in Lancashire, and a Hist
College Cambridge, he won a Trevelyan Sc
Marquis of Montrose in 1960. Between 196
of the Diplomatic Service and served in Jakart
Nairobi. His first book, *Montrose: Cavalier in Mourning*, was published in
1975. In 1980 he joined the forestry sector and is currently Executive
Director of the Forestry Industry Council of Great Britain – an occupa-
tion which allows him to travel extensively in Scotland and pursue his
interest in its history.

He was appointed OBE in 1991 and is a Fellow of the Royal Society for
the Encouragement of Arts, Manufactures and Commerce (FRSA). In
addition to Scottish history, he has a passion for fly-fishing and his interests include archaeology, photography, walking, travel and Real Tennis.
When not in Scotland, Ronald Williams lives in a small Hampshire
village in the valley of the River Test.

Ronald Williams's second book, *The Lords of the Isles*, was published in
1985 and is now reprinted by House of Lochar together with its sequel,
The Heather and The Gale.

THE HEATHER AND THE GALE

THE HEATHER AND THE GALE

Clan Donald and Clan Campbell during the Wars of Montrose

RONALD WILLIAMS

British Cataloguing in Publication Data
A catalogue record for this book is available from the British Library

The Publishers acknowledge subsidy from the Scottish Arts Council
towards the publication of this volume

ISBN 1 899863 18 4

First published by House of Lochar 1997

© Ronald Williams 1997

All rights reserved. No part of this publication
may be reproduced, stored in a retrieval system,
or transmitted, in any form or by any means,
electronic, mechanical, photocopying,
recording or otherwise, without the
prior permission of the publisher.

Typeset in Ehrhardt 10/12pt by
Posthouse Printing & Publishing, Findhorn, Forres
Printed in Great Britain by SRP Ltd, Exeter
for House of Lochar, Isle of Colonsay, Argyll PA61 7YR

Contents

List of Maps

PART I
PREMONITION

CHAPTER I

Invasion in the West

On 27th June, 1644, four ships set sail from the River Barrow in southern Ireland, bound for the west Highland coast of Scotland. They carried on board a force of 1600 Scoto-Irish troops and gallowglasses, sent by Ranald Og MacDonald, Marquis of Antrim, to fight for the royal cause against the Covenanting armies in the Scottish Civil War.

The commander of this expedition epitomised the ideal of an antique Highland fighting man – Alasdair MacDonald, 'the red-armed horse-knight, the brave and courageous son of Coll Kietache, son of Gillespie, son of Coll, son of Alexander, son of John Cathanach'[1] – and known to his enemies more simply as Alasdair MacColla, 'the Devastator'. He was a younger son of the fierce old chieftain Colkitto of Iona and Colonsay, a cadet of the Clan Donald of Islay and Dunyveg, whose ability to fight with either hand Alasdair inherited together with his name. This made him also a cousin to the Marquis of Antrim, and like other chiefs of the Clan Donald, he could claim descent from the Lords of the Isles and the great ancestors of the Clan Colla in the Western Isles.

In a hundred fights and skirmishes through Ireland and the Hebrides, the huge MacDonald had earned a ferocious reputation so that already his name was feared or famous in the western Highlands, and his deeds praised in the poems of MacVurich. Of heroic build, he was half a head taller than most men, with the great thews and shoulders of a swordsman. It was told that as a boy he had wrestled the wild bulls of Colonsay, and full-grown, he was accounted the finest warrior among his father's people. He was by nature violent and brave, but sullen tempered, impetuous, and proud as Achilles. In front of Antrim he had drawn his claymore to claim command of the expedition as of right – 'for this sword is wielded by the best hand in Ireland!' And when an Irish captain moved unwisely to dispute the boast and asked him which was next best then, Alasdair tossed the sword from right to left hand, and answered 'It is there!'

The titular leader was in fact Alexander MacDonnell, Antrim's brother, who did not accompany the force. As Alasdair's immediate

3

second in command, Antrim appointed Manus O'Cahan, who was his foster brother as well as being Alasdair's own kinsman by marriage. The name of O'Cahan was much respected in the Hebrides, since in the fourteenth century the great Angus Og, father of the first Lord of the Isles and who had established the power of the clan, married Agnes O'Cahan, and the O'Cahans could count themselves related. Her portion had been 140 men of every surname within her father's territory, and their descendants – the MacPhersons, Munroes, Beatons, Roses, and others who settled in the Highlands, were thereafter known collectively as 'the dowry of O'Cahan's daughter'. Manus O'Cahan was an experienced soldier, and had recently saved Alasdair's life when he was wounded at the Battle of Glenmaquin in Donegal.

The small invasion force comprised three regiments of foot – native Irish recruited in Antrim and Derry, and for the most part MacDonnells, together with a number of MacDonalds from the Western Isles of Scotland. The regiment of Antrim's brother was commanded in his absence by its Sergeant Major Thomas Lachtnan (or Lachlan); Manus O'Cahan commanded another with a Captain Mortimer as his second, while the third was led by Colonel James MacDonnell – officers who were all to distinguish themselves in the subsequent campaign. Their troops, while often accounted irregular 'Irishes' by conventional Lowland standards of the time, were, despite appearances, disciplined soldiers, battlehardened in the campaigns of the Catholic Federation, and some were veterans of the Spanish Netherlands and the Thirty Years War. In the Irish fashion, they were accompanied by an assortment of women, children, and other camp-followers, and since they were Catholics, a number of priests sailed also with the army.

Alasdair carried the King's commission, authorising him to raise the western clans to fight for the royal cause in Scotland, but the predominance of MacDonnells and MacDonalds among the officers and troops indicated a preoccupation with an older, longer feud. Among the enemies of Clan Donald, the Campbells were of all the tribes most hated. For generations, under their chiefs, the MacCailein Mor (the Earls of Argyll), they had encroached and scavenged among the ancient MacDonald dominions in the Isles, profiting from the fragmentation of the western clans, and using their influence with the Lowland government to drive them from their ancestral patrimony in Islay and Kintyre. But now, by irony of circumstance, although the Campbells had owed their advancement to the favour of the Stewart Kings of Scotland, the present

MacCailein Mor was one of the principal leaders of the covenanting party and thus in rebellion against the crown.

Alasdair had his own personal quarrel with the Campbell chief. Some time past, the MacCailein Mor had forced a claim to the MacDonalds' lands in Colonsay, and because Colkitto had often given him trouble, he lured the old chieftain and two of his sons under safe conduct to Inveraray and imprisoned them in one of the Campbell castles in Argyll. Alasdair himself had escaped across the Irish Sea to take service under his kinsman, the Marquis of Antrim, fighting in the Ulster wars and returning regularly to raid the Campbells' lands along the west Highland coast and in the Isles. When the Covenanting general, Alexander Leslie visited Ireland, he had marked the MacDonald for his courage and rising reputation, and seeing in him a dangerous and persistent adversary, had offered to negotiate with the Earl of Argyll for the release of his father. But the MacCailein Mor would disgorge neither the chief nor his lands, for having once confined Colkitto, he had no mind to set him loose again. Enraged by this implacable response, Alasdair had sworn to exact a vengeance in Campbell blood, and the expedition provided a long-awaited opportunity.

Antrim had originally promised to send an army of 6000 men into western Scotland, but his plans had been more extravagant than real. A prolonged raid against the Western Isles the previous year had been a costly failure, and the surviving MacDonalds had for the most part been cornered and killed by the Campbells on Rathlin. In the event, he could raise only some 2300 troops, and of these about 700 had to be left in Ireland for want of shipping to transport them. Alasdair was told that his 1600 Irishes were the advance force, his task being to establish a bridge-head in front of the main army which would follow. Because the mutual jealousies between the clans might cause them to reject his authority, he was also instructed to offer nominal command of the army to Donald Gorm of Sleat, who was the oldest and most respected of the MacDonald chiefs, and in addition he carried letters signed by the King to the Earl of Seaforth requesting his support, and to others among the Highland clans who would no longer tolerate the oppression of the Campbells and might rise in the royalist cause. The invasion was intended as part of a wider strategy, to coincide with a campaign in Aberdeenshire under the Marquis of Huntly, while the Earl of Montrose, who had been appointed the King's Lieutenant in the north was to lead a force across the border and rally the Scottish royalists against the Covenanters. After completing his commission in the west, Alasdair was to join the main royalist forces under Huntly or Montrose with all the clansmen he could muster. But if the venture failed, or if Antrim's invasion did not follow within the time agreed, he was merely to raid the western marches of the Campbells' country and then return to Ulster.

The four ships – two Flemings, an Irish merchantman, and an Irish frigate called the *Harp*, made fair passage through the dangerous waters of the Irish Sea. Parliamentary naval operations had been disrupted by the royalists' capture of Liverpool a short time before, and they were unmolested by enemy men-of-war. In mid-channel, the small fleet intercepted and captured a Covenant vessel bound from Ulster to Scotland and took a number of prisoners whom Alasdair possibly hoped to bargain against the freedom of his father and two brothers, and on 4th July, they paused at Islay to obtain intelligence of Campbell dispositions in the Isles. On the evening of 5th July, they anchored off Duart Castle at the entrance to the Sound of Mull.

Sir Lachlan MacLean of Duart declined to compromise himself by joining what he took to be another short-lived raid against the Campbell power in the west, but the following day brought a further success when the frigate *Harp* captured two English ships carrying supplies to the Parliamentary forces in Ulster which had been blown off course into the Firth of Lorne. On 7th July, Alasdair sailed up the Sound of Mull, and detached Manus O'Cahan with his regiment to reduce the Campbell defences at Loch Aline on the southern coast of Morvern.

At the moment of their landing, a strange phenomenon occurred, significant in an age when men believed in omens. One of the Catholic priests recorded that 'although the sky was cloudless and there was no sign of any disturbance in the atmosphere, there was suddenly heard a terrific explosion, so loud as to be heard in every part of Scotland [2], the effect of which was to make everyone feel as if his ears were stunned by a report behind him, from an enormous brazen cannon of unheard of dimensions.' It was a warning, the devout priest concluded, to 'the whelps of Calvin' that their enemies were come upon them.

On the headland, overlooking the Sound, the ancient Castle of Ardtornish, which had once been a favourite residence of the Lords of the Isles, was now a ruin, and the Campbells had occupied a fortified tower at the head of the Loch. O'Cahan's men took it by assault, and leaving a garrison marched overland through Morvern to rejoin the rest of the army at Loch Sunart.

Alasdair meanwhile, continued through the Sound of Mull, and landed on the peninsula of Ardnamurchan, where he established a leaguer and raised an earthwork or battery called the 'trench' in preparation for the arrival of a larger force later. On the northern shore of Loch Sunart, the Campbells held the fortress of Mingary which until comparatively recent times had been the ancestral stronghold of the MacIains of Ardnamurchan – a branch of Clan Donald which had succumbed to the predation of the MacCailein Mor. Mingary was strongly fortified, founded on solid rock at the edge of the sea, with a formidable curtain wall in the style of the old castles of the Lordship, allowing only two small entrances – one cut into the rock above the shore, and the other approached over a wooden bridge across a fosse on the landward side.

After ravaging parts of Ardnamurchan, Alasdair camped in front of the castle on 10th July, and having driven off a quantity of cattle which had been herded under the walls for shelter, laid siege to the place. Having no artillery, and because the castle was difficult to take by storm, he filled the ditch with wood stripped from the houses round about and fired the landward gate. Fortunately for the Irishes, the garrison was undermanned and short of water and the fortress surrendered on the second day with the loss of only nine Irish dead and a number of wounded.

Mingary became Alasdair's headquarters while he waited for O'Cahan to rejoin the army. On 16th July the Royal Commission was formally read before the troops, and Sir James MacDonnell was sent to deliver the King's letter to Donald Gorm of Sleat. Captain Mortimer and other officers were also sent to take the summons to the neighbouring clans – MacDonalds, MacLeans, MacLeods, and Camerons, while Alasdair repaired and reprovisioned the Castle, and consolidated his bridgehead.

On 17th July, a ship was sighted to seaward, and the frigate *Harp* put out to intercept it, only to return two days later closely pursued by two Parliamentary men-of-war. In a confined sea fight which followed, one of Alasdair's Flemish transports was captured, but the frigate and the other merchant vessels escaped by anchoring close under the castle walls. Blockaded from the sea but with his army ashore and intact, Alasdair chose to ignore the set-back and march overland. Having placed a strong garrison in Mingary, he also designated an island in Loch Sunart to corral the captured livestock against the day when, if Antrim failed to follow, they could be carried back to Ireland and show a profit on the venture. Satisfied then that his base in Ardnamurchan was secure, he turned his attention to the personal object of the enterprise, and turning inland, set out 'to bring a Highland vengeance against a Highland foe'.

PART II
THE HEATHER AND
THE GALE

CHAPTER 2

The Lost Lordship

Heather is the flower of MacDonald, and was worn by the several branches of that once great and powerful clan. They were a proud and factious people, calling themselves the seed of Somerled, and tracing their descent from the famous Irish High King, Conn of the Hundred Battles, who had ruled in the halls of Tara. The clan's genealogy was above all things dear to the Gael, and in Scotland their ancestor had been the chieftain Fergus Mac Erc, who in the year 500 AD, stood on the ancient crowning stone at Dunadd in the Crinan Moss and founded the Scoto-Irish kingdom of Dalriada.

During the ninth century, when Kenneth MacAlpin moved the High King's seat to Scone and established the claim to all of early Scotland, the progenitors of the Clan Donald remained in the west as rulers of Argyll. Shortly afterwards the Viking tide engulfed them, and the thread of ancestry claimed by the clan historians became indistinct and incapable of substantive proof, until in 1140 the warrior Somerled, claiming descent from the early Kings of Dalriada, drove the Norsemen from Argyll and carved out an independent principality in the Western Isles. His grandson Donald gave the clan its name, and through his heirs the succession passed to the later MacDonald Lords of the Isles.

In the first part of the fourteenth century, their chieftain Angus Og gave refuge to Robert the Bruce when the King was fleeing from his enemies, and in 1314 he led the fighting men of the Western Isles at the Battle of Bannockburn. His reward was further extensive territories in the Highlands, forfeited by the supporters of Balliol and Comyn, and when the Stewart dynasty succeeded to the throne of Scotland in 1371, the chief of the Clan Donald, by inheritance, marriage, and other acquisition, had come to control a vast dominion in the west, and began formally to style himself the 'Lord of the Isles'. During the period of the Lordship – from approximately 1350 to 1493, the entire Hebrides and the west Highland coastland formed a single Atlantic principality, and the MacDonald Lords of the Isles conducted their affairs and governed this dominion as independent rulers of a western Gaeldom.

Their greed for territory led them to challenge the Scottish crown for possession of the northern Earldom of Ross which they eventually acquired for a time, thus adding to their domain a great tract of land in the north-west Highlands. In maintaining their claims to independence they exploited the political divisions within Scotland and the constant wars against England, frequently entering into conspiracy and alliance with the English kings – a policy which ultimately contributed to their downfall. For at the height of their greatness the symptoms of decline were already becoming apparent, as feudal impositions and Lowland laws gradually undermined the early Celtic polity. In 1493, after an ill-advised and unsuccessful rebellion, John fourth Lord of the Isles, proved incapable of controlling the clansmen, and upon such excuse the Lordship was formally forfeited to the Scottish crown. Subsequent attempts to revive it failed, and after Donald Dubh, grandson of the last Lord of the Isles, died without heirs in 1545, the Clan Donald were never again united under a single chief. But although to their ruin, they could not repair the fragmentation of the Lordship, the old ambitions lingered still, and the memory of its former greatness continued to sustain them.

* * *

The forfeiture of the Lordship effectively removed the only focus of authority in the Western Isles, and the branches of Clan Donald and the many vassal clans embarked on a policy of individual aggrandisement, which caused them to feud against each other and rendered them vulnerable to the predations of the Campbells and other neighbours who long had envied the fabled wealth of the Isles. 'The islanders and the rest of the Highlanders were let loose, and began to shed one another's blood. Although The MacDonald kept them in obedience while he was Lord over them, yet upon his resignation of his rights – all families, including his own as well as others, gave themselves up to all sorts of cruelties which continued for a long time thereafter.'[3]

By abolishing the Lordship and making the Highland chiefs independent tenants of the crown instead of vassals of MacDonald, the Scottish government had thought to win their co-operation, but in the event this policy succeeded only in arousing their cupidity. The effect was to release the latent rivalries which had been held in check by the authority of the Lords of the Isles, while the Government's obvious desire to diminish the MacDonald's influence encouraged lawlessness and violence among the lesser clans.

The maintenance of order and the 'danting' or subduing of the Western Isles became the abiding preoccupation of the Lowland Government. But the Lowland authority was too remote to command respect, and successive Scottish kings followed a policy of contracting the task of subjugating the Highlands and islands to appointed Lieutenants – in particular the Earls of Argyll and Huntly – themselves Highland noblemen whose personal ambitions could readily identify with the performance of such public service. Since in many cases they were set to govern clans who were also their hereditary enemies, it was inevitable that they should abuse their authority. The Campbells were as rapacious and acquisitive as any, and the powers given them were an irresistible temptation. While it was their affirmed duty to enforce order, too often their interests were better served by promoting disturbance and reporting events in lurid colours as an excuse for seeking more extensive powers. Thus Sir Alexander Hay would comment in 1615: 'The frequent insurrections in the first fifteen years of the seventeenth century were encouraged if not originated by Argyll and the Campbells for their own purposes', – and numerous western chiefs on their way to execution made a similar complaint.

Stories of Highland disorder – false or genuine, instigated or spontaneous – were ever in the Government's ears, and during the second half of the sixteenth century, Lowland sentiment towards the Gaels grew progressively more antagonistic. It was coupled also with greed – for estates and revenues – and the barbarous inhumanity of the Highlanders was considered justification enough to deprive them of their hereditary lands, and even to exterminate entire populations. Thus in 1528 James V could sign an order to the Earl of Moray and others to put down disorders among the Clan Chattan and 'leave no creature living of that clan, except priests, women, and bairns' (who were to be deported to Shetland instead). In 1597 an Act of Parliament required all chiefs and landlords in the Highlands and the Isles under penalty of forfeiture to produce title deeds to their lands, although it was known that in many cases no such deeds had ever existed. In the Highlands, notions of landholding were various, so that some chiefs claimed possession by ancient sword-right and settlement, or by verbal grant in front of witnesses during the period of the Lordship, and only a few could produce a formal charter. This gave the crown Lieutenants a licence to pillage as they pleased, and through new tenancies, the buying up of debts, bonds of man-rent, the exploitation of dormant claims, and the intricacies of Lowland law – or more drastically by commissions of fire and sword – the Campbell power crept inexorably across the old territories of the Lordship.

In 1598 a grossly distorted report described the island of Lewis as 'the most fertile and commodious part of the whole realm... enriched with an incredible fertility of corn, store of fishing and other necessaries, surpassing far the plenty of any part of the inland'[4], and when MacLeod of Lewis failed to produce the required title deeds, James VI leased the island at a substantial rent to the company of Lowland colonists headed by his cousin the Duke of Lennox, who were known as the Fife Adventurers. In establishing their settlements they were authorised to employ 'slaughter, mutilation, fire-raising, or other inconveniences'[5] to expel the native population. An Act of Parliament[6] justified 'the rooting out of the barbarous inhabitants' on the excuse that they were 'void of any knowledge of God or his Religion' and had 'given themselves over to all kinds of barbarity and inhumanity'. In the same year, the Privy Council ruled that no part of the highlands and islands should thenceforth be 'disponit in feu, tak, or otherwise but to Lowland men'[7]. Hired colonists were landed at Stornoway, but the MacLeods justified their reputation by massacring the first settlers and burning their townships. The venture failed.

Nevertheless, in 1607, the Northern Hebrides except for Skye and Lewis were offered to the Earl of Huntly – 'not by agreement with the people of the country but by the extirpation of them'[8] – an atrocity which did not occur only because the feu duty was higher than Huntly was willing to pay, while the Presbyterians were not prepared to allow such an increase in power to accrue to a Catholic noble. In 1613 another intended royal grant of Morvern to Sir John Campbell of Lawers was not implemented solely because Lawers and Argyll felt that they might not be able to contain the resistance of the MacLeans who were established there. It was an irony of later Jacobitism that the clans should be loyal to a dynasty of kings who had done so much to accomplish their ruin.

Continued disorder and piracy in the Hebridean sea prompted Andrew Knox, the Bishop of the Isles, to suggest an alternative solution. In 1609 the Privy Council decided to seek the co-operation of the clans themselves – a policy which was implemented by kidnapping the chiefs aboard a government frigate and forcing them to approve *The Band and Statutes of Iona*. 'The special cause of the great misery, barbarity, and poverty into which for the present, our barren country is subject, (stated the preamble) has proceeded of the unnatural deadly feuds which have been fostered among us in this past age.' Chieftains' households were to be reduced in size and firearms to be expelled from the islands. Bards were to be put in the stocks as common thieves and likewise driven from the country. Every Highland gentleman (owning more than sixty cows) was to send his eldest son to be educated in the Lowlands, and the Gaelic language was banned in schools. The Highlanders were to become temperate. The wine trade which had developed with the continent during the sixteenth century had encouraged drunkenness among the Gaelic population, and therefore the importation of wine was prohibited. As a consequence, locally distilled whisky became the principal drink, while piracy and smuggling flourished. In an attempt to curb illegal trade, Highland chiefs were permitted to maintain only a single galley, and the once great sea power of the Isles was destroyed in consequence.

The chiefs when released largely ignored the new Regulations, which thus had little immediate effect. But the bellicosity of the clans contributed to their continuing decline. Their pride fed on a tradition which with time had grown more mystic than substantial, and while their contentiousness echoed the old ambitions of their tribe, the reality of these had crumbled long ago. They had dreamed while their dominion dwindled, and scavengers picked among the ruins of the Lordship for a share. Successive waves of Lowland greed and Campbell guile had eroded their once broad possessions in the Isles. Campbell tenants encroached the old MacDonald lands, and Campbell garrisons occupied their ancient strongholds. The Gaels were a people of long, long memory, and though their history had lost direction, they brooded still upon these things. 'Without Clan Donald there is no strength. It is no joy to be without them.' And as the power of that once great Clan diminished, there grew a legacy of bitterness and hatred, to which events would one day give release.

CHAPTER 3

The Campbell's Kingdom

The gale or bog-myrtle is the badge of the Campbells. The clan took its name from Sir Colin Cambeul or 'wrymouth', a knight of probable Strathclyde British descent, who in the thirteenth century married the heiress of an Irish chieftain called Duncan MacDuibhne, through whom he acquired the castle of Innischonnel in Loch Awe. From Sir Colin the later Campbell chiefs inherited their Highland appellation of MacCailein Mor – 'great son of Colin', and the clan were also known as the Children of Diarmaid, after their mythological Irish ancestor Diarmaid MacDuibhne, who in Fingalian legend slew the wild boar of Caledon and died from standing barefoot on its poisoned bristles.

In 1294, Sir Colin Cambeul was killed by the MacDougalls at the String of Lorne. His son, Sir Neil fought under Sir William Wallace, while his grandson, the second Sir Colin, was a supporter of Robert the Bruce and for his loyalty was awarded further lands in Lorne and Cowal which had been forfeited by the MacDugalls, the Lamonts, and other adherents of the Balliol and Comyn factions during Scotland's War of Independence. To this second Sir Colin the King granted 'the one free barony of Lochow' which at that time comprised the whole of mid-Argyll between Lorne and Loch Fyne excepting the districts of Glassary and Craignish. In Cowal, by the end of the fourteenth century the Campbell Lords of Lochow had come into possession of the additional baronies of Ardkinglas at the upper end of Loch Fyne, Ardgartan on Loch Long, and Kilmun on Holy Loch. During the fifteenth century, by marriage, charter, or more sinister acquisition, the family amassed a great chain of territory stretching from Cawdor in Moray through Breadalbane into the heartland of Argyll itself, and as far south as Ayr.

Duncan Campbell, brother of the second Sir Colin, married the daughter of Sir Reginald Crawford of Loudoun, Sheriff of Ayr, and when Crawford died in 1303, his lands passed to the Campbells together with the office of Hereditary Sheriff. The Campbells of Loudoun were elevated to the peerage in 1601. Within the principal branch of Lochow, Duncan, great grandson of the second Sir Colin, married the daughter of the Regent Albany who was ruling Scotland during the captivity of James I, and was made Lord Campbell in 1445. His grandson, yet another Colin, was created first Earl of Argyll in 1457, and obtained the ancient district of Lorne by marrying a daughter of the last Stewart incumbent and exchanging her property outside Argyll with the presumed heir-male to Lorne. This transaction was never recognised by the Stewarts of Appin who contended that the true heir to Lorne had been excluded, and continued to retain Appin itself by force. The Stewarts of Lorne had also owned Glen Lyon in Perthshire, and the marriage of a second daughter to the Earl of Argyll's uncle, Sir Colin Campbell of Glenorchy, would bring this further territory within the Campbells' domain.

Lowland honours followed this second marriage into the royal Stewart family. In 1464, the Earl of Argyll was made Master of the Royal Household (an office which became hereditary), and in 1473 he was appointed Justiciar of Scotland, Chamberlain, and Sheriff and Baillie of Argyll under Royal Charter. More ominous for the fortunes of the other western clans, James III also granted him a commission of Lieutenancy with vice-regal powers throughout Argyll, Lorne, and Menteith, where his ambition as MacCailein Mor encouraged him to intrude upon the territories of the Lord of the Isles and interfere with the vassals of Clan Donald. In 1474, the Campbells were granted Inveraray in Lochow, and this increasingly became their principal residence. From there, they were not only well placed to control their Highland territories in Argyll and Lorne, but its location on Loch Fyne gave ready geographical – and more significant, political – access to the Lowlands. The old castle of Innischonnel became a Campbell prison.

In 1488, the first Earl of Argyll was one of the nobles who hounded James III to death and placed James IV upon the Scottish throne. His reward was an extension of his vice-regal powers in the Highlands and an increasing influence at court. His son, Archibald, second Earl of Argyll, was appointed Justice-General of the kingdom – and promptly abused his power to acquire the ancient lands of Cawdor in Morayshire.

When John, last Thane of Cawdor died in 1495 leaving a baby girl, Muriel, as his sole heiress, the Earl of Argyll obtained the wardship of the infant from James IV and endeavoured by threats to secure her betrothal to his son. When the family resisted sixty Campbell clansmen broke into Cawdor and kidnapped the child. According to tradition, the girl's mother branded her with a red-hot key, and the nurse bit off one of the baby's finger joints so that she could later be identified, but the Campbells boasted that so long as there was a red-haired lass in Argyll they would not lack an heiress to Cawdor. She was kept in Lochow and eventually married to Argyll's third son John from whom the Campbell Earls of Cawdor are descended.

Marching with Lorne to the east was the district of Glenorchy, and beyond that again the region known as Breadalbane – a tract of land stretching from Glen Dochart and Glen Lyon east through Lawers and the old estates of Balloch at the further end of Loch Tay, and north into the wild country around Loch Rannoch. The expansion of the Campbells into this wide territory, and their dispossession of the Clan Gregor, was one of the blackest episodes in their history.

* * *

The MacGregors claimed descent from the royal house of Alpin, father of the Kenneth of Dalriada who in 843 had moved the High King's Seat to Scone and founded the kingdom of Scotland. For centuries they had occupied Glenorchy and the broad glens beyond, with their ancestral stronghold near the head of Loch Awe.

In 1292, Iain, son of Malcolm of Glenorchy, died, leaving an heiress, Mariota, who was married to Iain Campbell, a younger son of Sir Colin Campbell of Lochow. There was no surviving child of this marriage, and when the Cambpells claimed ownership of Glenorchy by right of inheritance through Mariota, the MacGregors found themselves feudal vassals under a family of strangers with whom they had no bridge of kinship. Under Celtic law, the clan would have elected a 'tanist' from among the kindred of the last chief, and consequently Gregor, grandson of Malcolm of Glenorchy, claimed the chiefship and continued to occupy the land by swordright in defiance of feudal imposition. This Gregor gave his name to the clan, and was succeeded by his son, John the One-eyed, who lived until 1390.

Nevertheless in 1432, Duncan Campbell of Lochow was in a position to grant lands in Glenorchy to his younger son Colin, who became the first Campbell Laird of Glenorchy and built the great castle of Kilchurn at the head of Loch Awe. Beyond Glenorchy in Breadalbane, the lordship of Glen Dochart had come into the hands of the crown, and parts of it had been granted to various new proprietors, including another cadet branch of Lochow called the Campbells of Strachur. East of Glen Dochart the lands north and south of Loch Tay were also crown property, while to the north, the Stewarts of Lorne, shortly to die out, were in possession of

Glen Lyon. By marriage, purchase, grant, lease or feu, the Campbells of Glenorchy gradually expanded into this vacuum.

In 1488, immediately following the death of James III in which the Earl of Argyll had played a conspicuous part, an Act of Parliament empowered Sir Duncan Campbell of Glenorchy and Ewen Campbell of Strachur to enforce law and order in Breadalbane. In 1498, Campbell of Glenorchy was appointed Baillie of the crown lands around Loch Tay, Glen Lyon, and the barony of Glen Dochart, and in 1502 he obtained formal charter to Glen Lyon by inheritance through his mother who had been a daughter of the last Stewart of Lorne. Cadet branches of Glenorchy were thereafter established in Lawers and Glen Lyon (it was a descendant of this latter family who actually carried out the massacre of Glencoe). It was a feature of the Campbells that they sired prodigious quantities of children, and this in turn encouraged their insatiable greed for new lands with which to endow the younger sons. The loyalty which all the branches of the clan displayed towards the MacCailein Mor, and their tendency (in stark contrast to the fragmentation of Clan Donald) to hunt in a pack also contributed to the development of their formidable power in the Highlands.

Meanwhile, having lost their ancestral lands in Glenorchy, the MacGregors had scattered throughout Breadalbane – in Glen Dochart, Glen Lyon, at Balloch and Roro near Loch Tay, and northwards into the rough country around Rannoch – wherever they could find holdings. The principal chieftain of the clan was MacGregor of Glenstrae whose residence was at Stronmilchan in the foothills between wild Glenstrae and Glenorchy itself, about a mile from the present village of Dalmally. He possessed legal title to Glenstrae as the tenant of the Earl of Argyll, but the other branches of the clan had no such security, and being remote from the authority of their chief, and yet recognising no other, they earned a reputation for lawlessness which would later be used to justify their extirpation.

In 1519, Sir Colin Campbell, third of Glenorchy, prevented the succession of the legitimate heir to MacGregor of Glenstrae in favour of the chieftain of a junior branch who had raped and later married his daughter. It was in the Campbells' interest thereafter to dispose of the true heirs, and the disinherited line became known as 'The Children of the Mist' – moving north into the lands of Rannoch where under their proper chief, Duncan Ladaslach (Duncan the Lordly), they raided the lands of Clan Menzies and terrorised half of Perthshire. A reconciliation was eventually effected, however, when Duncan Ladaslach became Tutor to the young, though not rightful chief, Gregor MacGregor, and the clan were relatively unmolested until 1550.

But in that year, Grey Colin became the sixth Campbell Laird of Glenorchy, and a more deadly persecution of Clan Gregor began. In 1552, under pretence of friendship, he invited Duncan Ladaslach and his two sons to Finlarig castle where on arrival, they were promptly beheaded. He then appointed his kinsman Red Duncan Campbell of Glen Lyon as guardian to the young MacGregor chief, who was kept at Carban Castle and betrothed to Red Duncan's daughter.

Widely dispersed though the MacGregors were, often holding land under alien landlords, their chief still owned responsibility for them and claimed their allegiance in time of war. For this reason they constituted a threat in Campbell eyes, and Grey Colin, who was proceeding to convert into feudal tenures leases which formerly had been held of the crown, was not satisfied with the rents alone, but demanded that his tenants gave him military service. The MacGregors refused to enter into bonds of manrent which would allow him such authority, holding that their loyalty belonged only to the head of their clan, and so to bring them to submission, Grey Colin bought the superiority of Glenstrae from the Earl of Argyll, and in 1560 refused to confirm Gregor Roy MacGregor as his tenant when the young chief eventually came of age. Deprived thus of their ancestral lands and reduced to the status of 'broken men', the MacGregors retaliated fiercely and the whole clan rose under their outlawed chieftain. Their resistance continued for nine years, until Gregor Roy was finally captured and after a short imprisonment executed on Grey Colin's order.

A period of further violence and disorder followed. In 1587, an Act of Parliament authorised reprisals, including summary execution, against any member of the clan if an actual offender could not be apprehended. Six years later the disorder in the Highlands was such that the General Band obliged landlords and Baillies to post sureties for their duty to arrest criminals, and it further enacted that in the case of 'broken men' like the MacGregors who lived on the property of various landlords but retained their loyalty to the clan chief, these obligations of arrest and reparation should apply also to such chiefs, who were therefore made responsible for the behaviour of their clansmen. But while a chief who was a feudal baron could deal himself with crimes committed within his area of jurisdiction, the MacGregor chiefs who owned no land, could only surrender their clansmen for trial, usually in a Campbell court, and this they refused to do.

Gregor Roy was succeeded as chief by his two year old son Allaster, who for his skill at archery and hunting, was later known among his people as 'the Arrow of Glen Lyon'. Throughout his youth the disorder among the outlawed MacGregors continued to spread as the Children of the Mist raided wild through Rannoch, and at the age of twenty he had scarcely assumed the chiefship when an atrocity occurred which nearly led to the immediate destruction of his clan. Some MacGregors in Balquidder were caught poaching deer in the royal forest of Glenartney, and instead of bringing them to trial, the King's Forester, John Drummond, mutilated them on the spot and then turned them loose with murder in their hearts. During the wedding celebrations of James VI and Anne of Denmark, Drummond was sent to the forest to get venison, and while he was hunting the MacGregors set upon him and cut off his head. Drummond's sister was married to Stewart of Ardvoirlich who lived nearby, and as an act of wanton cruelty, the outlaws called at her house and confronted her with the head of their victim on a platter, its mouth obscenely stuffed with the bread and cheese which she, unaware of the crime, had offered them to eat. The lady was pregnant, and the shock drove her mad. For some days she wandered raving in the forest until her husband eventually found her and brought her home to be delivered of her child. The baby boy to whom she shortly gave birth was John Stewart of Ardvoirlich, who seemed to inherit a part of his mother's madness and was instigator of another violent and tragic murder in 1644.[9]

When Drummond's death was reported to Allaster, he summoned the Clan Gregor to Balquidder to consider the likely consequences. The MacGregors realised that retribution for the crime would fall upon them all, and each man swore on the severed head (which had been brought to the meeting and set upon a tombstone) that they would defend the murderers to the death.

The Privy Council drew up a list of 140 MacGregors who were to be hunted down and brought to trial, but despite commissions of fire and sword, local landlords were reluctant to try consequences with the outlawed clan. Those MacGregors who were driven from their houses joined forces with other bands of broken men and raided along the Lowland fringe. Burning, killing, and cattle reiving became so widespread that in the words of the King: 'there were neither God nor man' to control and repress the rebellious clan.

This disorder, however, played into the Campbells' hands, and the seventh Earl of Argyll, appropriately known as Gillespie Grumach, or Archibald the Grim, obtained from the Privy Council a formal commission to control the MacGregors whom he now manipulated into ravaging the lands of his personal enemies. Chief among these were the Colquhouns of Luss, who occupied the western shore of Loch Lomond and were themselves a wild tribe by no means innocent of bloody crime. Nor were the MacGregors the first to deal them ruthless retribution, for only a short time previously the sixteenth Laird of Luss had been at feud with the chief of the Clan MacFarlane whose wife he had seduced. The MacFarlanes besieged the Colquhoun's castle, and when during the fighting, Luss was shot in the back by his own brother (who was later hanged for the deed), MacFarlane obtained access to the body and later served the genitals to his wife for dinner. Now, in 1603, the seventeenth Laird of Luss hanged a number of MacGregors for stealing and eating his sheep, and the clan retaliated by raiding the Colquhoun lands and killing a number of the menfolk who resisted them. The Colquhoun widows protested to the King, bearing the bloodstained shirts of their dead husbands (and a few which had been dipped in sheep's blood), and the Laird of Luss was given authority to pursue Clan Gregor with fire and sword. When he heard that Luss was mustering his people, Allaster promptly invaded Dumbarton with 400 of his clan and defeated a combined force of Colquhouns and Buchanans in the hills west of Loch Lomond. Colquhoun himself and some 140 of his people were killed in the fight which was thereafter remembered as the 'slaughter of Glenfruin'.

For this deed the MacGregors became the 'one doomed and unpardonable clan in all the Highlands'. Two months later, the Privy Council proscribed the entire clan and the very use of the surname MacGregor was forbidden under pain of death. All those who had taken part in the massacre at Glenfruin, together with any who gave them food or shelter, were sentenced to death. The fugitives were hunted with bloodhounds, and during the twelve months following, some fifty were captured and hanged at Edinburgh.

Allaster remained free for almost a year, until he accepted an invitation from the Earl of Argyll to discuss the future of his clan upon the promise that he would not be arrested. The guileless Allaster was welcomed at Inveraray with every sign of friendliness and gestures of good faith. Argyll offered to send two gentlemen to accompany him to England, and promised that he himself would plead his case to the King in London. 'He had no doubt' Allaster recalled later, 'but his Majesty would at his request, pardon my offence'.

Argyll kept his promise in so far as he allowed Allaster to cross the border into England, but he was then arrested at Berwick and returned to Edinburgh for trial. Argyll's part in the invasion of the Colquhoun's lands was never clear, but Allaster's defence was an eloquent testimony as to the Campbell's role in his destruction:

> 'I, Allaster MacGregor of Glenstrae, confess here before God that I have been persuaded, moved, and enticed, as I am now presently accused and troubled for. Also if I had used counsel or command of the man that has enticed me, I would have done and committed sundry murders more. For truly, since I was first His Majesty's man, I could never be at any ease by my Lord Argyll's falsity and inventions for he caused Maclean and Clan Cameron to commit hership and slaughter in my room of Rannoch, the which caused my poor men thereafter to beg and steal; also thereafter he moved my brother and some of my friends to commit both hership and slaughter upon the Laird of Luss; also he persuaded myself with message to war against the Laird of Buchanan, which I did refuse. For the which I was continually threatened that he would be my unfriend...'

On 20 January, 1604, the Arrow of Glen Lyon was hanged in Edinburgh with seven of his clansmen. Argyll was made the chief executor of justice against the outlawed MacGregors – for which he was later rewarded with a grant of the old Clan Donald lands in Kintyre. By 1613, the Campbells had largely attained their ends in Breadalbane. All MacGregors of consequence were either dead of had submitted. The name MacGregor was proscribed, and the clan itself had officially ceased to exist.

* * *

Throughout this period, the Earls of Argyll had continued to hold high office in the Lowland Government. Archibald, the second Earl, had been killed leading his Highlanders against the English at the Battle of Flodden. Colin, third Earl of Argyll, was Warden of the Marches and hereditary Justice-General of Scotland. Archibald, the fourth Earl, distinguished himself at the Battle of Pinkie. Archibald, the fifth Earl, became Lord Chancellor, but fainted at the Battle of Langside when commanding the army of Mary Queen of Scots. Colin, sixth Earl was

Lord Chancellor of Scotland. Archibald the Grim, seventh Earl of Argyll, was the government's chief agent in bringing the Highlands under Lowland writ, and was principally responsible for encompassing the destruction of the MacGregors and the ruin of Clan Donald of Islay.

By 1615, the Campbells controlled a vast but compact block of territory in the Highlands, knit together by a strong skein of kinship and clan loyalty to the MacCailein Mor. Secure in these mainland possessions, and in their influence with the Lowland government, it was inevitable that the Earls of Argyll should also contemplate the remaining lands of the Clan Donald, and within the old dominion of the Lordship, seek yet a greater extension to the Campbell's kingdom.

CHAPTER 4

The Ruin of
Clan Donald of Islay

In 1545, Donald Dubh, the grandson of the last Lord of the Isles, died without heirs. Of the other branches of the Clan Donald, the family of Lochalsh which might have claimed the seniority, was also extinct in the male line. In 1497, Sir Alexander of Lochalsh, nephew of the last Lord, had been murdered at Oronsay by his kinsman MacIain of Ardnamurchan (another sept of MacDonald), who had hoped thereby to gain the favour of the King. Sir Alexander's son, Donald Gallda, visited a bloody revenge upon MacIain for his father's death, but when he also died without heirs in 1519, the remaining inheritance of Lochalsh passed by marriage through his sister Margaret to Donald, sixth chief of the MacDonalds of Glengarry – who were themselves a sept of the Clanranald of Garmoran. Much of the old territory of Lochalsh had passed into the hands of the MacKenzies after the Lords of the Isles lost the Earldom of Ross, but in 1600 the MacDonalds of Glengarry still held the lands of Lochalsh itself on the northern shore of the loch, together with the district around Loch Carron and the fortress of Strome.

Across the narrow Sound, the Clan Huisdean – the MacDonalds of Sleat – were established along the coastland of southern Skye around their castle of Dunskeath on Loch Eishart. In the north of the island they also held the peninsula of Trotternish on the eastern shore of Loch Snizort, with the grim stronghold of Duntulm rising out of the coastal rock and looking westward over the Minch to their further possessions in the Uists. The rest of Skye was largely occupied by the Siol Tormod – the MacLeods of Harris – with whom, after the fall of the Lordship, the MacDonalds of Sleat were in constant dispute.

On the mainland of Garmoran, south of the sound of Sleat, the Clanranald – comprising the families of Knoydart, Glengarry, Moidart, and Morar – occupied a broad but inhospitable territory northwards from Loch Shiel through the 'rough bounds', and east up Glengarry to the Great Glen itself. By the beginning of the seventeenth century, the leadership of the clan had passed to the family of Moydartach of Benbecula, who styled themselves 'Captains of Clanranald' and occupied the ancient castle of Island Tioram which guards the narrows into Loch Moidart.

In the lands bordering the Clanranald to the south, the MacIains of Ardnamurchan and Sunart had also become extinct early in the seventeenth century. Failure of the male line resulted in a MacIain heiress resigning the superiority of Ardnamurchan in favour of the fourth Earl of Argyll, although the Tanist, or nearest heir-male, for a time continued to occupy the estates in defiance of Argyll's legal claim. In 1602, however, the MacIain claimant found it expedient to resign the land which he still held to the seventh Earl of Argyll against the promise that he would be regranted the estates in feu. But Argyll did not honour the contract, and instead leased Ardnamurchan and Sunart to one of his Campbell vassals. Thus completely dispossessed, the MacIains resorted to piracy and shortly ceased to exist as a clan.

East of the Clanranald beyond the Great Glen, the MacDonalds of Keppoch occupied a tract of Lochaber in the wild country around Glen Spean, and extending into the mountains of Corrieyarack. To their south, beyond the Cameron lands of Glen Nevis and Mamore, a small branch of the MacDonalds called the Clan Ian Abrach, were settled in Glencoe.

In the old days of the Lordship, the mainland possessions of the Clan Donald had stretched virtually uninterrupted from Strome in the north as far south as the Castle of Dunaverty on the point of Kintyre, but during the sixteenth century, much of the intervening territory had passed into other hands. The MacLeans held Mull and Morvern, no longer as vassals of the MacDonald Lord of the Isles, but as direct tenants of the crown. The Clan Cameron occupied a broad tract from Loch Eil eastwards across the Lochy as far as Ben Alder. A branch of the Stewarts still clung to Appin, while Lorne and Argyll – the very heartland of ancient Dalriada – was in the permanent possession of Clan Campbell. In the south, however, another major branch of the Clan Donald – the family of Islay and Dunyveg – still held Islay itself, part of Jura, and the southern half of Kintyre. Inevitably, the wealth of these lands, and their proximity to the Campbell dominions on the mainland, made them prey to the ambition of the MacCailein Mor.

The founder of Clan Ian Mor – the MacDonalds of Islay and Dunyveg – was John Mor the Tanister, brother of Donald, first Lord of the Isles, who had married Margery Bisset, heiress of the Glens of Antrim in northern Ireland, through whom the clan acquired considerable interests in Ulster. John Mor's son, Donald Balloch, achieved fame by leading the Clan Donald to victory over the Earls of Mar and Huntly at the Battle of Inverlochy in 1431, and his marriage to another Irish heiress, the daughter of the O'Neill of Connaught, further strengthened the clan's connections with Ireland.

In 1494, the male line barely survived extermination, when Donald Balloch's son Sir John Mor, and grandson John Cathanach, were seized by MacIain of Ardnamurchan (the same who had murdered Sir Alexander of Lochalsh) and delivered to the Lowland government for execution. Fortunately for the clan, John Cathanach's son Alexander was in Antrim at the time of his father's betrayal and in due course succeeded to the chiefship. This Alexander had nine sons, of whom three deserve mention: James of Dunyveg, who succeeded him; Coll, who founded the cadet branch of Colonsay and was the grandfather of Colkitto; and Sorley Buy, who was the ancestor of the later Earls of Antrim.

James of Dunyveg remained neutral during Donald Dubh's final and hopeless bid to revive the old Lordship, but because of their Antrim connections, the MacDonalds of Islay were drawn as allies into the rebellions of the native Irish against the English government in Ireland. This Irish involvement gradually drained the strength of the clan, so that by the end of the sixteenth century there was barely manpower enough to populate Islay itself. James of Dunyveg and two of his brothers were killed in battle in Ulster, and the clan's possessions in Antrim were eventually acquired by the younger branch of Sorley Buy.

In 1569, the chiefship of Clan Donald of Islay passed to Angus, second son of James of Dunyveg. His mother was a daughter of the Earl of Argyll, and his wife was the daughter of MacLean of Duart – dynastic connections which ought to have ensured his survival. But the first did not prompt Argyll to relent in his ambition, and the second did not prevent a deadly feud with the MacLeans which gave the Campbells their opportunity and contributed to the ultimate ruin of the southern MacDonalds.

In 1585, Donald Gorm, chief of the MacDonalds of Sleat, was sailing to Islay to visit Angus of Dunyveg, when storms forced him to find sheltered anchorage in MacLean of Duart's territory on the coast of Jura. Shortly before, Donald Gorm had outlawed two of his relatives, Hugh MacGillespie and MacDonald Herrach, men of bloody reputation both, who being in Jura at the time, saw an opportunity to reive a quantity of MacLean's cattle in the certain expectation that Donald Gorm would have the blame. The MacLeans attacked the MacDonalds during the night and many of the men from Sleat were killed, Donald Gorm himself escaping only because he had chosen to sleep on board his galley. He returned to Skye swearing that he would be revenged on MacLean of Duart.

When Angus of Dunyveg heard of this affray, he sailed to Skye where he attempted to pacify Donald Gorm, and then visited Lachlan MacLean of Duart in the hope of effecting a reconciliation. But MacLean was also in dispute with Angus over possession of the Rhinns of Islay, and against all rules of Highland hospitality he treacherously seized the MacDonald chief and refused to release him unless he surrendered the lands in question. This Angus was forced to do, and he was also obliged to leave his brother Ranald and his young son James as hostages to guarantee fulfilment of the agreement.

Shortly afterwards, MacLean went to Islay to receive sasine of the ceded lands, taking one of his hostages, Angus's son, with him. While he was staying at Lochgorm, he received an invitation – with pledges of good faith – from Angus to lodge at the chief's house at Mullintrae, and somewhat suspiciously, he accepted. Angus in the event, had decided to pay MacLean in kind, and during the night MacDonald swordsmen surrounded the building where he and his followers were sleeping, while Angus knocked at MacLean's door on the pretext of offering him a drink. Sensing danger, MacLean appeared in the doorway carrying his hostage on his shoulders. Seeing his father with drawn sword and obviously intent on murder, the boy begged him to spare MacLean's life. Angus relented, and apart from two men who were killed when they attempted to resist, MacLean and his followers were made prisoner and confined in the dungeon of the castle.

A few days later, Angus received a false report from Mull that the MacLeans had executed their other hostage – who was his brother Ranald. In Islay, retribution was swift and bloodthirsty, and the MacDonalds began to kill two of the captured MacLeans every day, Lachlan MacLean of Duart being spared only because Angus broke a leg in an accident while travelling to supervise his execution.

These violent proceedings came to the notice of the Lowland government through Archibald the Grim, seventh Earl of Argyll, who obtained a Commission empowering him to intervene and mediate between the parties. (It was alleged by some that, in pursuance of his policy of supporting the MacLeans against the old power of Clan Donald, he may have had a hand in instigating the original dispute over the Rhinns of Islay, and that MacLean would not have placed himself in such danger had he not had some surety from Argyll.)

The negotiations which followed resulted in a favourable settlement for Angus, who kept eight hostages, including MacLean's son and heir, and other prominent relatives of the Duart chief. This was not altogether satisfactory to Argyll, who had wanted the hostages to be transferred into his own keeping, and the government consequently did not ratify the agreement. But Angus had no intention of surrendering his prisoners, and having concluded that the matter had been settled, at least for the time, he departed for Ireland to pursue his family interests in Antrim.

No sooner had he left, than MacLean, without regard for the safety of the hostages, invaded Islay and Gigha, pillaging these islands and killing many of the people there. When Angus heard of it, with uncharacteristic forebearance he did not kill the hostages but retaliated by going to Mull with Donald Gorm of Sleat, 'and there killed and chased the Clan Lean at his leisure and so revenged himself fully of the injuries done to him and his tribe'. MacLean in his turn, responded by plundering the MacDonald territories in Kintyre, and 'thus for a while they did continually vex one another with slaughter and outrages to the destruction almost of the countries and people.' [10]

The Earl of Argyll represented these disorders to the government as being the responsibility of Angus of Dunyveg, and because he had not surrendered his hostages, in 1587 his lands were forfeited and the life-rent granted to his enemy MacLean. MacLean celebrated this mark of favour by next setting upon Angus's kinsman MacIain of Ardnamurchan, whom first he lured to Duart with the offer of his mother's hand in marriage, and then imprisoned in a dungeon where he was tortured daily by his gaolers.

Shortly after this incident (which became known as 'MacLean's nuptials'), the *Florida*, a galleon from the Spanish Armada, put into Tobermory for shelter, and in return for supplying the vessel with victuals and other necessaries, MacLean hired a hundred soldiers from the ship's complement to fight against the MacDonalds. With these reinforcements he ravaged the islands of Rhum and Eigg, Canna and Muck, and besieged MacIain's castle of Mingary. This provoked the MacDonalds in their turn to burn the MacLeans' lands in Jura and Ardgour. The general disorder spread northwards as other clans saw opportunity to pursue feuds of their own, until finally Angus and

MacLean accepted the mediation of Sorley Buy and the Countess of Tyrone, and an exchange of prisoners was agreed.[11]

It was probably a matter of some satisfaction of Donald Gorm of Sleat that the two renegades who had provoked the first massacre on Jura – MacDonald Herrach and Hugh MacGillespie – both came to violent deaths in the years which followed. MacDonald Herrach for a time seems to have been reconciled with his chief, but over-reached himself when, staying one night at Dunskeath he took objection to ten of his fellow guests and murdered them while they slept – hanging their corpses in front of his hostess's window before leaving in the morning. The lady was deeply offended by this abuse of her hospitality and her Chamberlain went after MacDonald Herrach and put him severely to death.

Hugh MacGillespie returned to Skye and built Castle Huisdean on the edge of the MacLeods' country. From there he harassed the fishermen of the north isles and earned a reputation as a pirate. In 1602 he was still conspiring to kill Donald Gorm whom he hoped to lure into Castle Huisdean on the pretext of agreeing to a reconciliation. By some careless oversight, however, he misaddressed the invitation, and instead of conveying to Donald Gorm his intended letter of loyalty and affection, he inadvertently sent him the instruction to one William Martin of Trotternish to murder the chief as soon as he arrived at Castle Huisdean. Donald Gorm's clansmen hunted him to Uist, and then brought him back to be imprisoned in the dungeon underneath Duntulm Castle. There he was starved for several days, and when his hunger was extreme, they lowered down a large salt beef on a pewter platter. After devouring this he was consumed with thirst, but his tormentors would not allow him anything to drink. He quickly went mad and died in a miserable condition, even tearing to pieces with his teeth the pewter plate on which the beef had lain.

* * *

The truce between Angus and MacLean of Duart was temporarily effective, and in 1589 they were both remitted for all the crimes laid to their charge during the course of the feud. In 1591, however, Angus, MacLean and Donald Gorm, were invited to Edinburgh to discuss their affairs before the Privy Council, and on their arrival, with the unscrupulousness which characterised Lowland dealings with the Highlanders, they were promptly thrown into prison to be released only upon payment of heavy sureties for their future good behaviour. Donald Gorm was fined £4000, but in Angus's case, allegedly because of his Irish interests, the bail was set at £20,000 – a truly huge sum which meant his complete financial ruin. It was no coincidence therefore that Campbell of Cawdor – who had already loaned him various sums in respect of lands in Gigha – offered to advance the money, thus acquiring a financial interest in the old Clan Donald possessions in Islay. Angus was eventually released in 1592, having in addition been obliged to surrender his two sons, James, and another Angus, to remain as hostages at the royal court.

He returned to Islay full of resentment at the treacherous behaviour of the government, and with little intention of fulfilling the conditions of his liberation. The Privy Council threatened him with forfeiture, and in 1593, when he failed to respond, he was summoned for treason. In the following year, since he still refused to compear, and because he remained an obdurate Roman Catholic, he was declared contumacious, and his possessions forfeited to the Crown.

In an effort to bring him to heel, the Privy Council next sent his son, Sir James MacDonald, who had become something of a favourite at court, to persuade his father to submit – thus sowing the seeds of a family quarrel which was to prove disastrous for the clan. Sir James appeared to have been successful in his mission, since in 1596 he presented to the Council a letter from his father Angus, authorising him to act on his behalf and, subject to suitable arrangements for his retirement, renouncing all this lands in favour of his son. The Privy Council accepted this submission on the conditions that Sir James would remain a hostage at court, while Angus should evacuate Kintyre and Gigha and confine himself to the islands of Islay and Colonsay. Angus was further ordered to present himself at the Council before the end of the year or else surrender the castle of Dunyveg to the King's Lieutenant at Kilkerran.

Angus complied with this last condition but failed to fulfil the rest, so that in 1598 Sir James MacDonald was again sent to Kintyre to negotiate his father's good behaviour. A serious quarrel now broke out, and, possibly incited by the government, Sir James trapped Angus in his house at Askomull and set fire to the building. The old chief, badly burned, was taken prisoner and confined in irons at Smerbie for several months.

But any hopes which Sir James may have had of enjoying his father's island possessions were shortly dashed when MacLean of Duart revived the old feud and laid claim to all of Islay. In a bloody battle at the head of Loch Gruinard MacLean was killed with most of his followers, but Sir James was also dangerously wounded by an arrow. He now sought an accommodation with the government, offering to evacuate Kintyre and to place the fortress of Dunyveg at the King's disposal – proposals which were agreed to by the Privy Council but never implemented, due to Campbell intervention.

At about this time, Sir James MacDonald married the sister of Campbell of Cawdor, and his brother-in-law advised him to hold out for better terms. In the meanwhile, the Earl of Argyll decided that his interests would be better served by promoting the quarrel between Sir James and his father. Angus was released, and induced to sign a bond of defence against his son with Campbell of Auchinbreck. Thus Campbell duplicity now destroyed any chance that Sir James may have had of securing his inheritance in Islay.

In 1604, Argyll traduced Sir James to the Privy Council and accused him of conspiracy against the Crown. He was captured and surrendered to the authorities by Angus himself, and was subsequently imprisoned for several years in Edinburgh Castle. From this confinement he watched helplessly as the Campbells set about the systematic destruction of his clan, for with Sir James in prison, Argyll promptly withdrew his support from Angus and secured the tenancy of Kintyre for himself. The legal Agreement deposited at the General Register House specifically provided that no lands in Kintyre were thereafter to be leased to anybody by the name of MacDonald or MacLean without the King's express approval. Angus predictably rebelled, and together with Donald Gorm of Sleat drove the Campbell colonists out of Kintyre, determined to defend his lands by swordright against the predations of the MacCailein Mor.

In 1607, Sir James MacDonald made an unsuccessful attempt to escape from Edinburgh Castle, and two years later he was formally condemned to death by a lowland court presided over by the Earl of Argyll. However, the sentence was not carried out and his imprisonment continued. In the meanwhile, fresh disorders in the Isles prompted sterner measures for their pacification, and in 1609 the western chiefs were kidnapped and forced to subscribe *The Statutes of Iona*[12]. The Bishop of the Isles, Andrew Knox, was appointed King's Lieutenant and Constable of Dunyveg, and he immediately set about collecting the arrears of taxes owed by Angus of Islay and other chiefs within his jurisdiction.

By 1612 Angus was so financially reduced that he was obliged to sell Islay to Campbell of Cawdor for the paltry sum of 600 merks, and the Campbells came into legal possession of the ancient patrimony of

MacDonald. Physical occupation was their next logical objective, and in 1614, shortly after Angus's death, the final tragic episode in the ruin of the Clan Donald of Islay, was enacted at the fortress of Dunyveg.

In that year, Ranald Og, a bastard son of Angus, and a 'vagabond fellow without any residence', seized the weakly guarded castle. With Sir James MacDonald still imprisoned, the leadership of the clan devolved upon his younger brother Angus Og, who entrusted the siege and recovery of the stronghold to Colkitto of Colonsay (the father of Alasdair). Ranald Og was driven out, and Angus Og offered to restore the fortress to the Crown. But for some reason the former garrison suspected treachery and refused to reoccupy it.

Bishop Knox was sent to mediate, but in the interim, Angus Og (as he later maintained at his trial) received a message through a gentleman called Malcolm MacNeill that the Earl of Argyll 'was afraid that he and his friends would give up the castle, and if they did so it would be to their utter wreck'. Angus Og therefore refused to submit to the Bishop unless he was promised a seven year lease of the crown lands in Islay, possession of Dunyveg itself, and a free pardon for all crimes which he had committed to date. The Bishop's own record of the negotiation confirmed the subterranean role of the Campbells in inciting Angus Og to resist his authority, since he reported to the Privy Council that: 'Angus Og their captain, affirmed in the hearing of many witnesses that he got direction from the Earl of Argyll to keep still the house, and that the Earl should procure him therefore the whole lands of Islay and the house of Dunyveg to himself'. The Bishop was no friend to the MacDonalds, whom he described as 'a false generation and a bloody people', but he warned the government against Campbell ambitions – 'Neither I nor any man who knows the state of that country (Islay) think it good or profitable to His Majesty or to the realm to make the name of Campbell greater in the Isles than they are already; nor yet to root out one pestiferous clan, and plant another little better'.[13]

His advice was swept aside, however, as were the pleas of Sir James MacDonald who, writing from prison, offered to pay 8000 merks rental for the lands of Islay, or failing that, to transport his kinsmen to Ireland if the government would give him money to rent lands in Antrim. Campbell of Cawdor was given a commission to proceed against Angus Og, and immediately fitted out an expedition (including a train of artillery for which he had to pay himself) to take Islay by force.

Angus Og might still have surrendered and survived, but other greedy men were also getting their fingers into the pie. The Lord Chancellor of Scotland, The Earl of Dunfermline, upon some ambition of his own, sent a secret messenger to Angus Og, advising him, as if with the authority of the Privy Council, that if he yielded up Dunyveg to himself, together with some hostages taken from the Bishop, all proceedings against him would be suspended. When Angus Og complied, Dunfermline sent a second message, instructing him to reoccupy the castle as its official Constable, and to refuse any demands for its surrender until he should receive further orders from the Chancellor.

Thoroughly duped and confused, Angus Og therefore defied Cawdor's summons, and the fortress was bombarded into submission. Colkitto of Colonsay escaped, but fourteen of the defenders were summarily executed, and Angus Og with some of his closest advisors was sent to Edinburgh for trial. The Earls of Argyll and Dunfermline both denied any part in the affair, and Angus Og was executed on 8th July 1615. The Campbells now had possession of Islay, and its subsequent dereliction bore witness to their occupation. The Castle of Finlaggan, once the administrative centre of the ancient Lordship of the Isles, was left to crumble until only some ruined masonry and the outline of its foundations in the earth remained to evoke a memory of the time when Clan Donald was great. Today it is a featureless place, the old walls grass-grown, and even the small chapel where once the children of the chiefs were buried, is no more than an empty ruin of nettles, tumbled tomb-stones, and neglect.

In May 1615, shortly before his brother's execution, Sir James MacDonald succeeded in escaping from Edinburgh Castle, aided by the Chief of Keppoch and the young Moydartach of Clanranald. At Eigg he was joined by Colkitto of Colonsay and others of the clan who in the interim had taken to piracy among the Hebridean islands. In June they returned to Islay and briefly drove Cawdor's creatures from the Clan Donald lands before sailing to Kintyre where they resolved to make a stand near the Island of Cara. But by August the government forces had mobilised, and Argyll, with the support of some English warships, recaptured Islay and outmanoeuvred the small MacDonald warband, to bring an end to their brief rebellion. Colkitto surrendered Dunyveg upon promise of being allowed to return to Colonsay, but Argyll had no mind to leave that troublesome pirate free, and a few years later he was captured again and imprisoned in the Campbells' dungeon at Innischonnel.

Sir James MacDonald and the Chief of Keppoch escaped to Spain.

They were later recalled by the King and pardoned for their offence, but while Keppoch was permitted to return to his lands in Lochaber, Sir James remained an exile in London and never saw Scotland or the Western Isles again. Sometimes called the last of the great MacDonalds, he died in 1626, leaving no heir to succeed him.

And 'thus ended the last great struggle of the once powerful Clanranald of Islay and Kintyre to retain from the grasp of the Campbells these ancient possessions of their tribe'; concluded Donald Gregory in his *History of the Western Highlands.* The Clan Donald were, forgivably, less dispassionate. 'You stole green pleasant Islay from us by trickery, and Kintyre with its fertile plains', wrote the hereditary bard, Iain Lom MacVurich. And for Alasdair, son of Colkitto marching from Ardnamurchan in that summer of 1644 with the lands of the Campbells at the point of his sword, there were many wrongs to be avenged.

PART III
LOWLAND ANTAGONISTS

CHAPTER 5

The Marquis of Argyll

In 1644, the MacCailein Mor and Chieftain of Clan Diarmaid was Archibald Campbell, eighth Earl and first Marquis of Argyll. Perhaps the ablest of his line, he was nevertheless a man of powerful contrasts whom history has variously portrayed. Part Douglas by blood, but Campbell by name and disposition; part feudal magnate, part gaelic chief; a Highlander yet trusted in the Lowlands; a skilful and pragmatic politician shackled to a fanatical Presbyterian creed; he was respected and loved by his closest associates, who found him mild and affable, inclined to simplicity and with a 'far reaching apprehension', while his enemies pronounced him 'the deepest statesman, the most crafty, subtle, and ever-reaching politician that this age could produce.'[14]

Physically, he was not cast in the heroic mould. He was slight of build; his hair light brown with the reddish tinge that was common among the Campbells. His nose was long, becoming pendulous with age; a heavy chin, thin lips and a pursed mouth, and his eyes, which were grey-blue, 'ill-placed' so that he was often called the 'gley'd Argyll'. Portraits of him differ considerably. As a young man, he appears dull and rather sour. The later Castle Campbell portrait (now destroyed) showed a tired and melancholic face, but in middle age a dour severity is the chief impression. Only the last portrait has a seeming malevolent aspect which might reflect the character which his enemies put upon him. The clothes of the nobleman have been exchanged for the black gown and skull cap of a Presbyterian cleric. The squint is more pronounced, and the mouth is twisted, giving him a sinister appearance as if the crooked face were somehow symbol of a crooked soul within.

In stark contrast to the Gaelic tradition, he had no joy or skill in battle, and was generally thought to be a coward. Bishop Burnet, who was not unduly biased against him, recorded in his Memoirs that the Campbell was cruel in cold blood, and events confirm that when he had the power to be so, he was brutally vindictive. Nevertheless, his authority was such that at no time was his leadership questioned by his clan.

He was probably born in 1607, the youngest child and only son among five daughters. By all accounts he had a bitter childhood, since his mother, a daughter of the Douglas Earl of Morton, died shortly after his birth, and his father abandoned him three years later. From the age of three he was placed in the hands of 'curators' – chief of whom was his uncle, the Earl of Morton – in whose care he underwent a secluded and solitary education in classics and the Protestant religion. At sixteen like other sons of the nobility, he entered the University of St Andrews, but events prevented him thereafter from making the usual continental tour which at that time was the fashionable conclusion to a university education. Consequently he was neither 'marred nor fashioned' by foreign influences or the English court, and the omission was later an important factor since as a result the Presbyterian ministers were more inclined to trust him. Nor did he ever display any interest in foreign affairs, and the concentration of his ability on domestic politics – in which he excelled – was also a principal reason for his later influence.

From an early age, albeit under the guidance of his curators, he was burdened with responsibility for the welfare of his House, and like his predecessors, he was extremely conscious of the Campbell power, regarding its preservation and extension as a duty as well as an ambition. But in those first years his inheritance was marred by scandal and encumbered with debt.

His father, Archibald the Grim, seventh Earl of Argyll, had been principally responsible for the extinction of the Clan MacGregor and the ruin of the Clan Donald of Islay. The Campbells' domain had been considerably enlarged in consequence, but despite his power, he had been less successful in the sphere of national politics. Three years after his first wife died, he went to London where he married a minor heiress, Anne Cornwallis (her mother owned Earls Court), and as she was an ardent Catholic, he also embraced the Roman faith. For this indiscretion he was declared traitor and outlaw, and in 1618 was forced to leave Scotland for Western Flanders, where he took service under Philip III of Spain. In 1627, however, Charles I had the sentence reversed, and he returned to London and spent the last ten years of his life in somewhat reduced circumstances in Drury Lane.

Before leaving Scotland, Archibald the Grim had conveyed the fee simple of his hereditary estates to his son, and thereafter enjoyed the income from the property as a life tenant. But while the seventh Earl survived in exile in London, father and son were continually at odds over the inheritance, and the chief preoccupation of the young Argyll – while he was still Lord Lorne – was to prevent the estates from falling into the hands of the children of his father's second marriage.

The quarrel made it politically advisable for Lord Lorne to visit the court in London. The King quite liked him, and the Queen, who had a shrewd appreciation of his potential power in Scotland, advised that the young man should be entered on the royal pay-roll – notwithstanding that he was a Presbyterian. A marriage was arranged with Elizabeth Stewart, daughter of the Duke of Lennox, but she eloped with Lord Maltravers, son of the Earl of Arundel – preferring, said the gossips, a crooked marriage to a crooked man. Instead, Lorne married Margaret Douglas, the daughter of his guardian, the Earl of Morton.

At the same time, his suit against his father progressed satisfactorily. In 1628, Lord Lorne was made Privy Councillor, and in 1631, Archibald the Grim was ordered to renounce his life rent in exchange for a fixed subsistence. Two years later, Parliament confirmed Lorne in his full inheritance, causing the old Earl to complain to the King: 'Sir, I must know this man better than you can do; you have brought me low that you may raise him; which I doubt not you will live to repent. For he is a man of craft, subtlety and falsehood, and can love no man; and if he ever has it in his power to do you mischief, he will be sure to do it.'[15] Father and son hated each other most cordially, and the remark was less prescient than splenetic. Secure in his estates, Lorne could now devote greater attention to events in Scotland where the political situation was rapidly moving towards a crisis.

Certain factors are of crucial importance if that distemper which was soon to convulse all of Scotland and ultimately provoke the Civil War is properly to be understood.

First, in contrast to England, the Reformation in Scotland was not led by the Crown, but by the nobles in opposition to it. Consequently it was the nobles and not the Crown who profited from the lands and wealth despoiled from the monastic foundations. Second, while in England the break with Rome was schismatic rather than heretical in so far as the English divines still recognised one Catholic and Apostolic Church under the monarch, the Protestant religion which was established in Scotland looked to the radical doctrines of Calvin for its genesis, and because it was introduced in opposition to a French Queen Regent and a French educated Catholic Queen (Mary), it developed a strongly nationalistic bias with anti monarchical undertones.

On ascending the throne of the two kingdoms, James VI and I had been gratified to lay his hands on the Tudor instruments of autocratic power, not realising that a despotism which might have seemed acceptable under Elizabeth I would prove an anachronism when administered by her inept successor. With the distasteful experience of his Scottish minority behind him, James set out to revive the power of the monarchy in Scotland as well as England – developing for the purpose a theory of 'Kingcraft' which, when he practised it, stood him in good stead, and a notion of Divine Right which was to prove fatal to his successor who believed in it. The anti-monarchical utterances of the Presbyterian ministers had convinced James that an episcopal form of Church government was essential to support the authority of the Crown, and for so long as his hierarchy of Bishops was little more than an administrative stratum grafted onto the main body of a Presbyterian polity, an uneasy accommodation was sustained. But as the apologetics of Presbyterianism hardened, notions of Divine Right became increasingly opposed to ideas of a King ruling under Divine Law, while theories of an absolute monarchy collided inevitably with the theocratic pretensions of the Scottish Kirk.

When James died in 1625, a stranger came to the throne of the two kingdoms. Although Charles I had been born in Scotland, he had left the country at the age of four, and did not return for nearly thirty years. Destined originally for the Church, he knew little about the land of his birth, its institutions, its life, or its people. His only contact was with the Scots who had migrated to the court, many of them sycophants, whom he knew only as individuals, with little understanding of their heritage, environment, or the family connections and other ties which held them and others of their kind together. Unlike his father, to whom experience had imparted a certain silly wisdom, Charles's horizon was bounded by the artificial limits of the court, where formal protocol protected him from harsh reality, and disguised the true abilities of the courtiers he trusted rather than his own. And like others of his ill-fated House, he was inclined to place his faith in men who were themselves unfaithful.

Charles I's initial blunder came at the very beginning of his reign. He had inherited an uneasy peace in Scotland, and one which had only been achieved by keeping the country divided. In practice, this had meant keeping the nobles and the Kirk (those original allies of the Reformation) apart. The key factor should not have been too hard to see. However much James VI may have exasperated the Presbyterians by his episcopalian proclivities, as long as he left the nobles' property alone, he was safe. But in 1625, Charles I attempted by an Act of Privy Council, to recall to the Crown all lands alienated since the accession of Mary Queen of Scots in 1542. Since this included most of the old Church property which had passed into secular hands, there were few among the nobility who did not stand to lose. No matter that tithes were an open scandal, or that the King only intended to provide a living wage to the ministry for whose support the system of tithes had originally been devised. The nobles were not interested in justice; nor did the Kirk wish to see money wrung back from the nobility in order to pamper an idolatrous and prelatical Church. The aura of popery which surrounded the pretensions of the English Archbishop, Laud, and his attempts to introduce what many considered to be the Romish practice, confirmed the worst rumours put about by Presbyterian extremists. Kirk and nobility were thus encouraged to make common cause and to renew their unnatural alliance.

In April 1637, the King's attempt to introduce the new Prayer Book provoked the famous riot in St Giles – although it was not quite the spontaneous event that many people at the time supposed, since the disturbance was planned and organised by some of the Presbyterian leaders on the previous evening. The momentum which developed was real enough, however, and the King's second blunder was to under-estimate the gravity of the situation. A further attempt to impose the Prayer Book caused a fresh riot in October, and when in November 1637, the Scots established the 'Tables' – tantamount to a Committee of Public Safety – the idea of revolution began to take a tangible form. Opposition to the King having thus become institutionalised, it was a short step to the framing of a formal Declaration or Band of Union, and on 28th January 1638, the National Covenant of Scotland was signed amid scenes of great popular emotion in Greyfriars churchyard in Edinburgh.

The King conceded so far as to permit a General Assembly of the Kirk to convene at Glasgow in 1638, but he instructed the Marquis of Hamilton, whom he appointed as Royal Commissioner to preside over the deliberations, to dissolve it at the first sign of trouble. He also told Hamilton to play for time, since his real intention was nothing less than a three-pronged invasion of Scotland – by land across the border, a seaborne landing in Aberdeenshire, and an Irish expedition against the Western Highlands – 'for I expect that not anything can reduce that people to obedience but only force' – and he needed six months to prepare.

The western clans still adhered to the old Roman Catholic faith, and although Presbyterian iconoclasts had vandalised some of the churches of the Isles, smashing ancient celtic crosses and other relics, the Highlanders had remained largely outwith the religious controversy that followed the Reformation. The Campbells alone as a clan had adopted Presbyterianism, and because of their greater access to the Lowlands and the involvement of their chief in national affairs, the leading families were more directly concerned with the developing current of events.

The Campbells had done moderately well out of the Reformation, but unlike the other Scottish Earls, Lord Lorne had few material ambitions in the Lowlands since the principal sphere of Campbell aggrandisement lay in the Highland north and west. The revocation of Church lands did not therefore greatly affect his interest. Moreover, as one of the great magnates and a member of the Privy Council, he remained somewhat aloof from the middle ranking baronage who formed the opposition.

He was, however, extremely anti-clerical, and strongly opposed to the secular pretensions of the prelates. This was partly due to his strict Presbyterian upbringing, and partly to political interest. In 1635, when the office of Chancellor became vacant, Lord Lorne had 'dealt' for it, but the King appointed Archbishop Spottiswoode, thus passing over the most powerful subject in Scotland in favour of a priest. The following year Lorne was involved in a violent dispute with the Bishop of Galloway who had fined and banished a Campbell client, and he also defended a non-conformist minister who had been arraigned before the Court of High Commission for preaching against the episcopal system.

Shortly after this, Lorne convened a meeting of the Earl of Rothes and other opposition leaders to discuss what steps should be taken to curb the importunities of the Bishops, but apart from this, his relations with the malcontents were generally discreet. Campbell of Loudoun was one of the foremost secular orators of the Covenanting Party, and he probably had his chief's permission and connivance. Moreover, Lorne drew closer to the Presbyterian ministry as their influence increased, and he was possibly a frequent though secret visitor to the house of Archibald Johnstone of Wariston – the brilliant but fanatical lawyer who was the chief architect and draftsman of the National Covenant. He probably had warning of the riot in St Giles and conveniently absented himself, while in the months that followed, he may have supplied Wariston with information concerning the secret proceedings of the Privy Council. But he did not sign the Covenant itself, and to most men he was enigmatic.

In May 1638, he accompanied the Earls of Traquair and Roxburgh to London to report officially on the situation to the King. There is no detailed record of this conference, but Lorne was said to have spoken his mind in criticism of the Bishops. The King was displeased and rumour had it that Lorne would be arrested – possibly on the advice of his father, who told Charles that his son 'would wind him a pirn'. He left ahead of the other members of the delegation, however, and returned safely to Scotland.

Charles is said to have distrusted him from this time, but indeed he had good cause to suspect that Lorne would join the opposition, since he was himself playing the Campbell false. His strategy of an invasion to subdue the Covenanters by force, included a plan whereby an army of Irishes under Ranald MacDonald, Earl of Antrim were to invade Argyle. Antrim's reward was to be the old Clan Donald lands in Kintyre which the Campbells had acquired in 1617. In Ireland, the Earl of Strafford, who was possibly the ablest of the King's administrators, vehemently opposed such a scheme, for (of Antrim) 'he is as much able to do it as I to take upon me the Cross with so many for the Holy Land' – and he argued that Lorne's doubtful loyalty should be strengthened and not under-mined. But Charles was beginning to display that callous and misdirected cunning which would bring them all to ruin, and Antrim was confirmed in his promise of Kintyre. It was indeed a foolish plan, and the first in a sequence of events which would lead to the Irish rebellion – that other great disaster of this King's career.

Inevitably, the secret got out, and in Scotland, Lorne complained to the Marquis of Hamilton, the Royal Commissioner, that if Antrim invaded Kintyre, he would defend it. In Argyll itself, the Campbells mustered in readiness, while Hamilton, in a characteristically serpentine and meddling way, wrote to Charles, encouraging him to use Antrim as an instrument to harass Lorne into declaring for the royalists! But the Campbell was a cautious politician. He signed the King's Covenant – the Government's response to the National Covenant – with other members of the Privy Council, and his further correspondence with Hamilton gave no indication of the action which he contemplated. Nevertheless, personal motive and political calculation prompted him to choose an opportune moment to declare his support for the Covenanters. Inherent in his position as the MacCailein Mor was the duty to protect his patri-mony against whomsoever might threaten it, and regardless of whether he had declared for the malcontents or not, the King had been prepared to rob him of Kintyre and grant it to his hereditary enemy – a scion of Clan Donald. Charles did not reward neutrality it seemed. At the same time, religious conviction now became a predominant motivating factor in his life, since although he had been brought up a strict Presbyterian, it was during these days that he was 'converted' in the full, emotive sense of the word, and the religious quarrel took on a prime importance. During the early sessions of the Glasgow Assembly in November 1638, the Moderator, Alexander Henderson, conducted nightly prayer meetings which the Campbell attended, and, according to his friends, it was at one of these that his conversion occurred. Royalists were subsequently quick to allege that the occasion was too convenient for to be genuine, but his private life thereafter did seem to confirm the sincerity of his professed belief. Others among the Covenanting nobles would drop the mask of piety as soon as occasion suited, but Lorne never did. As he grew older, his preoccupation with religion took on a more sinister aspect, and it was one of the strange contradictions in his character that a man with such a clear political acumen could be so chained to medieval intolerance and a fanatical creed. Yet it was this contradiction which now enabled him to become the leader of the Covenanting movement. Greater than any of the other secular lords who were ranged against the King, his interests were neither so similar nor so obvious as theirs, while his religious belief gave him more in common with the extreme Presbyterians who trusted him as they did no other noble.

Political calculation doubtless determined the detail of his actions. In the middle of 1638, his father Archibald the Grim died in London, and Lorne became the eighth Earl of Argyll. The need for caution was thus past. The decisive moment was approaching when his power might tip the balance. As the great distemper spread throughout the country, he knew the doubts and fears of the majority of Scots who shrank still from open rebellion, but he realised also the impotence of the King. He knew who among the Privy Councillors were secret Covenanters, and that of all of them, only he was ideally qualified to become the effective leader of the movement.

When therefore, Hamilton dissolved the Glasgow Assembly, the Earl of Argyll remained in his place, and when the uproar had abated, he asked leave to speak. He had been commanded by the King, he said, to attend the Assembly as one of the royal Assessors, and he had acted properly and honourably in that capacity. But he would never be moved by private ambition to flatter the King or persuade him to 'run violent courses'.

He begged the Assembly not to misunderstand his delay in declaring his position, since from the beginning he had been 'set their way'. By remaining a member of the Privy Council he had hoped to be more useful than he could have been otherwise. 'But now of late, matters had come to such a height that he found it behoved him to join himself openly with their society except he should prove a knave.'[16] From this moment the Covenanters began to defer to his advice, and he stepped naturally into the pre-eminent position among the other leaders of the opposition movement in Scotland.

But as Argyll later told his son: 'I never thought of those dire consequences which presently followed.'

CHAPTER 6

The Marquis of Montrose

James Graham, fifth Earl and later Marquis of Montrose, is one of the most romantic, and also controversial figures of seventeenth century Scottish history. Few men have been so admired or so vilified both in their own time and since. His contemporary, Clarendon, described him as 'one of the most illustrious persons of the age in which he lived'. For the French Cardinal de Retz, he recalled the great classical heroes of a bygone, better age, while Carlyle, when later considering the anatomy of heroes and hero worship, regarded him as the epitome of the 'hero cavalier'. To his enemies, however, he was a bloody murderer, who loosed the savage Highlanders upon his christian Lowland kindred; a man who contrary to his professed ideals, joined the Covenant out of pique and deserted it for ambition. And this caricature came to be perpetuated, partly through the bias of later Whig historians and the lasting effectiveness of Covenant propaganda, and partly because the Restoration for which he fought did not produce an heroic age.

The answer, if one is required, hangs on the question of whether a man who joins a Party for reasons which he believes initially to be right, is thereafter obliged to support it even to excess, or whether loyalty to faction is more important than loyalty to country – or an ideal. When the parties finally divided and the great Civil War began, the most effective protagonists on either side were often considerably less noble than the causes which they claimed to represent. The extremists had the easy choice, but the moderates – men whose loyalty belonged to neither extreme, who opposed what seemed unjust and obsolete, but would not commit themselves to the uncompromising structures which the revolutionaries attempted to impose – were trapped in a mortal dilemma. For if moderation was not to equate merely with apathy and silence, such men themselves were forced to choose, and as best they might, defend that principle against the extreme doctrines which threatened to destroy it. If, during the progress of a State, the constituted authorities resort to open war against each other, even the moderate may be compelled to draw his sword for what he believes to be the best inheritance of his country. There follows the further distinction of whether the hand that reaches for the sword is guided by determination – or despair. During the Civil War, the second alternative may be said to have found a brief expression in Lord Falkland. In Scotland, the first was personified in Montrose.

Many things have been claimed of him – some rightly, some exaggerated – but he was by common consent, one of the greatest soldiers of the age, and 'perhaps the most brilliant natural military genius disclosed by the Civil War'.[17] Above all, he was one of the very few Lowlanders ever to win the respect of the western clans and who could command Highland caterans in battle. And in the retrospect of causes lost and battles won, he assumed that peculiar, heroic quality, not least because of the antique cast of mind which lent a haunting and romantic aspect to his character. He rode to war like some paladin of medieval romance, and left behind 'an inspiration and a name which would survive the ruin of his hopes'.

He was not a political philosopher in the conventional sense of the term, although some have endeavoured to describe him so. He did not set out to design a new polity but to interpret the constitution as he believed it already existed, and the simplicity of his conception did not fit him for a statesman because he had no eye for the complexity of the situation in which he found himself. As a politician he was ingenuous and no match for his Campbell adversary. The idealist who could not equivocate with honour, he had little chance within the darkening corridors of revolutionary intrigue, where resolution blunted on the tortuous arguments of clever men's deceit.

This man, so different from Argyll in personality, talent, and belief, was to become the Campbell's mortal enemy.

Montrose was born in about 1612, the only son among five daughters. His mother was Margaret Ruthven, grand-daughter of the grim Earl who had led the murderers of Rizzio, and child of the Earl of Gowrie whose ill-fated house was associated with necromancy and dark deeds of violence. It was said that she consulted witches at his birth, who told that the baby would trouble all of Scotland, but she did not live to watch the prophecy mature.

The boy spent his childhood on the family estates of Old Montrose in Angus, and at Kincardine Castle, by Auchterarder in Perthshire. His eldest sister, Lilias, was married to Sir John Colquhoun of Luss, and so he was a frequent visitor to their house at Rossdhu and the hills around Loch Lomond, where he acquired some knowledge of the Highlands.

In 1626 he succeeded to the Earldom on the death of his father, and his education, like that of Argyll, was overseen by curators. Of these the most important, and the greatest influence, was Lord Napier, who had married another sister, Margaret, and was then Treasurer Depute of Scotland. Scholar, philosopher, and a public servant of rare integrity, Napier might have been a Scottish Clarendon and the historian of his time. Throughout his life, he remained the young Earl's principal mentor and closest friend.

The Grahams were a large family with numerous cadet branches – Inchbrakie, Braco, Monzie, Gorthy, Fintry, Claverhouse, Morphie, Tamrawer, Balgowan, and many others – while the Earls of Menteith and Airth were also cousins to the Graham chief. In their company, unlike the young Argyll, he had a pampered and privileged childhood; handsome, a natural sportsman, and popular with his many friends. At the age of fifteen he also went to the University of St Andrews, and at seventeen he married Magdalen, a younger daughter of Lord Carnegie of Kinnaird, who had had a distinguished career in the royal service as a member of the Privy Council and Parliamentary Commissioner for Fife.

When King Charles I eventually returned to Scotland for his northern coronation in 1633, Montrose was already regarded as a rising star of the younger generation and a certain candidate for preferment. At the end of 1632 he had attained his majority, and it would have been an excellent opportunity at the very start of his career, for him to be presented to the King. His antecedents seemed to assure him of the royal favour. His father, the fourth Earl of Montrose, had been President of the Privy Council, and his grandfather Viceroy of Scotland. His sponsors were to have been Lord Carnegie who was high in the King's esteem and about to be created Earl of Southesk, and Lord Napier who was one of the four peers chosen to hold the canopy over the King's head at the coronation.

But ironically for a man who was to become one of the most loyal servants of the Stuart dynasty, Montrose's early relationship with Charles I was singularly inauspicious. In 1633 he was not in Scotland, having left some months previously for the continent. The reason for his absence can only be guessed at, but it was probably on account of a particularly unpleasant scandal involving his younger sister Katherine, who was seduced and abducted by her brother-in-law, Sir John Colquhoun of Luss. But Colquhoun was charged with witchcraft not incest, since it was alleged that he accomplished his evil design through the agency of a German servant called Carlippis – 'ane necromancer' – who had used certain love philtres and a 'jewel of gold with divers precious diamonds or rubies which was poisoned and intoxicat', to bewitch the girl and bring about her ruin. The matter came to the notice of the King, and Montrose, shamed by the stain upon his family's honour, either decided, or was advised, to depart the country before the coronation, leaving his wife and two small sons in the care of his father-in-law, Carnegie.

Comparatively little is known about his travels in Europe, except that in France he attended the famous school of arms at Angers where he first began seriously to study military science. The Thirty Years War still raged in Europe, and the continent was a breeding ground for aspiring soldiers. This was where Montrose's inclinations lay, and his own campaigns would later indicate that he made a special study of the tactics of Gustavus Adolphus of Sweden, who had been killed at Lutzen only a short time before.

It was not until 1636, three years after the Scottish coronation therefore, that Montrose was first presented to Charles I. Returning to Scotland by way of London, he approached the Marquis of Hamilton as the senior Scot at court to be his sponsor, stating that he wished 'to put himself in the service of the King'.

Hamilton was to exert an obstructive and disconcerting influence over the early dealings between Charles I and Montrose, as indeed he was to play a disastrous part in the Scottish Troubles to come. The Hamiltons were the senior branch of the Stewart family besides the royal line – a fact of ancestry which made the Marquis prey to an uneasy but undefined ambition.

He and Charles I had grown up together, and after the assassination of the Duke of Buckingham, Hamilton had naturally succeeded to the position of Royal Favourite, as Master of the Horse and Gentleman of the Bedchamber. More recently he had become a member of both the English and Scottish Privy Councils, and the King's principal adviser on Scottish affairs. He was by nature melancholic, tortuous and pessimistic in his thought, and given to irresolute intrigue, but a natural taciturnity led many to think him wiser than he was. He thus became, in a sense, the victim of over-estimation, and Charles believed him to be more able and trustworthy than was true, while his enemies regarded him as being more dangerous than he deserved. This at least was the contemporary Clarendon's estimation of him, and so 'the world came to regard as a knave a man who was principally a fool'.[18]

Hamilton viewed Montrose's arrival with some alarm, since the young Graham was altogether too prepossessing not to be a potential rival in the King's affection. He therefore agreed to present Montrose at court but warned him that the King was prejudiced against the Scots – at the same time advising Charles that the young Earl was arrogant and conceited, and likely to endanger the King's interests in Scotland. When Montrose was presented to the King in front of the court, Charles merely extended him a hand to kiss and coldly turned away. The snub was worse in that it was public, and the young Earl's hopes of entering the royal service were thus dashed at the outset.[19]

It was afterwards alleged by Montrose's critics that, angry and disappointed at this personal affront, he returned to Scotland and at once aligned himself with the King's enemies. But the available evidence and the precise sequence of events would seem rather to indicate that such an interpretation reflects the bias of historians and not the principal. It was true that Montrose returned to find that he had become a figure of considerable interest to the Scottish faction leaders who hoped to secure for their cause the prestige of his name, as well as the talent and enthusiasm which Charles I had so misguidedly rejected. But initially he devoted himself to the administration of his estates, and it was not until a year later – in the autumn of 1637 – that he first appeared in company with the opposition leaders. It was generally held to have been his friend the Earl of Rothes and Robert Murray, the Minister of Methven, who converted him to the cause – and from the beginning his motivation seems to have been genuinely anti-clerical, a political view which he inherited directly from Lord Napier who had always held that to invest churchmen with power and office was to encourage corruption and disturbance. This was not a religious motive in the narrow sense, since throughout his life Montrose displayed a tolerance of belief which was unusual in the seventeenth century. Rather, on the one hand, he made a distinction between the things of God and of Caesar, while on the other, he held that the preservation of constitutional liberty and the King's prerogative were indivisible under the same Law – so that opposition if constitutionally justified was still compatible with loyalty to the King. Such a theory presupposed, however, that a King like Charles I could govern in peace with a Presbyterian Kirk, and naively overlooked the fact that no Stuart Monarch would ever share such an ideal. In this simplicity, he failed also to understand the ambitions of the malcontents, so that although he became ostensibly one of the leaders, he was in reality one of the led, since the opposition was neither as spontaneous as it seemed, nor the issues so genuinely constitutional as Rothes and others were at pains to suggest. Wiser heads like Napier recognised this truth and held aloof.

During the winter of 1637, Montrose became an enthusiastic and vocal member of the opposition, and together with Campbell of Loudoun, Rothes, and Lindsay of the Byres (another friend from college days), he was elected to represent the nobility on the Committee of the Tables. In February 1638, he was one of the first signatories of the National Covenant, and in the months that followed, he was active in touring the country and obtaining further signatures.

Having joined a faction, Montrose inevitably became factious, but to the end of his life he professed always to adhere to this first, 'true' Covenant – and his quarrel with the extremists was that they had broken it. For this reason, the famous document itself deserves a brief description.

It was intended as a Band of Union – not uncommon among a rebellious nobility – 'to be made legally'. It was, said Rothes, 'A band with Jehovah', and it was, said a later Kirk historian, 'an expedient admirably devised, the success of which exceeded even their own most sanguine expectations.'[20] The Covenant has also been described as 'a candid and straightforward document, temperately expressed and accurately directed to the grievances which it was designed to remedy. The claim was to both spiritual and religious freedom, and the formidable sanction behind it was at once ecclesiastical, feudal, and democratic.'[21]

The first part of the text was a repetition of an earlier Covenant against popery signed by King James V in 1580. The second part rehearsed all the Acts of Parliament passed since the Reformation in favour of the Reformed Church. The third part, which was the most important, contained a pledge to defend the true religion against all innovations 'already introduced' and all corruptions of public government 'till they be tried and allowed in the Assemblies and in Parliament', and it concluded with the following, apparently unequivocal statements:

'We declare before God and men that we have no intention nor desire to attempt anything which may be to the dishonour of God or to the diminution of the King's greatness or authority. But on the contrary we promise and swear that we shall, to the utmost of our power,... stand in defence of our dread sovereign, the King's Majesty, his person and authority, in the defence and preservation of the foresaid true religion, liberties, and laws of the Kingdom... as also to the mutual defence and assistance, everyone of us another in the same cause of maintaining the true religion, and His Majesty's authority...

against all sort of persons whatsoever... Neither do we fear the foul aspersion of rebellion... seeing that what we do... ariseth from an unfeigned desire to maintain the true worship of God, the Majesty of the King, and the peace of the Kingdom.'

The document was superscribed: 'For God and the King'.

It may be possible, in the retrospect, to ascribe an ambivalent interpretation to certain sections of the text, and to make a distinction between the spirit in which the Covenant was signed by thousands of people, and the intention with which it may have been drafted by the brilliant lawyer Johnstone of Wariston and the inner circle of the opposition. It might imply, for example, that the promise to defend the King's authority 'in defence and preservation of the true religion' was valid only if Charles himself espoused Presbyterianism. Did mutual defence 'against all sorts of persons whatsoever' legitimise resistance to the King? The Covenanters' use of ambiguous terminology became clear later – when they also justified a military alliance with the English Parliament and the invasion of England on the grounds of their 'unfeigned desire to maintain the true worship of God, the Majesty of the King, and the peace of the Kingdom'.

In February 1638, however, the vast majority of the subscribers took the Covenant as they read it, free of ominous interpretation. The Rev. Robert Baillie, for example, a Presbyterian minister whose letters and Diaries are one of the most enlightening sources of this period, could write with complete sincerity of the Covenant:

> 'I do not only believe that there is no word in it that makes against the King's full authority so far as either reason or religion can extend it... not only do I believe this, but have professed to say as much before the whole meeting at Edinburgh... If any presently or hereafter shall abuse any claims of this write – to overthrow the King's authority etc... I can make it evident before the world that the (document) has no such errors... else I should never have subscribed it.'[22]

Montrose therefore, was not alone, nor so singularly naive, in his interpretation of the original Covenant. The Rev. Baillie when the time came, lacked the courage of his convictions, but Montrose never changed his position and always claimed that his subsequent actions were consistent with his Covenanting oath.

At the Glasgow Assembly of 1638, prior to Argyll's sudden announcement, Montrose was a noisy and controversial participant, but although he was involved in the dubious work of packing the Assembly with Covenant supporters, even Hamilton could see that he was not among the real leaders of the movement. 'It is more probable that these people have somewhat else in their thoughts than religion,' he wrote to the King. 'Now for all the Covenanters, I shall say only this: in general they may all be placed in one roll as they now stand; but certainly Sire, those that have broached this business and still hold it aloft are Rothes, Balmerino, Lindsay, Lothian, Loudoun, Yester, Cranstoun. There are many others as forward *in show* – amongst them none more vainly foolish than Montrose.'[23]

CHAPTER 7

The Approaching Conflict

In the months following the Glasgow Assembly, King and Covenanters prepared for war. The Scots recalled the veteran General Leslie, who had distinguished himself in the German Wars, and with him returned a number of other experienced mercenaries, happy to find employment in their native country and in their national cause, who trained the fresh levies and formed the nucleus of a professional officer corps. Arms and equipment were shipped from Holland, and a cannon foundry established at Potterow. The Presbyterian ministers toured the country, persuading the people to shake out their purses and contribute to a war chest, while the nobility in the shires began raising local regiments among the tenantry.

In February 1639, Montrose obtained his first military command when he was sent to quell a royalist rising among the Gordons in Aberdeenshire. During this short campaign he displayed talent and energy as a commander, but also a characteristic impatience with the interference of the ministers and decisions by committee. His refusal to sack the city of Aberdeen caused him to be criticised for unnecessary leniency, but an incident involving the Marquis of Huntly, the principal catholic royalist and Chief of the Gordon clan, was to have more serious repercussions in the future. Precisely what happened is unclear, but after negotiating a truce on behalf of the Gordons and other northern Catholics, Huntly apparently went to Aberdeen at Montrose's request and on his personal guarantee of safe-conduct, in order to attend a Covenant committee which had been convened to 'take a course for the final settlement of the North'. After the meeting, however, Huntly was not permitted to leave, but forced to accompany the Presbyterian army to Edinburgh, where, on his refusal to sign the Covenant, he was imprisoned in the Castle.

Later historians described this as 'the only mean action' of Montrose's life, and Huntly bore a grudge against the Graham ever after. 'He could never be gained to join cordially with him nor to swallow that indignity... whence it came to pass that such as were equally enemies to them both...

in the end prevailed so far as to ruinate and destroy both of them and the King by consequent.'[24]

It is likely that the committee, intent on ruining the northern catholics, over-ruled Montrose's safe-conduct, and also the truce terms which he had agreed with Huntly a few days previously. Monteth de Salmonet, writing a few years afterwards maintained that 'Montrose opposed with all his might their determination to break the parole which had been given; nevertheless, his single authority being insufficient to prevent it.'[25] It is significant also that Huntly's sons, Lord George Gordon and the Viscount Aboyne, who were witness to the event, did not share their father's grudge since they later were among Montrose's close comrades in arms. It is equally for speculation whether Huntly's resentment stemmed from the belief that the Graham had personally betrayed him, or because he had been witness to his humiliation at the hands of the Covenanting nobles whom he accounted his inferiors. It is certain, however, that he never forgave, and the quarrel was eventually to have fatal consequences for them both.

In the meanwhile the King's plans to invade Scotland ended in fiasco, and in June 1639, with his army mutinous and unpaid, and facing a superior Scottish force across the Tweed, Charles was forced to negotiate. The Pacification of Berwick was little more than a temporary truce since neither side was genuinely prepared to honour the doubtful terms of the Treaty – and the King was determined to reverse the resolutions of the Glasgow Assembly which had banned the Bishops and declared episcopacy to be unlawful, since in England, this was a precedent which he could not permit. In this atmosphere of distrust and hostility, five Scottish Earls – Rothes, Loudoun, Lothian, Dunfermline, and Montrose – were summoned to confer with Charles at Berwick.

The conference itself was a complete failure, and deteriorated into an exchange of threats, but it was important in that Montrose's friends later averred that 'the King had turned him at Berwick'. Probably the change of heart was nothing so precise. He remained a Covenanter – until the objects of the Covenant should be achieved – and so he was left, as he afterwards recalled, 'to wrestle betwixt extremities'.

At the same time, however, Montrose was becoming a prey to doubts – engendered by the strength of the revolutionary undercurrents which he had not anticipated, and the growing arrogance of the Kirk which he had experienced during the Aberdeen campaign. Possibly he detected more sinister ambitions among the extreme Covenanters and was concerned at the apparent intention of reducing the central authority of the Crown which in his own, conventional view, had to be preserved as the fundamental basis of political order. He had also been exposed to that peculiar charm of the Stuarts – which could so attract men's loyalty and yet defied precise description – and the harassed man at Berwick was different from the imperious monarch who had snubbed him before the English court.

In the months that followed, this unease grew, and came to focus more and more upon the ambitions of the Earl of Argyll, who now appeared increasingly to be directing the Covenanters' policy towards his own advantage. The Campbell had raised two regiments of his clansmen and embarked on a profitable persecution of the catholics whose houses he systematically looted. 'The Campbells were so greedy of booty'. reported a Jesuit priest, 'that they searched even the graves of the dead, and groped with their hands in pools of water, and behind walls, and were always most savage in places inhabited by catholics!'[26]

Argyll further abused his authority to pursue a dynastic feud against the Ogilvie family, who were Montrose's close neighbours in Angus. Lord Ogilvie held Airlie Castle for the King, and on learning that Argyll had obtained a commission of fire and sword to take it, Montrose received Ogilvie's surrender and garrisoned the house with a detachment of his own Covenant troops. Argyll was incensed by this interference. He dismissed Montrose's garrison, stripped and burned the castle, and then proceeded to pillage other Ogilvie properties in the area, afterwards obtaining a complete indemnity from the government under the King's authority. When Montrose protested, Argyll demanded that the Graham should be impeached for leniency towards enemies of the Covenant. The charge was monstrous, and Montrose, arraigned before the Earl of Leslie as General of the army, was completely exonerated. But the enmity between the two men was now an open thing, and worse was to follow.

After dealing with the Ogilvies, Argyll arrested the Earl of Atholl, another principal supporter of the King, by luring him to a conference at the Ford of Lyon. A member of Atholl's train, called Stewart of Ladywell, who was present at this event, reported to Montrose that Argyll had boasted of being the 'eighth man from The Bruce', and spoke of certain circumstances in which a King might be deposed. In the Covenanters' camp, Argyll's clansmen claimed openly that they followed 'King Campbell'.

Shortly afterwards, while Montrose was with the army on the border, he was approached by one of the Campbell surrogates and asked to sign a Band, the purport of which was that the Committee of Estates was unsuited to the conduct of a war and the government of Scotland should therefore be vested in a Triumvirate, consisting of Argyll, who was to rule the country north of the River Forth, and the Earls of Mar and Cassilis, who would administer the area south of it, seconded by a new Committee of which Montrose could be a member. Montrose posted to Edinburgh were he had a significant conversation with his old college friend Lindsay of the Byres (a supporter of Argyll) who told him of a plan to make 'a particular man' Dictator of Scotland 'after the Roman fashion'.

Montrose was now thoroughly alarmed, and he convened a meeting of those other moderates who like himself believed that a point had been reached when some action was necessary to save the Covenant from the extremists. Accordingly, at Cumbernauld they signed another Band of their own, pledging themselves to the defence of the National Covenant – against 'the particular and indirect practising of a few'. There were nineteen signatories to the document, but this moderate party included no men of any great power, and it was an indication of their weakness that they pledged also to keep the Band a secret.

In August 1640, the Scottish army crossed the Tweed and advanced to Newcastle, where they reopened negotiations with the King from a position of even greater strength. The Covenanters now demanded the abolition of episcopacy in England also, and although their 'Root and Branch' Petition was rejected in the English Parliament, Puritan support for it gave the Presbyterians cause to hope – and indeed, the provision was later inserted in the Solemn League and Covenant. Montrose argued against the Petition on the grounds that it was 'contrary to the minds of the most part of the subscribers of the National Covenant', but at Newcastle he was himself arraigned on charges of corresponding with the enemy because of a letter which he wrote to the King. Such charges if proven could have led to his impeachment for treason, but he defended himself on the grounds that since the same Articles of War also provided that any man 'who opened his mouth against the King's Majesty's person or authority... shall be punished as a traitor', by whose interpretation was the King to be deemed an enemy?

The charges were dropped, but Montrose was now highly suspect in Covenant eyes, and when in November 1640 the secret of the Cumbernauld Band also leaked out, he was again summoned before the Estates to answer fresh charges of treason. Some of the Presbyterian extremists demanded the death penalty, but the number of signatories, and in particular the inclusion of the Earl Marischal who was popular with the army, caused Argyll to hesitate. The wording of the Cumbernauld Band could not be called treasonable, and the Committee had to be content with censuring it as a 'divisive movement'. The document was ordered to be burned, and the destruction of the only evidence enabled Covenant propagandists to put whatever interpretation they liked upon this 'conspiracy', so that it was portrayed as a wicked and treacherous plot against the cause of religion and liberty. Many later historians followed this description, and it was not until a handwritten copy was discovered among Lord Balfour's papers two centuries afterwards that the true, moderate content of the Cumbernauld Band was revealed.

The Band at least persuaded Argyll to postpone any plans he may have had to make himself Dictator, but its discovery was a serious blow to Montrose's hopes of forming a moderate constitutional party in Scotland willing or able to oppose the extremists. In his dilemma, he sought the advise of his old guardian, Lord Napier, and from about Christmas 1640, a small family group consisting of Montrose, Napier, Sir George Stirling of Kier and Sir Archibald Stewart of Blackhall, took to meeting in Edinburgh in order to discuss the deteriorating situation in Scotland and debate what should be done. They concluded that the only remedy lay in persuading the King to visit Scotland in person, both so that he could assess the situation at first hand, and at the next Parliament satisfy the Covenanters on the question of religion and liberties. Charles should be warned of Argyll's plotting, and those suspected of treason should be formally charged before Parliament. Finally, certain important offices of State – notably the positions of Chancellor and Lord Treasurer – which had fallen vacant, should not be filled until the King arrived in Scotland and could appoint persons loyal to both himself and the principles of the Covenant, and who would fulfil their duties correctly in the interests of the Crown and the country.

The first problem was to establish communications with the King, and the group attempted to achieve this through the Duke of Lennox, by using a certain Colonel Walter Stewart – an acquaintance of Blackhall and a cousin of the Earl of Traquair – who claimed to have entry to the English court. By this means, Montrose now wrote at length to the King, setting out the causes of the distemper in Scotland, and advising Charles to come north and settle the religious question without delay. The letter reached the King, and accepting its advice, he replied to Montrose that he would attend the next session of Parliament – 'having a perfect intention to satisfy my people in their religion and just liberties' – and looked to the Earl for support.

Unfortunately, the plan miscarried. In March 1641, Montrose again met Stewart of Ladywell to confirm the latter's account of Argyll's treasonable utterances at the Ford of Lyon, but in a subsequent argument with the Minister of Methven – who had been one of his original sponsors but was also a Covenant busybody and bent on mischief – he foolishly revealed his suspicions and proofs against the Campbell. The whole was repeated to Argyll, who violently denied the accusation, and the Committee of Estates began a full inquiry into the allegations made by Montrose.

The Covenanters' intention was to dismiss the charges and discredit Ladywell's testimony on which they were based, but when Ladywell refused to retract his evidence he was arrested and imprisoned on a charge of 'leasing making'. The Committee passed a resolution stating that Montrose had 'misunderstood' the proposition put to him concerning the Triumvirate, and the Band which he had been asked to sign was conveniently forgotten. Other potential witnesses such as Mar and Cassilis were not called to testify.

In prison, and probably under torture, Stewart of Ladywell was eventually forced to withdraw his statement, but he consistently refused to admit that the charges against Argyll had been deliberately fabricated by Montrose. He did disclose however, that copies of his deposition had been sent to the Earl of Traquair in London by hand of the courier, Colonel Walter Stewart, and thus presumably had been seen by the King. Knowing through their spies at court of Montrose's correspondence with Charles, the Covenanters intercepted and arrested Walter Stewart while he was returning to Edinburgh. A search revealed the King's reply to Montrose, stating his intention to visit Scotland, together with some curious strips of paper containing cryptic notes in an elementary code of Stewart's devising which probably referred to verbal messages with which he had been entrusted. There was enough here, if not to prove a conspiracy, then at least to create suspicion of one, and in June 1640, Montrose, Napier, Kier, and Blackhall, were imprisoned upon Argyll's order. Covenant propaganda meanwhile, broadcast lurid reports of sinister plots against the National Covenant, which incriminated also the Earl of Traquair and the King himself.

Argyll's object was to keep Montrose and his friends in prison until after the King's visit to Scotland, so that he would have no opportunity to meet Charles or repeat his accusations in public. To prolong the process against the 'plotters', a huge indictment was drawn up by Wariston, accusing Montrose of perjury, oath-breaking, conspiracy, criminal leniency, military inefficiency, leasing-making, seeking preferment, and almost every other crime which he could conveniently devise – charges which the Graham dismissed as a 'pack of senseless lies' and 'a rhapsody of aforethought villainy'. Argyll took the additional precaution of executing Stewart of Ladywell so that the principal witness against himself was also ruthlessly removed.

In August 1641, therefore, Charles arrived in Edinburgh to find himself deprived of support, while the Covenanters were intent on nothing less that his complete capitulation. 'There was never a King so insulted over', wrote Sir Patrick Wemyss to the Secretary in London. 'It would pity a man's heart to see how he looks; for he is never at peace among them, and glad he is when he sees any man that he thinks loves him.'[27] There followed also an unseemly wrangle over the vacant offices of State. Charles adamantly refused to appoint Argyll as Chancellor (the office went to Campbell of Loudoun) , but he was created a Marquis, and other honours scattered among men who in reality were the enemies of the Crown.

At no time were Charles and Montrose permitted to meet, although it is likely that a number of messages were passed between them. Some years later, it was alleged that Montrose offered to assassinate Argyll, but had such a charge been true, the Campbell would have acted on it, since there were genuine fears among those around the King that the Graham would be executed upon the least excuse. A curious 'incident' in which Hamilton, who at this time was 'very careful of his own person' (the King's phrase), complained about plots to murder himself and Argyll, is still largely unexplained, and was more likely indicative of the tension which Covenant propaganda was endeavouring to sustain. Charles was very sensible of Montrose's dangerous situation, but although he considered it a point of honour to secure his release, he was too weak to insist on justice. Only after news of the Irish rebellion obliged the King to return to London, were Montrose and his friends discharged from prison, without trial, and their innocence unproven. In later years Argyll must have regretted that he had not killed them while he had the chance.

In January 1642, Charles wrote to Montrose in terms of personal sympathy and friendship, but after the Scottish debacle he inclined once more to Hamilton on whose dubious diplomacy he relied to keep the Covenanters neutral in the war which he knew was coming. He was the more deceived, for Hamilton was now on terms of intimacy with Argyll, and the royalists in Scotland received neither encouragement nor direction.

As the situation deteriorated, in May 1642, Montrose, with Lord Ogilvie and Stirling of Kier, tried to obtain an audience with the King at York. But Charles had promised the Covenanters, as a condition of the Graham's release, that he would have no further dealings with him, and he could only write that it was Montrose's duty to endure. On 25th August the King raised his standard at Nottingham, and the English Civil War began.

In February 1643, after the Battle of Edgehill, Montrose met the Queen at York and tried to convince her that the Covenanters were only awaiting a favourable opportunity to join the English rebels. He argued that only a bold, pre-emptive stroke in Scotland might prevent such an alliance, but Hamilton hurried south from Edinburgh with contrary evidence to dissuade the Queen from action. Montrose was dismissed with curt thanks for his loyalty and good intentions, and Hamilton was appointed Royal Commissioner in Scotland and promised a Dukedom for his service.

Amazingly almost, in view of all that had passed, the Covenanters now tried to entice Montrose back into their own party, even offering him a commission as Lieutenant General of the army second only to the Earl of Leslie. It was a cynical manoeuvre, calculated possibly to retain the benefit of his talent and popularity with the army, but as a means also of creating the suspicion in the minds of other royalists that the Graham could be bought. Montrose did not deny such rumours, and knowledge of an argument between himself and Huntly, together with his open contempt for Hamilton, persuaded the Covenanters that he might indeed be induced to desert the King. This seemed confirmed when Montrose agreed to meet the Moderator, Alexander Henderson, whom he knew and respected, in order, as he said, to remove 'certain doubts' and resolve his scruples.

In fact, Montrose was now convinced that nothing less than proof positive of Hamilton's incompetence – or collaboration – would persuade the King. With Napier, Ogilvie, and Kier as witnesses, he therefore met Henderson, from whom he elicited information concerning Scottish negotiations with the English Parliament and the intelligence that the Covenanters planned to send a powerful army to the assistance of 'their brethren in England', since the Presbyterians of both countries had resolved to bring the King to terms 'or die in the attempt'. Once in receipt of this information, Montrose stalled for time, and when, in July 1643, he learned that an English delegation had arrived in Scotland to solicit a Scottish invasion of northern England, he did not await the issue, but hurried to Oxford to warn the King.

Charles was at Gloucester, and the Queen absolutely refused to believe his intelligence, since it conflicted with all the reports that she had received from Hamilton. Montrose rode on to Gloucester, but the King did not believe him either, and the courtiers of the Council attributed his actions to a jealousy of the royal favourite. When he was finally vindicated by events, it was too late. In the autumn, a number of Scottish royalists came south and endorsed Montrose's suspicions of Hamilton, and eventually, at the end of the year – and only after the Scottish army had reached the border – Hamilton wrote to admit that he could not prevent the Covenanters from joining with the Parliamentary forces in England. There followed the news that between August and October of that year, the Scots had agreed and signed the Solemn League and Covenant with the English Parliament – and that Hamilton's brother Lanerick had even affixed the Royal Signet to the Treaty and the consequent commissions of array. When Hamilton and Lanerick themselves arrived in Oxford with 'a fair though lamentable tale' and numerous excuses for their behaviour, they were arrested on the depositions of the Scottish royalists. Lanerick escaped and joined the Scots Commissioners in London. Hamilton was imprisoned at Pendennis and later at Cariston Castle in Cornwall.

The King's eyes were finally opened, and he gave Montrose two days in which to submit proposals as to what was to be done in Scotland.

The plan which he presented had several, hopefully co-ordinated, elements. With a small force of royalists, he himself would fight his way through the border and raise the Royal Standard in Scotland. Orders were drafted for the Marquis of Newcastle, who commanded the loyal forces in the north of England, requesting cavalry and any other support which he could give, while commissions were sent to the gentry along the border requiring them to join the army with whatever men they could muster. Among the Scottish cavaliers with Montrose was the Viscount Aboyne, second son of the Marquis of Huntly, through whose agency he hoped to obtain the support of the Gordons, since alone among the royalist clans, they could supply the cavalry essential for a campaign. The invasion was to coincide with a Gordon rising in Aberdeenshire, and a special commission was sent to Huntly, naming him Lieutenant in the north, in the hope that this might satisfy his temperamental sense of dignity. Finally – although it was the slimmest chance of all in what was at best a doubtful venture – the Marquis of Antrim had renewed his promise to send an army of Irish gallowglasses against the west coast of Argyll.

Montrose's commission as King's Lieutenant in Scotland was signed by Charles on 1st February 1644. The preparations took several weeks, and at the end of the month he rode north with his little band of cavaliers to win Scotland for the royal cause.

PART IV
HIGHLAND CAMPAIGNS

CHAPTER 8

The Gathering at Atholl

It was afterwards said of Alasdair MacDonald, that if his knowledge of strategy had equalled his valour in battle, he would have been one of the best generals in Europe. The supreme fighting man who could inspire his soldiers to follow him wherever the combat was most fierce, he was less able to plot and direct the conduct of the campaign itself.

After establishing the bridgehead in Ardnamurchan, he marched eastwards to ravage the Campbell territories in Lorne and North Kintyre. Having at first the advantage of surprise, the MacDonald visited his enemies with fire and sword, reporting to Ireland that he had devastated forty miles through Argyll's lands, 'burning, pillaging, killing, and spoiling all the way'. 'He carried away all the cattle', recorded the *New Statistical Account*, 'with the exception of one dun cow that happened to escape his notice', being hid in a thicket of birch in a hollow beside Kilmartin. This cow is still known by the natives by the name of *Bo-mhaol othar achabean* – the humel dun cow of Achaven. It was this cow, by lowing for her calf, which had been carried away with the rest of the cattle of the strath, that is said to have sounded the first note of lamentation and wailing among the inhabitants when they ventured from their hiding places in the hills to behold the destruction of their dwellings, and the devastation of everything valuable that belonged to them. The lands of the Campbell's tenants were ruined along the line of march, the livestock butchered or driven off, the houses burned, and the people killed or forced to flee up the barren mountain-sides.

But news of this depredation and the war-smoke drifting over the hills forewarned others, and resistance began to stiffen as the local clansmen gathered for defence. At Craignish, Alasdair was beaten off with some loss, and at Duntroon in the Bay of Crinan, he failed to surprise the garrison and lost his personal piper. According to local tradition, this man had been sent ahead to obtain entry to the castle to spy out its defences, but he found the place strongly held, and when his behaviour aroused the suspicions of the guards, he was imprisoned in one of the upper turrets. From there, through a shot hole, he watched Alasdair's approach, and warned him of danger by playing on his pipes a pibroch which the MacDonald was certain to recognize:

> 'Dearest Coll, shun the tower, shun the tower,
> Beloved Coll, shun the sound, shun the sound,
> I am in hand, I am in hand.'

Alasdair understood the message, and believing the stronghold to be impregnable, he left the piper to his fate and continued his career of devastation along the shores of Loch Awe.

But although the Campbell lands yielded up a great store of plunder, Alasdair was not strong enough to storm the main castles in the region – Skipness, Tarbert, Sween, Innischonnel (where old Colkitto was possibly held), Dunstaffnage, or Dunollie – which were garrisoned by Argyll's troops. To these strongpoints the Campbells rallied in the wake of his march, and before long the forces of retribution were gathering in pursuit. Recalling then his commission to raise the western clans and the messages sent to Clan Donald and other chieftains in Garmoran and the western Highlands, Alasdair therefore marched north out of Campbell heartland and through Appin to Kyle Rhea.

At Skye, however, he discovered that Donald Gorm of Sleat had died some six months earlier, and his successor, with other established chieftains, were unwilling to join what experience advised was merely another raid by exiles and desperate men who would escape to Ireland when their venture failed – as all had done before – leaving them to face the vengeance of Argyll. MacDonald of Glengarry, from whom Alasdair had counted on obtaining at least a company of bowmen, offered beef for the army but few recruits. Nor did letters to the MacLeods, the MacLeans of Skye, the Stewarts of Appin, or the Clan Cameron, produce any positive response. While some held back for fear of the Campbells, others would not condescend to follow a junior MacDonald chieftain and one who was no more than a younger son of the Cadet of Colonsay. Having lingered for some weeks, Alasdair now thought to return to Ireland with his plunder before he could be drawn into a fight with Argyll's approaching army.

But it was already too late. The remaining vessels which had sailed north from Ardnamurchan to rendezvous with Alasdair at Skye, were surprised on 10th August by three Parliamentary men of war while they were at anchor at Loch Eishort. In a short engagement, the Flemish crew struck their colours at the first broadside, but the Irish, knowing that they could expect no quarter, put up a fierce resistance until their commander was killed and their ship sank under them. Alasdair now had no means of returning to Ireland, while on land, the Campbell forces moved to hold the passes and cut him off from the sea.

In this rapidly deteriorating situation, Alasdair considered the broader objective of the King's war in Scotland, and on hearing rumours that the Marquis of Huntly had raised an army in Aberdeenshire, he decided to try to join forces with the Gordons. Turning his back on the coast, where the Campbells now blocked his retreat, he again crossed Kyle Rhea and marched over the mountains of Quaich in the direction of Lochaber, only to receive fresh intelligence that the Gordon rising had failed. By this time the Irishes were running out of ammunition, and the Campbells' pursuit was drawing daily closer. Looking next for a loop-hole to the north-west, Alasdair doubled back through Glengarry, sending a messenger ahead to the Earl of Seaforth with the King's letter formally requesting help from the MacKenzies. But Seaforth, who might have held Ross, Caithness, and Sutherland in the royalist cause, had lost his nerve with the failure of the Gordons' rebellion, and defected to the Covenant. The Clan MacKenzie recalled past feuds with the MacDonalds and regarded Alasdair's approach with conspicuous hostility. Seaforth appeared civil enough at first, but excused himself 'with the malignitie of the time'. As all men could see, the King's cause in Scotland had been lost in the spring, and any association with this rene-gade band of Irish would be an act of grave imprudence.

Alasdair had almost reached the end of his resources, and his troops were becoming increasingly dispirited. In particular, the women and chil-dren who followed the army were by now in a sorry condition, ragged, weakening from hunger, exhausted by the relentless marching and knowing that they were beyond hope of Campbell mercy. Alasdair begged Seaforth to allow him free passage to the north and safety, but the MacKenzies became increasingly threatening, and when Seaforth himself raised the country against them, the Irish wearily prepared to fight. At the last moment, however, Seaforth's natural prudence caused him to realise that Alasdair's men were sufficiently desperate that they would fight to a finish, and he hesitated to attack. At a parley between the two forces, he agreed finally to provide Alasdair with beef and other necessities, and allowed him passage into Badenoch, which adjoined Lochaber to the east and had been part of Huntly's territory. The Irishes turned around once more, and trudged back over the mountains, fortified by the food in their bellies, but with the bitter knowledge that there was no chief in the

Highlands willing to assist them or cheat the MacCailein Mor of his revenge.

Since they could only look to themselves for survival, and because the King's letters obviously had such little effect, Alasdair now resorted to coercive methods to obtain recruits. During the night, he sent patrols into the neighbouring villages and settlements to kidnap the chief men of the district to whom he presented the Royal Commission with the choice that they could either provide men and assistance or see their property destroyed. By this means he acquired some 500 'volunteers'. He was also joined by the MacDonalds of Keppoch, some men of Glengarry, and also by 300 MacPhersons of Cluny under their young chief Ewen Og with the Finlays of Braemar and their captain Donald Og who was Alasdair's distant kinsman. These, together with a number from Badenoch, and 'broken men' – MacGregors for the most part – swelled his numbers to over 2,000, and he decided, optimistically, to strike east again and try among Huntly's tenants along the fringes of the Gordon country.

In Strathspey, however, his way was blocked by the Laird of Grant who held the river crossing in strength against him, supported by a force of Covenanting gentry from Moray and some horse and foot out of Ross. Seaforth also reappeared with 1000 of his clansmen as proof that he had indeed switched his allegiance to the Covenant.

Alasdair was obliged to retreat south again, and wandered hopelessly through Badenoch. A steel net was closing inexorably around his little army. To the west the MacCailein Mor was bent implacably on his destruction, and his Campbells held the only passes to the sea. Grant and Seaforth prevented any escape towards the north. The Gordons had been beaten and Aberdeenshire cowed into submission, while to the south, had Alasdair any thought of entering the Lowlands, the Covenant forces were mustering at Perth. Between their converging enemies, as the area of freedom steadily contracted, the Irishes would finally be cornered, and could expect only one last and hopeless battle in which they would get and give no mercy.

As Alasdair later told the royalist historian of the time, Patrick Gordon of Ruthven, the only chance now lay in 'Divine intervention', for there was nothing left that he or his soldiers could do. He had appealed to the MacDonalds but they had prevaricated. He had sent the fiery cross around the western clans, but the cause had foundered on their traditional jealousy of a minor Clan Donald chieftain. He had been led to expect a royalist army already in the field, but the Gordon rising had been crushed and their territory overrun by the forces of the Covenant. And of the promised help from England there had been no sign, nor intelligence of Montrose except that he was rumoured to be somewhere near the border. It was as a last resort therefore, that Alasdair sent a message to Carlisle in the faint hope that it might reach the King's Lieutenant, and that he might have forces enough to answer the appeal for help.

In fact, the situation was if anything worse than Alasdair knew, since the truth was that Montrose had reached Tullibelton in Perthshire. But he was in hiding, and he had no army.

Proceeding from Oxford, he had discovered the royalist forces in the north of England retreating before a strong Scottish army under Leslie, and falling back on York. The Marquis of Newcastle could offer little help, and some 800 levies whom Montrose managed to raise in Cumberland deserted as soon as he crossed the border. Reaching Dumfries, he raised the Royal Standard, but the border Earls – Home, Roxburgh, Hartfell, Annandale, and Carnwath – on whom he had counted, declined to accept the King's commission, and the approach of another Covenant army under Callander (by strange irony an erstwhile moderate and a signatory of the Cumbernauld Band) obliged him to retreat again to Carlisle.

Montrose now realised that winning through the borders would be virtually impossible without some diversion in the north. His column was too large to pass unchallenged through the Lowlands, yet too weak to risk any major engagement with the Covenant forces which barred the way. He therefore spent two unprofitable months skirmishing in the north of England, laying siege to Morpeth, and convoying supplies to help relieve the Scottish stranglehold about Newcastle. On 6th May he had the consolation of receiving word that he had been created a Marquis.

In late June, while still engaged in harassing the enemy along the border, he got an urgent summons from Prince Rupert, who had marched north to fight the combined Scottish and Parliamentary forces around York. Montrose hurried south, but arrived the day after the disaster at Marston Moor. He met Rupert at an inn near Richmond, and the Prince, who was himself now desperate for troops, commandeered all the recruits whom Montrose had raised, leaving him with less than 100 cavaliers.

The small column rode slowly back through Lancashire to Carlisle. There was still no news of Antrim's force, but they now caught a disturbing rumour that a Gordon rising in Aberdeenshire had miscarried. Scouts sent across the border returned with a dismal account. The

Gordons had indeed risen for the King and had been savagely put down by Argyll. All passes, towns, and castles throughout the Lowlands were in Covenant hands and strongly held against any attempt to win through towards the north. The Scottish royalists were cowed or beaten. None dared say a word for the King through fear of Argyll. The cavaliers were too few, and Montrose had come too late.

Confronted with this intelligence at Carlisle, Montrose called a Council of War, and listened in silence while his remaining followers urged him to abandon the enterprise. On 12th August, the small band of cavaliers began the long retreat south.

But unknown to any except his closest friends, Montrose was now resolved on a more desperate plan. He was haunted by the grim knowledge that if the present venture failed, there could be no second chance. Amid the growing pessimism at Oxford after the defeat at Marston Moor, the King would waste no more resources on another forlorn expedition against Scotland. He therefore ordered Lord Ogilvie to lead the column back to Oxford and inform Charles of what had happened, while he, together with two friends – Sir William Rollo and a Colonel Sibbald – attempted to slip undetected through the borders and reach his friends in Perthshire.

When the cavaliers started south, Montrose and his two companions kept to the rear – leaving his servants, horses, and personal baggage with the main body so that no-one should suspect their intention. On the second day the three dropped still further behind, until, when the rearguard was also out of sight, they turned their horses' heads about, and galloped back towards Carlisle.

The rest of the cavaliers continued southwards unsuspecting, and, as it happened, to disaster. On 15th August they joined up with some 400 of Prince Rupert's troopers who had been scattered after Marston Moor, and together attacked and carried a roundhead position at the Ribble Bridge near Preston. Almost immediately, however, they were themselves surprised by a detachment of Fairfax's army and captured to a man. The prisoners included Lord Ogilvie and also Harry Graham, Montrose's natural brother. The despatches which they carried to the King were also seized, and consequently were in the Covenanters' hands within the week.

In the meanwhile, Montrose paused in Carlisle to negotiate with the Viscount Aboyne, second son of the Marquis of Huntly. Despite the failure of the northern rising, he was still convinced that any campaign in

Scotland would have to depend on the Gordons, around whose nucleus, and particular their cavalry, he might rally the loyal gentry of Angus and the Mearns. Since Huntly was beyond reach, it seemed proper to consult with Aboyne, who agreed that Montrose should carry the King's commission to his father, and that rather than risk putting two heads in the one noose, he would remain in Carlisle until Montrose sent him word.

On 18th August, Montrose and his two friends left Carlisle and struck north across the border, Rollo and Sibbald dressed in the buff jackets of Covenant officers, and Montrose following some distance behind, disguised as a groom. Some miles into their journey they passed a deserter from Newcastle's army, who unfortunately recognised Montrose, but the man did not betray them and, riding hell for leather across the middle march and up Liddel Water to Roxburgh, they made it, incredibly in four days, to Tayside and the house of Patrick Graham of Inchbrakie at Tullibelton.

By now the hunt was up, and Montrose hid in a small cottage in Methven wood while Rollo and Sibbald scoured the country for news. The better part of a week dragged by and the signs grew steadily more discouraging. As ever in war, there was rumour and much that was unreal. Men claimed to have heard the 'touking of drums' at dead of night. Phantom armies fought on Manderlee, and at the Muir of Forfar some thought they saw contending hosts, mustering for battle in the air. People took such visions as dreadful omens of a conflict to come, but in the daylight Argyll's grip was tight around the land. Rollo and Sibbald could tell only of ruinous fines, imprisonment, or even death, meted out to those who might have stood for the King, and how the rest, dismayed, had either submitted to the Campbell or withdrawn into a terrified neutrality. They also brought the depressing details of the rising in the north: how Huntly had fumbled, and fled 'without a stroke stricken'; and the Gordon strength had been frittered away in a series of pointless and unco-ordinated raids.

The Cock of the North had, it seemed, strutted prematurely, and his crowing had been sadly out of tune. Without waiting for the King's instructions, in March 1644 he had issued a typically eloquent yet tentative declaration and set to calling up his clan. But having rattled his broadsword and made his speech, Huntly could not control the young fire-eaters among the Gordon lairds. Nor did the whole clan heed the muster, since the Lord George, Master of Gordon, was at this time on the Covenant side – somewhat unwillingly and to all intents a hostage of

75

Argyll – and a reckonable portion of the Gordons' fighting strength went with him. Other royalists were unwilling to follow until Huntly could produce a formal commission from the King.

The young Gordons raided the lands of their Covenanting neighbours, looting houses, lifting horses and cattle, and kidnapping prominent citizens and worthies of the Kirk. They occupied Aberdeen, which offered them no resistance, but apart from acquiring a quantity of arms and supplies, they did nothing to exploit the situation while the Covenant armies were unprepared. After vacillating for almost a month, Huntly called a muster at Inverurie where a rough count put his strength at 400 horse and 2000 foot. But despite intelligence that the Covenant forces were gathering to the south, he maintained his troops in arms and idleness and took no initiative of his own. This inactivity took severe toll of the Gordons' morale. The younger officers began to complain and quarrel among themselves. A number drifted away from the camp and returned home.

By the end of April 1644, Huntly was made to recognize that while Argyll's forces were said to be growing in numbers and confidence every week that passed, his own army was starting to dwindle away. At a second muster in Strathbogie the royalists numbered less than 300 horse and 1500 foot. With growing frustration, the Gordon lairds pressed him to issue some positive orders for a campaign, but a feeling of hopelessness seemed to have overtaken him, and he answered that he could not fight Argyll with so few men as he had left. The young Gordon commanders – Drum, Haddo, Gight, and Nathaniel Gordon (who was perhaps the most experienced soldier with the army) – were thoroughly disillusioned and rode away from the camp. 'We have shown ourselves foolishly and will leave the field shamefully. We thought never better of it', Drum shouted at Huntly as they left.

Huntly now looked at his own safety in the face of the approaching Argyll. Collecting several chests of treasure from his castle at the Bog of Gight, he sent the keys of his properties to his son, Lord George Gordon, who was still with Argyll, and sailing to Caithness, took refuge in Strathnaver. Such had been the ignominious end of the Gordon rising in the north.

Argyll was now master of the situation, and deployed the considerable forces at his disposal to stamp out each ember of revolt, and to make an example of the Gordon Lairds as would deter any other royalists who might be rash enough to contemplate rebellion against the Covenanting government in Scotland. His Campbells went through Deeside, and plundered Covenanter and non-Covenanter alike with Highland impartiality. The Gordon lairds were isolated in their strongholds and singly brought to book – some to be imprisoned, and some to be executed with the bare preliminary of a drum-head trial. A few escaped, including the soldier of fortune, Nathaniel Gordon, and gathered in the hills. But there was little that so few could do while the Argyll's garrisons held the countryside to heel. For the most part they took to brigandage and retired to the safety of the high country with other sorts of broken men.

When Montrose understood the full extent of the Gordons' ruin, he must have realised that his earlier plans to fight a conventional war in the east of Scotland would have to be abandoned. The Gordon force could no longer be a military nucleus around which to gather the Angus gentry and their small bands of retainers. Yet without such a nucleus there could be no royalist army in Scotland, and moreover, without cavalry – which would have been the Gordons' most valuable contribution – no army could hope to campaign successfully or even survive in the Lowland plains where any decisive battle against the Covenanters would undoubtedly be fought.

It was possibly now that Montrose began to contemplate the unconventional alternative of a Highland campaign. He knew the Grampians. His own estates bordered on the Highland line, and his guardian, Lord Napier, had inherited a quarter of the Lennox. The Highland clans looked on Charles I as their titular chieftain, and though remote from the constitutional struggle, their common hatred of the Campbells might foster a unity where this had hitherto been lacking. To bind the clans together for a political object was theoretically an impossible task, since none would defer voluntarily to its neighbour, nor one chief submit to the command of another. Yet given a leader, the authority of the Royal Commission, and their consuming envy of the MacCailein Mor, they might find it no dishonour to fight under the King's Lieutenant in a cause which equally served their own. Perhaps such a possibility had already been in his mind when he included Antrim's offer to invade the west as part of his original plan submitted to the King at Oxford. But such a scheme had failed before, and Antrim had a reputation for promising more than he could perform.

Yet there had been vague rumours that a band of Irish caterans had landed in the west and were laying waste the Highlands, although till now he had allowed them little credence. It was a significant coincidence therefore that quite fortuitously Inchbrakie should intercept Alasdair's message addressed to the King's Lieutenant at Carlisle, confirming that Antrim's force had indeed landed, but was in a desperate situation.

Montrose replied, as if from the vicinity of the borders, directing Alasdair to march with all speed to a rendezvous at Blair Atholl. Six days later, a government courier passing Methven Wood brought the news that a force of Irishes had entered Atholl, and that he had been sent to alert the Covenant authorities at Perth and raise the countryside for defence. Montrose promptly seized this last chance of the hour, and in Highland dress of plaid and trews, with the Royal Standard wrapped round his waist, and the King's Commission in his pocket, he set out with Inchbrakie's younger son, Black Pate (so called after an incident with gunpowder) to walk the thirty miles over the hills to Atholl.

Events now took on the quality of high drama. Alasdair had received Montrose's message, and guided by a Clanranald man, he marched south to Atholl and seized the castle. Thereafter he could only wait upon the arrival of the King's Lieutenant. But the local clans – Stewarts and Robertsons – who occupied the valleys of the Garry and the Tummel, had little cause to welcome the Irish, and although no Covenanters, they had an inalienable right to protect their land against all intruders. They prowled around the Irish leaguer, uttering threats which hourly grew more hostile, and as word spread and the clansmen banded, they took to shaking their weapons in grim earnest. Some Badenoch men under Donald Robertson, the Tutor of Struan, tried to mediate, or at least keep the two sides apart, but the situation grew steadily worse. The Irish were too desperate and too far gone to yield their ground. The women and children were in rags and near starvation, outlandish and wild eyed from travel. The men were lean as wolves, past hope of safety, and prepared to fight to a finish.

By 29th August, matters had come to a head, and the two forces confronted each other across the red waters of the River Tilt. Montrose's arrival saved the situation by a hairsbreadth. As the tension grew to flash-point, two figures were seen hurrying over the heather, down to the Garry and into the tumbling waters. As they passed between the threatening clansmen, the peering Robertsons recognised Black Pate Inchbrakie, and as realisation dawned and word spread that the man with him was none other than the King's Lieutenant, men on both sides started tossing their bonnets in the air and shouting for Montrose.

The huge MacDonald and the slighter Graham met beside the waters of the Tilt. It is not recorded just what Alasdair had expected of the King's Captain General when he came – a vision perhaps of a cavalry escort and trumpeters to herald his approach, or a snorting warhorse beneath the royal oriflamme. He settled for one aide de camp, and a smallish man in Highland dress, with grey eyes and command in his voice, who walked out of the hills in answer to a prayer. The next morning they raised the Royal Standard on a small mound called the Truidh, not far from Blair Castle, and called the muster.

There were three regiments of Irish, the remains of Huntly's broken men from Badenoch, and 800 Athollmen under the Tutor of Struan – a force of something under 3000 men. It was hardly the army that Montrose had planned for – not the Gordons with the Angus gentry, nor the full 10,000 troops whom Antrim had so easily promised him at Oxford. Instead he had a warband out of the mist, uncouth, half-armed, and marked for destruction. But there could be no margin for delay. There was the value of the moment – the heroic instinct of the Gaels, and the reserves of courage which the Royal Standard could conjure from the Highlanders. If it was to attempt the impossible, the army needed confidence, and what better than a swift blooding to unite its varied elements? It needed also to survive and they were ringed around by enemies. The Campbells were coming over the hills to avenge their burning homesteads. The MacKenzies, resentful of their cattle given to the Irish, were banding with the Forbeses, Frasers, Grants, and others north of the Grampian range. The Covenant General, Lord Burleigh, was at Aberdeen with a strong force, and closest of all, the Lord Elcho commanded the Lowland regiments at Perth. There were few tactical alternatives to ponder. The first defeat would be the last. But courage may rise with the occasion, and a great General can understand how fortune demands that a man should be prompt upon his hour.

And it was time to begin a legend. At Perth, the Covenant forces of Lord Elcho were their nearest enemy and so Montrose pointed his half-pike to the south, and in companies, to the fierce skirl of the pibroch, set his ragged army marching down the brae.

CHAPTER 9

The Battle of Tippermuir

Montrose did not march to Perth by the straightest route, but made a detour to the west, perhaps to listen for news of the approaching Campbells, or possibly in the hope of obtaining more recruits along the Highland fringe. The army swung down the Strath of Garry and past the narrow gorge of Killiekrankie before striking west through the gap in the hills where the River Tummel flows into the valley by the falls at Fascally, and skirted the northern shore of Loch Tummel until they reached the bridge at its further end. From there they turned south along the old raiding road over the flank of Schiehallion, and with Fortingall and Glen Lyon on their right hand, descended through the Strath of Appin to the Tay and the lands of Clan Menzies of Weem.

Alexander Menzies of Weem was one of Argyll's creatures, and when formally asked to submit to the Royal Commission, he maltreated Montrose's herald almost to death. His clansmen also began to harass the royalist rearguard as it passed, and having neither time nor the artillery to besiege Castle Weem itself, the Highlanders took a summary reprisal by firing all the homesteads in the brae and destroying the corn which had recently been harvested. By nightfall, the bulk of the army had crossed the River Tay at Aberfeldy, and the next morning, Grandtully Castle, the other strongpoint in the district, surrendered without a fight.

On the second day, (31st August 1644), they marched over the hills into Glen Cochill and down through Strath Braan, Amulree, and by the Sma-Glen into Glen Almond. As the vanguard of Athollmen under Black Pate Inchbrakie approached Gorthie Moor, they saw the sun glinting on a body of several hundred armed men drawn up across the slope of Buchanty Hill, and Sir William Rollo rode forward under a flag of truce to learn whether they were friend or enemy. He discovered that they were a force of 400 bowmen commanded by Montrose's cousin, Lord Kilpont, who was the eldest son of William Graham, Earl of Airth and Menteith. With him were others of the Perthshire gentry, including Sir John Drummond (a younger son of the Earl of Perth). Graham of Gorthie, the Master of Madertie (Montrose's brother in law), and James Stewart of

Ardvoirlich with his son. Kilpont told Rollo that they had been summoned by the Covenanting authorities to repel a band of marauding Irish, but had known nothing of Montrose's arrival in Scotland or his junction with Alasdair. Having seen the Royal Commission, the entire force came over to fight under the King's Lieutenant.

Kilpont's intelligence concerning the Covenant dispositions at Perth made it very likely that they would have to fight a major battle on the morrow, and the army rested overnight at the Moor of Fowlis. The next morning, Sunday 1st September, they crossed the Almond and marched down the fertile valley of Strathearn. On the wide plain between Tippermuir and Cultmalindy, the Covenant General, Lord Elcho, was waiting for them with 7000 men.

The troops which had mustered at Perth under David, Lord Elcho, were technically second-line regiments, and less experienced than the pick of the Scottish army who had marched south with General Leslie. Nevertheless they had been trained and drilled on the same model; they were paid, and well equipped. Each regiment was divided between musketeers and pikemen in the ratio of three to two. The latter wore steel corslets and helmets, and carried both pike and sword – their business as heavy infantry being to deliver the charge or repel the attacks of enemy cavalry. The musketeers wore no body armour, and carried matchlocks, each with an elaborate firing rest, which could shoot a 1¼-ounce ball a distance of something over four hundred yards. A regiment in order of battle was usually drawn up in files six deep, with the pikemen in the centre and the musketeers on either flank – their drill being for each rank to fire in turn and then fall back to reload – one rank at a time – until the enemy closed and the pikemen moved forward to begin a hand to hand melée.

The footsoldiers numbered about 6000 and were recruited from the Covenanting communities of Fife and Perthshire, but the flower of Elcho's army were 800 troopers from the Carse of Gowrie who formed the cavalry division under Lord Drummond. In Scotland, the cavalry were still equipped in the old style, carrying a lance, four pistols, and a carbine. They were trained to advance four deep at the trot, and deliver a volley from the saddle before peeling off in 'caracole' to reload, wheel, and advance again. The tactic of cavalry charging home, reintroduced by Gustavus Adolphus of Sweden and developed by Prince Rupert in the English Civil War, had not been adopted north of the border.

Elcho's strength on the day was further augmented by the local Perth militia, who marched under the banner of The Ancient Corporation of Glovers. In addition he had an artillery train of seven small cannon, each probably capable of firing a five pound ball.

The morale of the Covenant army was understandably high. The men were staunch in their ideological belief, well drilled, with the Lowlanders' contempt for the Gael and a fierce faith in the justice of their cause. They marched out of Perth that Sunday to exterminate a 'pack of naked runagates', ill-armed, undisciplined, and beyond hope of God's redemption. They were confident in their superior weapons, their drill and training, and in the overwhelming odds of three to one in their favour. Finally, the presence of the cannon – the 'musket's mother' – which the Highlanders were known to fear above all things, would resolve the issue beyond doubt. The presbyterian ministers moved among the army urging the troops to the Lord's work and the burghers and citizens of Perth also travelled to Tippermuir in small parties to watch the battle from the comfort of their carriages and enjoy what promised to be the spectacular annihilation of a beggar's army.

On learning of the Highlanders' descent into Glen Almond, the Covenanters had left Perth in the small hours of the morning, and in the early light the foot regiments marshalled in three divisions near the base of Methven Hill and facing across the open ground called Tippermuir, about three miles from Perth itself. Lord Elcho commanded the right wing of the army. The centre he entrusted to James Murray of Gask, while the left wing was led by Sir James Scott of Rossie, a professional soldier of considerable reputation and experience who had fought in the service of the Venetian Republic. While the centre was comprised entirely of infantry, each wing was reinforced by 400 cavalry stationed on the extreme flanks to allow them the maximum scope for manoeuvre. In front of the army, Elcho placed his seven cannon and a line of supporting skirmishers.

The Highlanders deployed onto the plain and without hesitation began to approach the Covenant army. The Gaels had risen that morning in expectation of battle, and the savage skirling of their bagpipes carried across the moor in the clear autumn air. In the forefront, the Robertsons under Donald, Tutor of Struan, displayed the *Clach-Nam-Brattich* on the point of their standard – the stone of the banner which made them invincible in the fight. Among the clansmen there had been talk of the *Taghairm* – the Oracle of the Hide – and it was told years afterwards that in accordance with this old superstition, they had killed a herdsman earlier that morning to ensure the first blood of the day. The sight of the Covenant host and the terrible odds in the enemy's favour did not dismay them. The wild clans had no fear of the pease-eating Lowland *bodachs* who had fattened on years of peace and ease. They had set their hopes on the spoil of Perth, and the spirit of the army was fierce and high.

Montrose's force now numbered something under 3000 men and three horses. His immediate problem was the greater length of the Covenanters' battle-line which forced him to extend his own front in order to prevent both his flanks from being overlapped by the opposing wings of Elcho's army. This could only be achieved by drawing up his men in a long thin line, three deep as against the enemy's files of six. On the left wing, confronting Lord Elcho, he stationed Lord Kilpont's force of 400 archers together with a company of Highlanders from Lochaber, armed with the deadly *Tuagh* – the Lochaber axe – which had a pike and a hook as well as a blade, and was an excellent weapon against cavalry.

Alasdair commanded the centre, wielding the great claymore which had forged his reputation. He is said to have modified this formidable weapon by attaching a steel rod parallel to the blade on which a heavy steel ball slid free, riding down to the hilt when the sword was raised, and hurtling forward with skull crushing force as the downward stroke was delivered.[28] The Irishes, numbering about 1100, were armed with the old matchlocks and an assortment of makeshift weapons. Powder and ammunition were down to a single pound per man. They were supported by the Keppoch MacDonalds who had thrown in their lot with Alasdair, but although some could boast a claymore or a dirk, many of the irregular caterans were unarmed except for rude clubs which they had fashioned on the march, and in the first encounter would have to rely on hurling stones gathered on the moor.

Montrose drew up the three Irish regiments side by side in the unusual formation which had been pioneered by Gustavus Adolphus – with the front rank kneeling, the second stooping, and the third standing erect. The men were ordered to hold their fire until the last moment, and on the command, all three ranks were to shoot simultaneously at point-blank range and then charge the enemy with clubbed muskets or whatever else they had to hand. The unarmed Highlanders would have to take their weapons from the enemy. He thus counted on a single, devastating volley to check the Covenant advance and turn the battle in the middle of the field. Placing the Irish in the centre was the practical course, not only because without massed pikes they were not equipped to meet the cavalry attacks but also because, in an army of irregulars they were the most expe-·rienced troops he had, and the centre would be required to hold fast under heavy and sustained pressure. Nor, if the line broke, did the Irish have anywhere to run.

Montrose led the right wing in person, and thus opposed himself to the experienced Sir James Scott of Rossie. He had elected to fight on foot at the head of the clansmen – the Stewarts and Robertsons of Atholl and Lochaber – and carried a half-pike (at that time esteemed the 'Queen of Weapons') and a Highland targe. A proportion of the Gaels were armed with claymores and Lochaber axes, but as on the left wing, many had only makeshift weapons. The Highlanders had no artillery.

By the time the Montrose had made these dispositions it was almost noon. The day was very fine, with hardly any cloud in the sky, and quite hot but for a light breeze off the mountains. When the preparations on both sides had been completed there was a pause, while in the classical manner, the respective leaders addressed their troops.

On the Covenant side, the Ministers of the Kirk had been preaching for some hours, exhorting the Army of God to its sacred duty of inflicting Heaven's punishment upon the heathen with the promise of certain victory. But in front of the shabby little Gaelic army, Montrose's speech was more practical and to the point. The Highlanders had few weapons. The Covenanters had plenty. Let the fight be at close quarters then, and each man arm himself with a sword which he had wrested from an enemy. The Gaels began to yell the *Cathghairm* – the battle-shout – and started to press forward in their eagerness to get to grips, but Montrose could not unleash them until one other formality had been completed. The Master of Madertie was sent forward under a flag of truce to ask in the King's name that Lord Elcho and his soldiers should return to their rightful allegiance. Montrose also asked if the battle could be postponed for one day so as to avoid the shedding of blood on the Sabbath.

But the Covenanters recognized neither the convention nor the immunity of the herald. Madertie was seized and sent to Perth in chains, to be hanged when the battle was over. As to the request for postponement, the ministers declared that they had chosen the Lord's Day for doing the Lord's work – no doubt suspecting that, faced with such odds, the Highlanders hoped to slip away into the hills under cover of darkness.

While the Covenanters were still abusing Madertie, Montrose began to realign his own division slightly further to the right in order to take advantage of a rise in the ground. Thinking perhaps that this might be the beginning of a general withdrawal, or wishing to harass the undisciplined Highlanders while they performed this manoeuvre, Elcho advanced two troops of horse and a company of foot to engage them. However, Alasdair saw the move develop, and ordered an equal number of his Irishes to intercept them. A sharp fight ensued, and in the smoke and confusion, the Covenant troopers were driven back in disorder against, and partly across, their own main battle-line. Quickly seizing this opportunity, Montrose gave the signal for a general attack, and with a great shout the entire Gaelic army surged forward and began to run towards the enemy.

The Covenant soldiers who served the artillery panicked before the solid mass of screaming caterans charging at them across the open ground, and discharged their pieces ineffectually over the heads of the attackers. Seconds later the cannon were over-run, and the Highlanders hardly paused to kill the gunners before racing on to assault the main Covenant position. Elcho's musketeers, who had been moving forward to meet the charge, had barely time to fire a single volley, when the Gaels ran at them out of the smoke, stooped under the bullets with their heads down and the targes high, and hurling rocks, clubs, and other missiles, burst into the Covenant files to grapple individual opponents in a savage melée of knives and teeth. In the centre, the Irish paused a spear's length from the enemy line to pour a concentrated volley into the dense mass of pikemen, before clubbing their muskets and breaking through the great gaps which their shot had torn in the Covenant ranks. Following them, the unarmed clansmen ran in behind a shower of stones, clawed men down to throttle them on the ground, and snatched up their swords to join the execution going on around them.

Simultaneously, on the flanks, the brute strength of the Gaels brought them almost immediately to close quarters, and their claymores scythed a path through the pikes to where the unprotected musketeers fell easy victims to the slaughter. Where the press was thickest, the axemen of Lochaber howled their terrifying war cries, and swinging the huge *tuaghs* in great arcs, hacked their way through the mass of shrinking flesh and bone. In front of them Elcho's regiments recoiled, as in the smoke and din, confused soldiers looked for officers who had already fallen, and young Perth apprentices, transfixed with terror, saw their friends die frightfully beside them and familiar faces whom they knew disintegrate in a hideous mess of brains and blood.

Now the weeks of formal drill dissolved in the terrible ordeal of battle.

Elcho's army had learned the rituals of war; to load, present, and fire at the command, and to march and wheel in the formations of the parade ground. But the dreadful savagery of this close quarter fighting surpassed the scope of any simple practice for melée. If in their imagination they had contemplated death, heroically in battle, it had been fancifully removed from the barbarous reality which engulfed them now. A comrade cloven to the teeth, skull bursting under a Lochaber axe, or the screams of a human being disembowelled, were horrors beyond their most fearful preconception. The Covenant line reeled under the ferocity of the Highlanders' attack, and within minutes began to break apart as terror seized the Fifeshire levies, and in whole companies they started to throw down their weapons and turned to run. The road to Perth became jammed with a frantic, sobbing herd of fear-crazed men whose only thought was to escape the carnage of that ghastly battlefield, for as the panic spread the whole battle-line disintegrated and the foot soldiers ran to save themselves if they could, while the cavalry, more fortunate, spurred through the rabble and galloped for their lives. Behind them, the maimed and wounded were deserted to the fury of the Gaels, and the doubtful mercy of the cateran women who came later to strip the corpses and leave them naked on the moor.

Only on the left did the Covenanters attempt to stand and fight – where Sir James Scott of Rossie rallied his troops and desperately tried to reach the shelter of some ruined cottages on the higher ground. But Montrose anticipated his intention and led the Athollmen in a race for the crest. Scott's men were decimated on the slope and driven back into the disorganised mass of fleeing enemy.

A terrible slaughter now took place. Some of the Irishes had hauled the captured guns around to blow away at point-blank range the little that was left of Elcho's army, but the rout was already so complete that Montrose counter-manded the order to fire. The Highlanders went after the fugitives in a pack, and pulled them down or killed them as they ran. Those who left the track to seek safety in the scrib were hunted out like beasts and dragged back to be butchered along the road. Fear itself killed some. Terrified burghers who could not survive the exertion, ran till they tore the tissues of their lungs, or haemorrhaged and fell retching blood like gutted fish until the Gaels finished them off. Others died of apoplexy, or were 'bursten in their corslets' so that after the battle they were discovered dead without a mark upon them. One of Alasdair's officers later recalled that a man could have walked from Tippermuir to Perth on the bodies of the slain.[29]

The town was invested later in the afternoon. Its walls were capable of defence, but only twelve men could be found to hold the ramparts and these were reeling drunk. The survivors of the battle hid in the cellars and could not be induced to face the Gaels who howled exulting at the gates. Perth surrendered without a fight, but in the countryside around, the Highlanders continued to pursue the fugitives till nightfall.

Elcho's army had ceased to exist, and one source later computed the Covenant casualties to be in the order of 2000 dead and 1000 taken prisoner[30]. The Irishes and Highlanders had many hurt, but only one man was killed outright. Among the officers, Henry Stewart, Ardvoirlich's son, died of his wounds a few days later, though what part his death might play in the tragic consequence to follow, at that time none could know.

CHAPTER 10

The Battle of Aberdeen

Montrose entered Perth on the evening of 1st September with a token force of 600 men. To their disappointment, Alasdair's Gaelic troops were not permitted to loot the town, since one of the conditions of surrender was that 'no Irishes should get entry or passage', and the King's Lieutenant hoped to reconcile the people to the royalists' cause by a display of clemency. The Irish regiments were quartered across the river in the old church of St Constantine at Kinnoul, where they broke up the seats and communion tables for firewood, but were somewhat mollified to receive 400 merks worth of cloth, exacted from the citizens to replace their worn out rags. The army spent three days in re-equipping themselves from the town's arsenal and collecting weapons and ammunition from the battlefield.

But any hopes that the victory at Tippermuir might induce numbers of the local gentry to declare for the King were quickly dispelled. Few recruits of note rode in, and 400 of the Athollmen left the standard to return home. At the outset of the campaign Montrose was thus confronted with the greatest problem attendant on a Highland army. Whatever the outcome of a battle, it was the clansmen's custom to carry the booty home, and because they were irregulars who fought without pay and were not sworn to the colours, they could not be prevented. It was therefore always difficult for a general in Montrose's position to exploit a victory, and in the longer term it cast grave doubts on the feasibility of leading a Highland force against the borders. The courage of the clansmen was superlative in battle but their endurance outside their immediate geographical area of interest was generally suspect.

The 400 departed with the spoils of Tippermuir and a vague promise to return when the harvest at Atholl had been gathered in, and Montrose had to resign himself to the loss of their claymores and let them go. It was not prudent to linger at Perth in the unlikely hope that some might return, and he decided to march north into Angus in order to seek recruits among his own neighbours in the Mearns. The army left Perth late on Wednesday 4th September, and having destroyed all the boats in the

88

vicinity of the town to impede Argyll's pursuit, they crossed the Tay and marched seven or eight miles in the direction of Coupar-Angus, and camped for the night near the kirk of Collace by the stream at the foot of Dunsinane Hill.

As they lay at Collace, in the early hours of Thursday 5th September, a tragedy occurred which later inspired Sir Walter Scott to write his novel 'The Legend of Montrose'. Shortly before dawn a tremendous commotion broke out in the camp, and fearing some quarrel between the Irishes and the local Highlanders, Montrose and his officers snatched up their swords and hurried towards the uproar. Pushing their way through the press until they reached the source of the confusion, they discovered the royalists clustering round the mutilated body of Lord Kilpont, who had been stabbed to death only a short time before and two of the Irish sentries with him.

The killer was James Stewart of Ardvoirlich and the crime was the more frightful in that he had been Kilpont's closest friend and companion. The motives behind the murder were never altogether clear and the royalist account of the incident suspected Ardvoirlich of a sinister but thwarted intention to assassinate Montrose himself.

'While he was on his march, one morning by the break of day, Captain James Stewart did withdraw the Lord Kilpont to the outermost sentry, where he had a long and serious discourse with him; at the end whereof, my Lord, knocking upon his breast, was overheard to say these words: "Lord forbid man, would you undo us all?" Upon which immediately the Captain stabbed him with a dirk, and my Lord, falling upon the first stroke, he gave him fourteen more through the body as he lay on the ground, that he might be sure presumably that he would not reveal what had passed between them: for it is conceived that he had intended so much for the Marquis, and that he had disclosed his purpose to my Lord Kilpont whom he thought to have engaged in the plot in regard of the familiarity that was between them. After the villain had committed this barbarous act, he ran to the sentry and shot him through the body; and so by reason of a thick fog, made his escape to the rebels by whom he was well received.'[31]

This allegation was also reported by Wishart in his contemporary biography of Montrose, and Bishop Guthry in his Memoirs, explicitly charged Ardvoirlich with intent to kill both Montrose and Alasdair.

The account of the affair as it came to be handed down within the

Ardvoirlich family (and subsequently reported to Sir Walter Scott) ascribed Stewart's motive to be a deep-seated grudge against Alasdair.

According to this version, the Irishes, during their wanderings had pillaged lands belonging to Ardvoirlich, who, shortly after joining the army at Buchanty, had formally asked Montrose for redress. The King's Lieutenant, unwilling to antagonise Alasdair, had returned an evasive answer, and Ardvoirlich, growing more dissatisfied, challenged the MacDonald to single combat. Acting on Kilpont's information, Montrose then placed both men under arrest until they agreed to a reconciliation. They were eventually persuaded to shake hands in his presence – which they did with ill grace, and Ardvoirlich, who was also a very powerful man, gripped Alasdair's hand so hard that he drew blood from beneath the MacDonald's finger-nails. Ardvoirlich, however, was by no means satisfied:

'A few days after the Battle of Tippermuir, when Montrose with his army was encamped at Collace, an entertainment was given by him to his officers in honour of the victory – and Kilpont and his comrade Ardvoirlich were among the party. After returning to their quarters, Ardvoirlich, who seemed still to brood over his quarrel with the MacDonald, and being heated with drink, began to blame Kilpont for his part in preventing his obtaining redress, and reflecting against Montrose for not allowing him what he considered proper reparation. Kilpont of course defended the conduct of both himself and his kinsman Montrose, till their argument came to high words; and finally from the state they were in to blows, when Ardvoirlich with his dirk struck Kilpont dead on the spot.'[32]

This version of the story is said to have been originated by the natural son of Ardvoirlich called John Dhu Mor, who was with his father at Collace, and thus may have actually witnessed the murder. John Dhu Mor lived until the Revolution and passed on the story to his grandson, himself a centegenarian, who in due course recounted it to the father of Sir Walter Scott's informant. However, the veracity of the tale is doubtful on a number of points.

From what is known about the movements of Alasdair and his Irishes after their landing in Ardnamurchan, they do not appear to have marched or pillaged in the vicinity of Ardvoirlich's lands. Rather, what Ardvoirlich may have objected to, was the presence among Alasdair's following of a number of MacGregors – outlaws with whom his family had long been at feud. Ardvoirlich was the son of that wretched woman who, while preg-nant, had been confronted by the head of her murdered brother, John Drummond, the King's forester in Glenartney[33], and driven mad in consequence. He was himself a man of violent tempers and mentally unstable, as if his mother's dreadful shock had somehow affected her unborn child.

The Ardvoirlich lands bordered on the Campbells sphere of influence and James Stewart himself may have been a reluctant recruit to Montrose's army at Buchanty, joining against his inclination only because he deferred to the wishes of Kilpont. The choice had cost him dear, since his son had died of wounds after Tippermuir, while Argyll, with an almost uncanny apprehension, singled him out for especial pressure in the days that followed. Among the Breadalbane manuscripts are two letters from Argyll to Campbell of Glenorchy dated 4th and 5th September (thus coinciding with Kilpont's murder), directing that Ardvoirlich's goods were to be seized and brought along with the army. It seems therefore that Argyll may have had some special hold over Ardvoirlich, and the alleged plot to assassinate Montrose and the murder of Kilpont when he resisted, may have resulted from pressure or black-mail by the Campbell. Immediately after escaping from Collace, Ardvoirlich joined Argyll, who appointed him a major in his own regi-ment, and he served with some distinction on the Covenant side throughout the Civil War.

The covenanting authorities praised Ardvoirlich for killing Kilpont and formally pardoned him for his actions at Tippermuir since:

'... heartily thereafter repenting of this error in joining with the rebels, and abhorring their cruelty, (Ardvoirlich) resolves with his friends to forsake their wicked company, and imparted this resolution to the late Lord Kilpont. But he, out of his malignant disposition, opposed the same, and fell in struggle with James Stewart, who for his own relief, was forced to kill him at the kirk of Collace, with two Irish rebels who resisted his escape... and so came straight to Argyll and offered his service to his country. Whose courage in this particular being consid-ered by the Committee of Estates they... did find and declare that the said Stewart of Ardvoirlich did good service to the kingdom in killing Lord Kilpont and two Irish rebels being in actual rebellion against the country, and approved of what he did therein.'[34]

The favourable reception given to Ardvoirlich indicated that any person who joined the royalists might be assassinated with impunity and the Committee of Estates now put a formal price on Montrose's head and offered a bounty of £20,000 (Scots) for his capture dead or alive.

Lord Kilpont's followers carried his body home for burial at Menteith, and thus, in addition to the personal loss of a close kinsman, the incident cost Montrose a further 400 men. He broke camp, and marched towards Dundee, but the town was well defended, and having neither the time nor the artillery to conduct a protracted siege, he turned north into Angus where his own lands lay in the hope of raising support among the gentry of the Mearns. In this he was again disappointed. Some who had promised help, now withdrew. The majority continued to wait cautiously upon events. Amidst the almost universal defection, only the Ogilvie family declared openly for the King, and Lord Airlie rode in with his two younger sons[35] and forty well-armed cavaliers. Another welcome recruit was Nathaniel Gordon, who had taken to brigandage since the northern rising and now brought thirty troopers to fight under the King's General. In all, the army at this time numbered some 1500 foot soldiers, and about 80 horse, together with baggage animals, camp followers, and a number of prisoners taken after Tippermuir. In the north, news of Montrose's march into Angus caused the Estates to commission Lord George Gordon to gather an army for the defence of Aberdeen. Gordon was a reluctant Covenanter, and although he called a muster at Kildrummy, the local Covenanting lairds – Forbes, Frazer, Crichton, and their kin – suspected him of latent royalism (he was Huntly's heir after all) and preferred to gather their own forces at Aberdeen. Lord Gordon was probably relieved at their refusal to serve under him, and as a somewhat equivocal gesture of good faith, he sent his youngest brother, Lord Lewis Gordon with twenty troopers to enlist as a gentleman volunteer. He then disbanded his force at Kildrummy, and keeping only 300 horse, rode south at a leisurely pace so that the Committee could not later accuse him of desertion.

The Covenant army mustering at Aberdeen numbered about 2500 foot and 500 horse, composed of the Clans Forbes and Fraser, with the lairds of Banff and Aberdeenshire, elements of the Fifeshire regiments withdrawn from garrison duty, the town militia, and conscripted citizens of Aberdeen. It became quickly apparent, however, that the problem was one of leadership, since none of the northern Covenanters had any previous experience of military command. In the event, responsibility devolved upon Lord Burleigh as President of the Provincial Committee of Aberdeen, with the Lords Fraser, Crichton, Frendraught, Lewis Gordon, and Sir William Forbes of Craigievar as his principal lieutenants. They took the precaution of sending their money and 'best gear' to Dunnottar Castle for safe keeping, and planned to stop Montrose at the Bridge of Dee.

News of their muster reached the King's Lieutenant while he was in the Mearns. Clearly, it was necessary to strike at one of the two covenanting armies that were now in the field against him, and to do so without delay. If Argyll and Burleigh joined forces their resulting superiority would make the odds too great, while if he hesitated and allowed Argyll to get close, there was the obvious danger that the Covenant commanders would concert and trap his small force between them. He decided, logically, to attack Burleigh at Aberdeen. The apathy of the Angus gentry, and his failure to win any appreciative following in the Mearns, made it imperative that he should gain access to the Gordon territory. If the royalist cause in Scotland was to triumph, or indeed to survive, the key to success or failure lay ultimately at Huntly. Although the Gordons were leaderless with the Marquis absent, and Lord George Gordon in apparent association with the Covenanters, the Gordon lairds executed, in prison, or outlaw, this had always been the breeding ground of opposition to the Covenant. If he could defeat Burleigh at Aberdeen before Argyll arrived, the road to Huntly would be open, and the Covenanters' military grip on Banff and Aberdeenshire at least temporarily broken – long enough perhaps for him to appeal to the Gordon clansmen to rise again, and with some hope that they might obey the summons.

Accordingly, he struck north, through Fettercairn in the lee of the hills, and by a pass called the Cryne's Corse Mounth to Deeside. Suspecting correctly that the Bridge of Dee would be held in strength, he marched swiftly up-river to a ford near the Mills of Drum, and by 11th September camped in the ground of Crathes Castle. Meanwhile, the Covenant detachment which had been outflanked at the Bridge of Dee retired hastily upon the main army, and the Covenanters prepared to fight at a place known as the Crabstane, a short distance outside Aberdeen.

Conscious of his obligations as the King's Lieutenant, Montrose was determined to adhere to the formalities, and on the morning of Friday, 13th September, as the armies prepared for the battle, he sent forward a messenger and a young Irish drummer boy to beat a parley and demand the surrender of Aberdeen in the King's name. The small delegation approached the town and were conducted to the Bowbridge where Lord Burleigh and his officers together with the Provost and city magistrates, were holding a council of war. The Covenanters were civil enough and 'caused the commissioner and drummer drink hardly' and one of the magistrates even gave the boy a coin valued at £6 Scots. But they were determined to fight and refused to evacuate the old men, women, and children as Montrose had also suggested.

As the deputation returned, the Covenant regiments were marching out of the city to the Crabstane where the army was being marshalled into line, and as they passed the Fife regiment, a soldier, regardless of their flag of truce, callously shot the young drummer boy. This act of wanton cruelty took place in full view of the royalist army, now drawn up by the How Burn, and a growl of anger spread along the ranks of Irishes at the pitiless killing of a child in flagrant breach of any accepted code of war. It was told afterward how Montrose, who was incensed, swore aloud in the hearing of his officers that the boy's death would be avenged.

The Covenant army took up a strong position along the crest of the brae in front of the town, facing south towards the How Burn. The road from Aberdeen ran parallel to their rear, and on the right flank it continued behind the crest down to the Upper Justice Mills. From the centre of the position, a lane (the Hardgate) descended the slope to their front through a number of detached cottages and gardens, which were occupied by a strong force of skirmishers. On the left, the ground levelled out slightly and was eminently suitable for cavalry. The foot regiments were marshalled in three divisions with 250 horse on each flank. The Aberdeen militia were probably to the right of the line displaying the famous banner of 'Bon Accord' which had been their ancestors' battle standard at Harlaw two hundred years before. Lord Burleigh commanded the right hand division, and Lord Lewis Gordon the left. The cannon were sited in front of the main battle line where, having the advantage of the higher ground, they could direct a plunging fire on the royalists massing by the How Burn.

Alasdair led his Irishes across the stream and attacked the cottages that straddled the Hardgate, dislodging the Covenant pickets and driving off a body of lancers who had been posted in support. The royalists then advanced some way up the slope and deployed into line facing the Covenant army. The Irish regiments again formed the centre, with Alasdair's small band of MacDonalds and the remaining clansmen of Atholl and Lochaber. Montrose divided his slender cavalry force into two

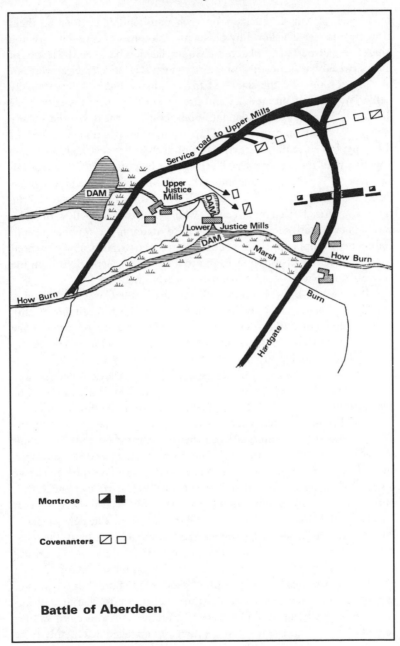

Battle of Aberdeen

squadrons, placing 40 cavaliers on each flank and strengthening them after the manner developed by Gustavus Adolphus of Sweden with 100 musketeers dispersed by platoons chequer-fashion between the troops of horse. Because of Burleigh's superiority in cavalry, shock tactics were out of the question, and the stance of the royalist wings was intentionally defensive – relying on mobility and fire-power to protect the vulnerable flanks of their shorter battle line, and repulse attacks by the enemy lancers. The cannon captured at Tippermuir were positioned in front of the army, but since they were trained uphill their fire was likely to be less effective than the Covenant artillery on the heights. Nathaniel Gordon and Colonel James Hay commanded the left wing with Captain Mortimer directing the musketeers. Sir William Rollo and Colonel Sibbald had the right wing. Alasdair led in the centre, while Montrose himself, with Airlie and a small staff remained mounted to maintain a mobile, overall command. Equipped with the spoils of Perth, the royalists now presented a more conventional appearance, and to distinguish themselves from the enemy, each soldier wore a rip of oats in his bonnet.

The action began with a stand-off cannonade, the Covenanters having slightly the better of it, before Lord Lewis Gordon led his twenty troopers down the hill in a gesture against Montrose's right wing. They came on in the old style, advancing in line to fire at a gallop before peeling off 'in caracole' to reform and repeat the manoeuvre. It was a gallant sight, but although it was done with courage and panache, they did not get close enough for their volleys to trouble Rollo's men. The Lord Lewis withdrew, having made no impression, but with Gordon honour satisfied.

Behind him, however, a more serious attack was developing, as the Lords Fraser and Crichton ordered their squadrons for a major assault against the royalist right. But their 200 dragoons advanced at a slow trot, checking to fire their carbines and reload, and showed no spirit to charge home. Rollo's musketeers stood them off with regular volleys, and as they milled indecisively around the perimeter, the 40 cavaliers counter attacked and drove them back up the hill in confusion. The deficiencies in the Covenant leadership were becoming apparent. On the bluff, the other lairds of Forbes and Buchan, who might have charged at the critical moment to support the first attack, continued to look on; as the Gordon historian later recalled, 'not for want of good will to fight, but for want of experience, not knowing that it was their right time to charge; and this error came chiefly for want of a General Commander whose orders they should obey'.[36] Fraser regrouped his men and attacked again, only to be repulsed with loss. This time he withdrew altogether, and Rollo's men could lean on their arms and await the next move in the battle.

The danger was not past. The Covenant right and centre had remained inactive while their cavalry attacked on the left, but under cover of this diversion, a force of 100 horse and 400 foot had been detached from the main body with orders to march along the service road behind the crest, and work their way round to a position a little to the rear of Montrose's left flank. Having arrived at this point unseen, a determined assault might have rolled up the royalist line and decided the battle there and then. But the Covenanters halted on a slight eminence, apparently awaiting a general order to attack. In these brief moments of hesitation, Nathaniel Gordon saw the threat, and while Mortimer swung his musketeers into a line to stand them off, he sent urgently to the general for help. On the right, Rollo had by now beaten off the last of Fraser's attacks, and having no reserve at all, Montrose promptly ordered the whole of his right wing to cross over to the left at the double. Once they had been reinforced, Nathaniel Gordon and Mortimer stormed the hillock and dislodged the Covenanters from their position of vantage on the flank. The Covenant cavalry fell back in confusion, but the foot were caught scrambling in the open and the royalist troopers cut them to pieces before they could retire to safety.

On the Covenant side meanwhile, Sir William Forbes of Craigievar, who had studied war on the continent and knew the value of shock tactics in battle, had watched impatiently as Fraser's squadrons withdrew in disorder. Seeing that Nathaniel Gordon and the bulk of the royalist cavalry were heavily engaged on the flank, he called out his own troop of horse and led them at full gallop into the royalist centre. Alasdair's seasoned Irishes had faced cavalry before, however. When Forbes's horsemen charged home, they opened their files to let them through, and facing quickly about, shot the Covenanters down as they passed. Unsupported, Craigievar's single troop lost their momentum and were swallowed up by the royalist centre as the Irishes closed ranks behind them and the Highlanders gaffed the troopers out of their saddles with their great hooked Lochaber axes. Craigievar himself was dragged off his horse and taken prisoner.

There was now a pause in the manoeuvering while the cannonade continued. Due mainly to the inadequacies of the Covenanting commanders, the battle so far had been unco-ordinated and episodic. The Covenant horse were disorganised and slow to regroup, and their centre had not moved from the crest of the ridge. Nevertheless, although the royalists had successfully beaten off each attack, the issue was still in the balance, since sooner or later the Covenanters would learn their lesson and attack both flanks simultaneously, and their superiority in numbers would turn the battle. The royalists had no reserves, and their cavalry, having fought on both flanks were already exhausted and the horses blown. In the centre, the Irish regiments had endured a galling cannonade for almost two hours. Irregular infantry were always nervous before cannon, and their steadiness and fortitude under fire had been remarkable. Almost every account of the battle mentions the heroism of one Irish soldier in particular whose leg had been shattered by cannon ball, and calmly leaning on his neighbour, had called for the surgeon's saw and severed his own limb – joking that he hoped that the General might find him a place in the cavalry.[37] He then handed the amputated leg to a friend with instructions to 'bury that, lest some hungry Scot should eat it.' But even the Irishes could waver under continuous bombardment, and this conventional battle stance would result in steadily mounting casualties and eventual defeat. Their way of fighting was to attack, and the Highlanders in the centre were shouting at Alasdair to lead them to close quarters with the enemy.

The Covenant cavalry were temporarily out of action – though possibly massing behind the Covenant position – and their absence presented the best opportunity for rushing the crest. Montrose galloped along the line, calling to Alasdair, O'Cahan, and the other Irish officers that there was nothing to be gained from fighting at a distance, 'for resolution must do it'. At the sound of the trumpet, the Irishes began to run up the slope and hurled themselves at the Covenant formations along the summit. Burleigh's regiments received them standing, took the shock of it, and began to recoil as the royalist attack splintered their files and broke the defence. When once their lines were pierced the Covenant divisions started to fragment as units broke and ran, and the Irishes clubbed their way through the press and boiled around the isolated groups who tried to stand and fight. Within a few minutes all order had disappeared, as the Lowland regiments disintegrated, and the Covenant army was in full flight.

The cavalry did not return to salvage anything from the rout, but having seen the foot soldiers over-run, turned and galloped for their lives. Lord Burleigh and his staff, being well mounted, fled across the Bridge of Don and into Buchan and left the Fifeshire levies to be decimated on the field. The last to retreat were the regular garrison of Aberdeen, who alone withdrew in some order and tried to break out southwards by crossing the Dee. But Alasdair saw their intention and 400 of his Irishes cut them off and killed them at the river.

The town militia, to the grief of Aberdeen, fled back towards the city with the Highlanders bounding after them, so that the running slaughter continued through the gates, and the streets of the town itself became part of the general killing area. Covenant casualties were afterwards put at about 1000 men killed – the majority of them during the rout. The royalists claimed to have lost less than a dozen men killed outright, with rather more than a score of badly wounded.

Yet within Aberdeen, the aftermath was remembered with greater horror than the battle itself. The Irishes and the Highlanders burst into the town:

> ... hewing and cutting down with their broadswords all manner of men they could overtake (within the town, upon the streets, or in their houses, and round about the town as our men were fleeing) without mercy. The cruel Irishes, seeing a man well clad, would first strip him and save the clothes unspoiled, and then kill the man. We lost three pieces of cannon with much good armour besides the plundering of our toen houses, merchant booths and all, which was pitiful to see... (Montrose) had promised to them the plundering of the town for their good service. However, the Lieutenant stayed not but returned back from Aberdeen to the camp this same Friday night, leaving the Irishes killing, robbing, and plundering the town at their pleasure. And nothing could be heard but pitiful howling, crying, weeping, mourning, through all the streets.
>
> Thus the Irishes continued Friday, Saturday, Sunday, Monday. Some women they raped and deflowered, and others they took by force to serve them in their camp. It is lamentable to hear how the Irishes who had got the spoil of the town abused the same. The men they had killed they would not suffer to be buried, but stripped them of their clothes and left the naked bodies lying on the ground. The wife dared not cry nor weep at the slaughter of her husband before her eyes, nor the mother for the son nor the daughter for her father; for if they were heard then they were presently slain also.[38]

This is one of the most graphic passages in Spalding's *Memorials*, and written by an Aberdonian who was probably an eye witness – and a royalist as well – it has proved damning evidence and left an indelible stain upon the honour of Montrose. It is possible that Spalding exaggerated, and that having lived through the event he continued to survive off the horror of it. Parliamentary propaganda, particularly when describing the unspeakable barbarity of the Catholic Rebellion, had caused the Irish to be regarded with especial abhorrence in Scotland. They were considered sub-human and worse than animals, and during the Civil War on both sides of the border, Irish prisoners were generally hanged or shot without compunction. Thus to an Aberdonian, atrocities at the hands of an Irish army may have seemed inevitable, and in some degree the subsequent account justified the expectation.

In fact, Spalding also recorded that the bulk of the royalist army remained 'standing close unbroken' on the battlefield, so that only a small portion probably went on the rampage inside the town. Later testimony to the Committee of Estates was more cautious. On this evidence it is certain that the later stages of the battle extended into Aberdeen itself, and during the subsequent fighting in the streets, numbers of innocent citizens were caught out of doors and killed along with the fleeing militia. Although the main royalist force remained outside the city, some elements at least – Irishes and Highlanders – started looting, and in the process, numbers of townfolk were maltreated, robbed or raped, or murdered during the night that followed, but the accounts do not suggest a general massacre – representative of the horrors which had become commonplace during the Thirty Years War in Germany. Aberdeen was not Magdeburg, and Montrose was no Tilly. Significantly, even the Covenanters when taxing him with needless slaughter, acquitted him of 'any but what was done in the field', and the Cromwellian Richard Frank, who visited Aberdeen in 1657, when recording the battle took occasion to praise the 'incomparable conduct' of the King's General.[39]

Montrose's fault was as much one of delay. He did not enter Aberdeen himself until the day after the battle, and was appalled by what he saw. The remaining Aberdonians – for the most part women, and the very old and young – were still in a state of shock, hiding in their houses and too terrified to show themselves outside or to remove the corpses that stiffened in the streets. Many had fixed a sprig of oats to their doors, hoping that by such a token they might be spared the savagery of the Highlanders who would recognise the royalist badge and not molest them.

Montrose ordered the main body of his army to Kintore and Inverurie, sixteen miles off, while with a number of senior officers he set about restoring order in the city. The prisoners in the tolbooth who had been gaoled for their part in Huntly's rising, were released. The citizens were commanded to bury the dead and clear the mess of battle off the streets, while looters found scavenging in the town were whipped off and charged to rejoin their regiments under pain of summary execution. However, all further activity was brought to an end by news that a large Covenant army under Argyll was already at Brechin and within two days march. On Monday, 16th September, Montrose rejoined his troops at Inverurie, and marching through Strathdon, reached Kildrummy Castle in the shelter of the hills. From there he sent out patrols to seek recruits among the local Gordon gentry, and waited to see what Argyll would do.

CHAPTER 11

The Fight at Fyvie:
Alasdair at Mingary

The Covenant army under the Marquis of Argyll straggled into Aberdeen during 18th and 19th September. Having been joined along the march by the survivors of Tippermuir and Aberdeen, the Campbell now commanded some 6000 troops, including three regiments of his own clansmen, Lothian's regiment, Sir Mungo Campbell of Lawers' regiment of musketeers which had been withdrawn from the Covenant force in Ireland, Buchanan's regiment, and 1000 cavalry under the Earl of Dalhousie. On 21st and 22nd September, he held councils of war in Aberdeen at which it was decided to divide the army, retaining the cavalry and Lothian's and Lawers' regular troops but deploying the rest to 'keep the country'. Then taking the Lords George and Lewis Gordon with him – as much hostages as allies – Argyll moved into Strathbogie after Montrose.

The Covenant march was cautious and unhurried, but if the Campbell's methods were unspectacular, they were nevertheless effective. His primary aim was to prevent Montrose from obtaining the support of the local population, and in implementing this design he was able to benefit from the experience of his previous pacification of the Gordon lands earlier in the year. Concentrations of regular troops deployed to police and punish within their areas of influence kept the power of the Covenanting government very much in evidence throughout the main centres of the Gordon territory, and were an essential first step towards containing any likely rebellion. In the meanwhile, his own column of cavalry and foot continued to pursue the royalist army itself.

The Covenant inquisition followed in close attendance. Any persons thought to sympathise or have communicated with the enemy were closely interrogated, and along the line of march, any area or community which had helped or supplied Montrose was punished with exemplary severity. The unfortunate population, caught in the path of both armies, suffered most. As the contemporary Aberdonian Spalding commented:

'The country was also holden in under continual fear, none knowing whom to follow, and gladly would have (seen the issue) resolved by a battle between them'. But without Gordon support Montrose could not risk battle against a vastly superior Covenant army, and while the royalists were forced to retreat the balance of fear remained in Argyll's favour. The season also suited him. The harvest was in; stooks ready for burning, grain for seizing, and men who lost their crops and cattle in the autumn could starve during the winter months to follow. Royalist sympathisers faced total ruin, and to make certain that the Gordons would have neither the will nor the resources to support Montrose, Argyll continued systematically to ruin their lands.

The success of these tactics may be measured by the fact that not one of the Gordon lairds rode in to join the King's Lieutenant. Despite his Royal Commission, Montrose was still no more than the leader of what to all intents and purposed was merely a small insurgent movement. He had no secure base, no fixed support, no supply line. He was dependent on the country for provisions, but since his purpose was to win recruits from the Gordon gentry he could not afford to lose the good will of the potentially royalist population. Nor could he defend those who had helped him, since his army, in contrast to Argyll's heavy front-line regiments, was composed of lightly armed troops – fast and mobile, but unsuited to a static defence of territory and demonstrably not strong enough to protect his supporters from the revenge of the Covenanters. Those lairds who helped or supplied him today must face an inevitable reckoning with Argyll tomorrow, and it was easy for others to blame the royalists – foreign Irishes as most of them were – for bringing down yet further suffering on people who had already suffered enough for the politics of their own chief. It also became apparent that the Marquis of Huntly himself still bore a grudge against the Graham for his alleged 'betrayal' in 1639, and from Strathnaver was actively deterring the Gordon gentry from joining the army – 'forbidding his friends and clansmen even with threats to have nothing to do with Montrose or help him by word or deed.'[40]

Because of their deficiency in cavalry, the royalists dared not risk being caught in the open by Argyll's regiments of horse, but were obliged to keep close to the shelter of the hills. In a morass somewhere in Strathdon they buried the cannon captured at Tippermuir and Aberdeen, and relieved of this weight, climbed through Glen Ernan to Tomintoul, and then by Glen Avon and the Braes of Abernethy to Rothiemurchus where they camped on the shore of Loch An Eilean. Montrose's intention was to put the Spey between himself and Argyll, but when he approached the crossing, he found a force of 5000 men – Grants, and the levies of Moray, Ross, Caithness, and Sutherland – mustered on the opposite bank. He therefore marched downstream and camped in Abernethy wood. It was by now 27th September.

In the region of Strathbogie, Argyll continued to sap the Gordon wealth. The Covenanters burned their way through Cromar, Aboyne, and Abergeldie on Deeside, then north to waste the country around Huntly itself, and on to the spoil of Enzie and the Bog of Gight. All horses and livestock were driven off, arms seized, the newly harvested corn eaten or destroyed. These depredations were carried out under the resentful eyes of Lord George Gordon, who as heir to this damage, saw only too clearly that Argyll intended nothing less than the ruin of his clan. But he could only rage at his own impotence and await a later opportunity for revenge.

Seeing how the Campbell was lacerating the Gordon lands, Montrose realised that the Covenant army would have to be lured away from Aberdeenshire before the country was devastated beyond recovery and the people altogether subdued. He therefore calculated that if he was to leave the area and strike south again, Argyll would be obliged to drop his prey and follow, and in the rugged mountainous country where cavalry was no advantage, the Covenanters, with all the impediments and encumbrance of a Lowland army would not be able to keep pace with his fast-moving Gaelic troops. In this way he might win time enough to circle back and try the Gordons once more.

Thus began 'that strange coursing... thrice round about from Spey to Atholl, wherein Argyll and Lothian's soldiers were tired out!'[41] The royalists marched south into Badenoch, up Spey and Truim, by Drumochter and across the high wilderness of the Grampians. Somewhere in the mountains Montrose fell ill of fever brought on by strain and fatigue, and the Covenant propagandists optimistically gave out that he was dead. But he recovered, and by 4th October, the army had swung down Glengarry and reached once more the fertile valley of Atholl.

Montrose garrisoned Blair Castle which from now on became his headquarters, a prison for the hostages whom he hoped to exchange and a hospital for the royalist wounded. The Atholl and Badenoch men who had fought at Aberdeen for the most part now returned to their homes, and their places were filled by another 300 local recruits and some 400 of the Clan Chattan who hitherto had remained cautiously obedient to

Argyll. But while the army paused at Atholl, Alasdair received news of trouble in Ardnamurchan, where the Campbells were besieging the Irish garrisons whom he had left at Mingary and Lochaline. He at once asked permission to go to their relief, and took nearly 1000 of the Irish troops with him. It was agreed that he should also try again to raise the Clanranald and others among the western clans whom rumour said grew restive, and then rejoin the army before the year's end.

O'Cahan's regiment of Irish remained with Montrose as the nucleus of his now much depleted force – amounting probably to a mere 800 foot and 80 horse. Leaving Atholl, they marched through Killiekrankie and by Loch Fascally along the River Tummel. Continuing then by Tayside to Dunkeld, Montrose now ordered the systematic destruction of Covenanters' property – an indication perhaps that Argyll's depredations were effectively discouraging the local royalists from offering support, and he judged it expedient to retaliate in kind. Avoiding a Covenant force at the Bridge of Dee, the small column continued through Monymusk and Strathbogie and by 21st October had reached Huntly. Montrose camped in the vicinity of the Castle and renewed his attempts to open negotiations with the Gordon Marquis. But Huntly was still absent, and the clansmen were either in hiding or reluctant to move without the approval of their chief. The royalists raided around Strathbogie, gaining confidence from minor successes, but as it became clear that Huntly was not prepared to co-operate with the King's Lieutenant – whom he took for an upstart with no claim to authority in the north – the campaign again lost momentum. A week's effort yielded only 200 recruits of doubtful calibre, and it seemed that little would be gained by lingering in Strathbogie. To the west, the dark ridges of the mountain line offered a safe retreat into the Cairngorms, but Montrose, either reluctant to accept defeat, or possibly because his men were again short of ammunition which could not be replenished in the Highlands, seemed unwilling to abandon the Gordon country. The royalists wandered eastwards through Tollie Barclay to the River Ythan, and on 27th October, occupied Fyvie Castle, the ancestral home of the Earls of Dunfermline.

In the meanwhile, Argyll's army had followed heavy-footed, eight to ten days behind Montrose. But the royalists' pause at Huntly enabled the Campbell to close the gap. By 26th October he was at Aberdeen, where he was reinforced by twenty one troops of horse sent north by General Leslie, Earl of Leven, and on 28th October, the Covenanters' advance cavalry screen found Montrose at Fyvie.

The royalists were taken by surprise. Bad intelligence in doubtful country had led Montrose to underestimate the closeness of the pursuit and he had assumed Argyll to be still struggling in the Grampians. When the outlying pickets came running in to Fyvie to give the alarm, the Covenant horse were barely two miles away and approaching fast. Taken unawares and with their own single troop of cavalry temporarily absent on a foraging expedition, the royalists could not retreat across the open country to Strathbogie since the enemy dragoons would have caught them long before they reached the shelter of the hills. The small force of Irishes and Highlanders therefore had no choice but to stand at bay where they were. While the royalists prepared to defend the castle, the Covenant force began to deploy into the valley, and the appearance of a great black banner with a golden cross and the motto 'For Religion, Country, Crown, and Covenant' confirmed that they were commanded by Argyll in person.

Fyvie Castle stands within a loop of the River Ythan. At that time the valley bottom was marsh and watermeadow, undrained bogland accessible only along spits of hard ground by which any attacking force would be obliged to approach. The castle itself stood on a terrace of firm ground surrounded on three sides by water-logged scrub, and connected with the small village to the south by a narrow causeway, where again, a small force might hope to hold off a stronger attacker. But the castle was a trap. It had originally been the baronial keep of the Thanes of Fortmartyine, but the present more elaborate structure with its drum-towered entrance to the south, its rich heraldic decoration, corbelling, angle-turrets, and crow-stepped roofs, dated from the beginning of the seventeenth century when Alexander Seton, Earl of Dunfermline and Chancellor of Scotland had converted it into a magnificent residence. His architectural alterations had weakened its fortifications, however, and Montrose, perceiving that it could not withstand a prolonged siege, did not make it the centre of his defence.

To the east was a small loch, marsh-banked, while behind the castle, and rising slightly above it between the river and the loch, a low bluff or ridge climbed steeply for about a hundred feet. This hill-face was broken by ditches and turf dykes once raised by farmers to fence off their allotments, and the slope was also thickly wooded. Montrose hurriedly positioned his men up the side of this bluff where the trees and coppice would hinder an enemy attempting to advance in formation, and the musketeers started digging trenches and raising breastworks to improve the position as best they could. Nathaniel Gordon and the troop of horse, who had

Montrose's first march ———————→

Montrose's second march ---→--

SCALE

Campaign of Tippermuir & Aberdeen

Miles

0   6   12   18   24

returned at the sound of the alarm, were posted to the rear, where the bluff merged with the high ground behind it and might be reached by troops who crossed the river lower down the valley where the ground was firm and attempted to attack from this direction. A further body of soldiers was probably stationed to hold the narrow causeway south of the castle entrance. The royalists were still short of ammunition, and the Irish armourers were set to work melting down the castle pewter and chamber pots to make musket balls. The shortage of powder, however, could only be remedied by capturing quantities from the enemy.

The main body of the Covenant army halted out of range, while Lothian's regiment of foot were sent forward to force the position or draw the royalists into the open. These were regular infantry who attacked with spirit, and as their initial charge went home, the 200 Gordons whom Montrose had newly recruited, promptly threw down their weapons and fled, so that the earthwork which they were defending was captured in the first rush. The other royalists were also demoralised by their defection, and began to give ground as the perimeter of their position was overrun, and the Covenanters began infiltrating the firing points further up the bluff. Montrose saw that the situation had suddenly become desperate, and called on O'Cahan and Donald Farquharson of Deeside to lead a vigorous counter-attack and dislodge the enemy from the captured trenches. The Irishes and Highlanders rallied to their officers, and stormed down the slope in a wild charge that drove Lothian's men clear out of the wood and onto the flat marsh below, leaving the royalists to strip the dead and wounded of their precious powder horns and augment their dwindling supply.

Argyll, unwisely, next ordered forward a regiment of horse, who struggled through the boggy valley bottom and tried to charge up one edge of the wooded slope. But the royalists had recovered their nerve with O'Cahan's charge, and this time withdrew intentionally to lure the horsemen into the wood among the dykes, where the musketeers waited behind cover to shoot them down as they pecked and floundered in the ditches. In the event the new Atholl recruits in their excitement opened fire before the trap was properly sprung, and the Covenanters were able to extricate themselves, albeit with considerable loss. An attack on the flank by 500 horse who had circled the position to engage Nathaniel Gordon's troop, rode into the concentrated fire of the Irish Musketeers whom Montrose had posted with his few horse to stiffen the defence.

As they milled about in confusion and the fallen horses entangled the others spurring in behind, the small body of royalist cavalry counter-attacked and chased them off the ridge. By nightfall, the Covenanters had gained no permanent foothold at any point on the royalist perimeter, and Argyll withdrew his forces two miles and made camp.

However, aware that Montrose's men were short of ammunition, he returned to the attack next morning, and the pattern of fighting continued much as on the day before. The boggy ground prevented the Covenanters from advancing in any regular order, and before going into action, each attacking unit had to pick its way across the open marsh under a galling musket fire until it could deploy and assault the bluff itself. But the ridge was a natural bastion, and among the ditches and earthworks the Covenant troops were unable to keep any disciplined formation. Irish musketeers among the trees shot them at close range as they scrambled up the incline, and the fighting in the trenches was savage and bloody with the Highlanders having the advantage in the close-quarter killing round the dykes. Covenant infantry and cavalry continued to attack at intervals throughout the day, but their morale began to weaken as the casualties mounted, and as each assault failed the troops grew disheartened at having constantly to abandon the trenches which they had temporarily won at a dreadful cost in dead and wounded. At length, badly mauled, Argyll withdrew and since his army had already consumed all the available provisions in the immediate neighbourhood, he ordered his troops to fall back a further two miles and leaguer at Crechie.

Montrose promptly seized the opportunity to slip away from Fyvie during the night. The royalists marched swiftly through Turriff and Rothiemay back to Huntly Castle, since Montrose still entertained hopes of persuading the Gordon chief. But he was again disappointed. A rumour that the Marquis of Huntly had returned to Enzie proved to be false, and the proud Gordon was still insisting that he would recognize no other authority in the north without express instructions from the King himself. The royal cause in Scotland was going down because Huntly, out of his old grudge against Montrose, would not allow another to have the glory which he himself had so signally failed to win while it might have been in his power to do so. Montrose sent Huntly a copy of the Royal Commission by hand of the Gordon's baillie, but he was now despairing of that nobleman's support – and yet without it, the Gordons would not stir.

On 31st October, Argyll pursued Montrose to Huntly Castle. After his experience at Fyvie, however, he was reluctant to launch a general attack, and instead, proposed a conference under a flag of truce. During this respite, he attempted to suborn a number of royalist officers, until Montrose grew alarmed at the possible extent of this subversion, and having nothing to gain by staying at Huntly, decided to make a break for the hills. The baggage had been sent off under convoy and the troops were ready to march when it was discovered that Colonel Sibbald – the very friend who had accompanied Montrose in his dash across the border – had deserted to Argyll and possibly betrayed the plan to withdraw during the night. Montrose immediately recalled the baggage train, and, as if he had changed his mind, remained at Huntly for another four days. Finally, on 6th November, having lit fires through the camp as usual, the small royalist force slipped away under cover of darkness along the moorland roads to Balvenie Castle on the Fiddich.

And at Balvenie the campaign ended. The Lowland royalists would not fight through a winter in the Highlands, and argued that so small an army without cavalry support could not hope to survive on the plain. The nights were drawing in with the approach of winter, the weather was growing colder, and the hills were inhospitable and forbidding. Many had estates and families at the Covenanters' mercy, and they accepted Argyll's promises of pardon and peace with his safe-conduct to return home. Since Badenoch offered the best refuge, where cavalry would only be a hindrance, Montrose also disbanded his troop of horse, detaching Nathaniel Gordon with orders to try to win over Lord George Gordon and other likely royalists before the spring. Only Black Pate Inchbrakie with Lord Airlie and his sons remained with the army.

Argyll no longer marched after them. In mid-November he sent his cavalry to winter quarters, and with the remaining infantry occupied Dunkeld. In a daring raid, Montrose tried to surprise him there, covering twenty four miles over broken country in a single night, but despite the incredible speed of his march, Argyll got word of his coming and withdrew to the safety of Perth. Thereafter the Campbell went to Edinburgh and resigned his commission to the Committee of Estates, who gave him a formal vote of thanks with the rather malicious comment – no doubt due to his failure to finish Montrose at Fyvie – that it was more deserved because there had been so little bloodshed. Feeling perhaps that his efforts had not been fully appreciated, the Campbell returned to his castle at Inveraray for the winter season.

And at Blair Atholl, Montrose was left to repine at the failure of his enterprise. Two victories snatched against the odds and a brilliant defence at Fyvie had accomplished nothing in real terms. He had failed to raise the Gordons whose support was crucial to success. He had failed to win over his own neighbours in Strathearn and Angus on whose royalism he had counted. Above all, he had failed to alter the course of the war in England. Some front-line troops had indeed been withdrawn from Leven's army to reinforce the Covenant power in Scotland, but Newcastle and Tynemouth had fallen in October, and with them Charles I had effectively lost the north of England.

Montrose's army had dwindled to O'Cahan's single regiment of Irishes and a few hundred Highlanders. Messages to the Marquis of Antrim had failed to produce any Irish reinforcements and a descent on the Lowlands was impossible. As wet autumn turned to freezing winter, he waited disconsolately in Atholl, and sent patrols foraging up the Garry and over the bleak moors of Badenoch. But at the same time his scouts were also ranging to Rannoch and beyond for news in Lochaber of developments in the west. For if he was to have help from anywhere, it would have to be from the Highland clans.

Alasdair had marched to the relief of his garrisons in Morvern and Ardnamurchan. Following the Irish landing in July and the subsequent pillaging of the west Highland coast, the Campbells had swiftly concentrated their power at Dunstaffnage Castle, and three regiments of clansmen were sent to campaign in pursuit. During the first week of August a force of Campbells arrived before Mingary and laid siege to the castle. Argyll himself came to direct operations, but when developments soon required his presence elsewhere, the siege was entrusted to Sir Donald Campbell of Ardnamurchan. The Irish garrison refused all demands to surrender, but opened negotiations to effect an exchange of prisoners, principally to obtain the release of old Colkitto and his sons. Since Sir Donald Campbell received no reinforcements and dared not attempt a direct assault, the investment of the castle dragged on for two months. During this time, the garrison were completely cut off, knowing nothing of the victories at Tippermuir and Aberdeen, and by the end of September morale was low.

At the beginning of October, Argyll learned that Alasdair had separated from Montrose at Atholl, and orders were sent to Dunstaffnage that the Campbells should concentrate and intercept him at Inverlochy. However, word had already reached the force at Mingary, and on 6th October, Sir Donald Campbell suddenly struck camp and abandoned the siege. The following day the garrison itself got definite news of Alasdair's approach.

The resistance at Mingary had in the meanwhile been watched with sympathetic interest by the neighbouring Clanranald, under their Captain, John Moydartach of Castle Tioram, who now seized the opportunity to raise the clansmen of Uist, Eigg, Moidart, and Arisaig and raid unopposed through Sunart. The Clanranald stripped the land of every cow in the byre and other four-footed beast, and when they drove the *creagh* back in triumph to Island Tioram, John Moydartach sent his son Donald with forty cows to relieve the defenders at Mingary.

Alasdair avoided the Campbell force at Inverlochy, and marched first to the relief of Kinlochaline, which being only a small fortification, he judged to be in the greater danger. Rather than commit a fresh garrison to its defence, he abandoned the tower, having first set it on fire, and reached Mingary on 16th October. There he met the young Donald Moydartach, and taking a liking to each other, they went together to Castle Tioram where Alasdair told the Captain of the Clanranald of the recent victories in the Lowlands, and proposed a major rising in the King's name against the MacCailein Mor. Having just incurred Argyll's wrath by destroying the Campbell wealth in Ardnamurchan, John Moydartach readily agreed, and after installing a fresh garrison in Mingary, they marched their combined war-band to Arisaig and Morar, gathering in the fighting strength of Moidart on the way. From Morar they sent to MacLeod of Dunvegan, inviting him to join the venture, but when he declined, they continued into Knoydart to seek out Aeneas MacDonald, the heir of Glengarry, who was the effective leader of the clan. Aeneas did not join them himself, but his uncle, Donald Gorm of Scotus brought in many of the clansmen, and having collected also a number of MacLeans from Coll and Lochbuie, Alasdair decided that it was time to return east to keep his tryst at Atholl. Accordingly he led the force from the head of Glen Nevis, gathering up the MacIans of Glencoe, and passing through Lochaber he was joined by Donald Glas with the MacDonalds of Keppoch, the Stewarts of Appin, and the Clan Cameron from east of the Lochy.

Alasdair now commanded a formidable war-band – indeed possibly the finest force of Highlanders since the great Donald, Lord of the Isles, had fought the battle of Harlaw. Winding through the hills, they would have presented an outlandish and inspiring spectacle. Chieftains and petty chieftains under the Gaelic battle banners, with eagle plumes and heather in their bonnets, and multi-coloured plaids brooched with silver:

each with body-guards and gillies as befitted his degree, sword-bearer and foster brother, *blathair* to speak his will, piper with the drones full spread, and bard to sing of battles past and fashion the praise-songs of forays yet to come: and behind each chief, the train of henchmen, tacksmen, and tenants – fierce, hairy red-shanked kerns from the Western Isles, in yellow shirts and ancient habershones, armed with steel-spiked targes, broadswords, muskets, longbows, dags, and huge Lochaber axes. Almost 1800 strong they marched into Badenoch and over Drumochter to keep the rendezvous at Atholl.

CHAPTER 12

The March into Argyll

Alasdair reached Atholl in the first days of December, to receive a rapturous welcome. At a moment when the morale of the small royalist force was at a low ebb, with winter upon them, and their leaders disheartened by the desertion of friends, the arrival of the huge MacDonald with the Clanranald at his back brought hope of a new chance and a fresh campaign.

Now that the three Irish regiments were reunited as the original nucleus of the army, when counted with the small Ogilvie contingent, Struan's Robertsons from Atholl, 300 men of Deeside under Donald Farquharson of 'Strathawin', and some Gordon renegades who had remained, this reinforcement from the western clans meant that Montrose could muster nearly 3000 men. Moreover, because it was largely composed of men accustomed to all weathers, it was a force capable of marching and fighting in any season, and while the Covenant cavalry were dispersed for lack of fodder and the regular troops rested in careless security to await the spring, it presented Montrose with an opportunity to mount a winter offensive.

There was time first to welcome Alasdair and the western chieftains, and for feasting in celebration of their alliance. But when the formal greetings were done, the toasts drunk, and the stories told, Montrose called a council of war and proposed an immediate invasion of the Lowlands.

The western Gaels rejected the idea utterly. They were aware of the Civil War in England and of the Covenanters' league with the Parliament, even though the constitutional issues were only dimly understood. But while their own sense of tradition, the respect for kingship, or indeed their religion – for many of the Highlanders were still Catholic – inclined them to the royal cause, their over-riding motive was to be revenged upon the Campbells, and they had not risen in hatred of MacCailein Mor only to raid into the Lowlands. They were intent on plunder beyond the frozen passes of Breadalbane, and they confronted Montrose with the unequivocal statement that they would march to burn Argyll or they would not march at all.

The King's General was appalled. His own proposal had been bold and unconventional enough. He had suggested a winter campaign in the Lowlands on the basis that, although it would be a hazardous undertaking, it would be so unusual as to take the Covenanters by surprise. But the western chiefs were resolved on a march over some of the wildest and most desolate country in Scotland, through inaccessible mountains and trackless bogs, without food or support, and at the mercy of the Highland winter.

The risk was enormous. 'It is a far cry to Lochow' was the Campbells' boast, and it was not an empty one. At any season, the Campbell country was virtually impregnable – a compact block of territory defensible on every quarter. To the south it had the protection of the sea and a coastline guarded by a string of fortresses such as Dunskeig, Skipness, Tarbert, and Armaddie. Eastwards, it opened on the Covenanting Lowlands, the approaches barred by the strong castles of Roseneath and Dunoon, while to the north and north-east stretched the strongest natural barrier of all – a thick knot of mountains ranging from Glenorchy in western Perthshire through Breadalbane to Loch Awe: rock walls and secret paths to which only Argyll held the key and swore 'he would rather lose 100,000 florins than that any mortal should know the passes by which an armed force might invade his country'. In times past, small bands of raiders from Lochaber might have slipped over the pass of Meran on a wild night, but no-one could remember an enemy to have penetrated to Loch Awe in force. In the narrow defiles, a hundred might hold back two thousand, and in winter, an army stopped and bogged down in that desolate place would surely starve. And within these frontiers, the whole was knit by a chain of castles of which Argyll had legal or illegal possession – even as he held Dunstaffnage as 'Governor' for the King. The power of the Campbells aroused would exceed 3000 claymores – and these Gaelic fighting men also, for all their wealth and fat black cattle, with their own warlike tradition and pride of race. In their own Highlands they would fight savagely and to advantage. If the royalists survived the long march through the mountains, and were not lost or buried in the winter blizzards, there was the likely chance that their watchful enemy would ambush and cut them to pieces as they struggled through the passes. Failure or defeat could result in the destruction of the entire army.

The western chiefs would not be dissuaded, however, and so it was resolved to decide the matter by calling a general council of war at which each side might present its argument and abide by the vote of the majority. The Gaels, confident in numbers, accepted this solution, while for the King's General, the formal vote of a majority offered a means of saving face.

At the council, Montrose spoke first, and he endeavoured to outline the practical difficulties which the army would face. The first problem would be that of food. Having no regular system of supply, the column would be living off the country; but it was winter, and the region to be traversed was largely uninhabited and barren. Driving along their own meat on the hoof was out of the question, since even if there were enough cattle in Atholl (and there were not) they had eighty miles to cover over a route which was largely unknown, and speed would be of the essence. The going would be extremely hard – impossible even – and the soldiers would have to travel light and fast, each man carrying provisions for a few days only. Once committed therefore, their survival would depend on their getting through and finding sufficient food on the other side of the mountains. If they failed to penetrate Argyll before their food ran out, if they became lost or stopped in a storm, or if the land beyond did not yield up the expected provisions, they could possibly perish of starvation and exposure.

Furthermore, they had to assume that the Campbells would be alerted as soon as they entered Glenorchy, and the passes would be defended. If they pushed on blindly they would risk ambush, or the defiles behind them would be sealed, so that they would find themselves trapped 'in the vast bowels of those deserts until famine had consumed every man'.

If they did succeed in breaking into Argyll, Montrose continued, the geography of the country was such, and so to the advantage of the defenders that the army might still gain little, while the risk of some disaster would remain extremely grave. The Campbell heartland led into a series of peninsulas separated by the long sea-arms of the western lochs so that from the mountains to the sea, the country was divided 'like the teeth of a comb'. For the Campbells, each peninsula was a refuge along which to withdraw with their goods and cattle, destroying all the ferries, so that an enemy traversing the country would have to take the long route around the head of every sea-loch. For the royalists, however, each peninsula was a potential trap which could be blocked to their rear, while the Campbells, having sufficient boats and control of the coastal waters, could harass them continually and cut off their escape.

The chieftains conceded that all this was no doubt true and of great consequence, but there was much more to be said in favour of the attempt. For their speaker they deferred to Alasdair, of whom they were in some awe, and who, as Major General of the army, might best be able to persuade the King's Lieutenant.

Alasdair declared that they knew the country well enough, and one of the Glencoe men, Angus MacAlain Dubh, would guide them through the passes. It was important not to over-estimate the Campbells. It might be true that the land of Argyll was held to be inaccessible and that within memory no regular army had attempted to penetrate the mountains, but for this reason there would be more honour in the trial and glory to those who first achieved it. Indeed, the very legend of Argyll's impregnability would work to their advantage since the Campbells had come to trust the MacCailein Mor in everything, and they would find the enemy in 'careless security'.

Turning to Montrose, Alasdair argued that it would be superfluous to dwell on the Highlanders' desire for revenge, or to rehearse the list of wrongs perpetrated against the western clans by the Campbell race. There was a wider issue which must appeal to the King's Lieutenant, since it touched on the whole balance of power in Scotland. The Marquis of Argyll was the mainstay of the rebellion against the King. His private ambition and wealth, coupled with his public influence and authority had cast him as a prime mover in advancing the Covenant cause. His Campbell swordsmen enforced the writ of the Covenant government in the west, and assured his prominent position in the direction of affairs. To smash his power in isolation when opportunity offered would be strategic common sense. Destroy Argyll himself and the Covenant would never recover. Beat him in his own Highlands and the western Gaels, freed from Campbell tyranny, would rise as one to fight for the King.

Alasdair, predictably, carried the day. The Glencoe man who was to be their guide confirmed that 'there was not a township under the lordship of MacCailein but was known to him, and that if tight houses and fat cattle to feed on would answer their purpose, that they would procure them'.[42] And one of the Catholic priests who was accounted something of a meteorologist, squinted up at the sky and pronounced that as long as the wind blew from the east the weather would hold – but that they ought to set out at once. Montrose was forced to accept the vote of the council, and he ordered the army to prepare to march next day.

They left Atholl on 11th December, along the familiar hill road of that first march to Tippermuir, turning up the Tummel and round the loch by the shoulder of Schiehallion to the Tay. To approach Argyll by Benderloch would risk being stopped at Brander, but once through Breadalbane they hoped to pick up the old raiding road out of Lorne, although the MacCailein might think he had the keys of it. On Tayside they visited once more the castle of Weem, caught Argyll's creature Alexander Menzies, and burned his lands, before striking west into Breadalbane itself. At the head of Loch Tay the army divided, with John Moydartach taking the Clanranald to burn the Campbell dwellings along the southern shore while the rest of the army attacked the island castle of Eilean nam Bonnaimh where Sir Robert Campbell of Glenorchy had taken refuge on hearing of the royalists' approach. The garrison held out for several hours and Montrose, who was directing the assault from the castle orchard on the shore, narrowly escaped being killed when a musket ball struck the pear tree under which he was standing. After the island had been subdued, the Highlanders and Irishes savaged the entire glen around from the Ford of Lyon to the point of Lismore before continuing their march along the wooded slopes of Ben Lawers.

Now the going became difficult. There was no track to follow and it took a long time to cover only a short distance. The army progressed by endless detours, ascents and descents, from rock to rock against the frozen pools along the water's edge, through bogs and mossland covered in snow and ice. With every mile the country grew more desolate. They moved through an awful stillness across a landscape, majestic and terrible in its natural grandeur, and the narrow column of men struggled and clawed their way along the steep mountainsides under the great convulsions of rock that loomed above them. But it did not snow, and the intense cold was to their advantage since bogs which would otherwise have been impassable were frozen hard enough to bear a man's weight. Painfully and slowly, the army continued through this wilderness, marching doggedly through the freezing wind until eventually they reached the broader strath of Dochart and could see the conical peak of Ben More beyond. But here they encountered another kind of obstacle, and the forward companies came to a sudden and disconcerting halt.

A Campbell castle stood on a small island in Loch Dochart, within a pistol shot of the land and overlooking the shore at a point where the track narrowed between the rocky hillside and the water's edge. The forward scouts reported that it was well fortified and inaccessible except by boat, and that it mounted heavy cannon commanding the narrow ground over which the army would have to pass. A siege was out of the question. The castle would hold victuals to last the winter, and the royalists had neither boats nor artillery to mount an assault. Yet while its guns bore on that vital stretch of shoreline, the way into Argyll was closed.

While Montrose and his officers were considering the problem, help came opportune and unexpected. In older times, the lands of Glen Dochart had belonged to the small Clan MacNab, before they too had been subjugated by the Campbells. Now one of the local MacNab chiefs with some of his clansmen, approached Montrose and volunteered to join the enterprise. Montrose was distrustful of any who were vassals of Argyll, but since they knew the area and claimed to be familiar with the routine of the garrison, he offered them an opportunity to prove their genuine intent by finding some way to neutralise the castle.

The small band of MacNabs went down to the lochside shortly before daybreak, and identifying themselves to the watch, called to the guard to send over the boat since they carried a letter from MacCailein Mor to the garrison commander. The sentry, knowing them for local Highlanders, duly warped the boat across and the MacNabs ferried themselves to the island. Once inside the castle, they cut the throats of the guard and surprised the Campbell commander in his bed. At sunrise they delivered the fortress to Montrose, and the army passed through the narrows, gratefully leaving the MacNabs in possession of their ancient stronghold to guard the line of retreat.

Their way now was along Glen Fillan and up towards Ben Doran, the Hill of Storms, until at Tyndrum they were poised within striking distance of Loch Awe itself. Somewhere in Glen Lochy it was decided that the army should split into three separate war bands. Alasdair was to take the Irishes and ravage the north from Glenorchy to Glenoe, and then swing back by Dalmally and Cladich to rejoin the main army at Inveraray. The Clanranald, the Camerons, and the Appin Stewarts under John Moydartach were to strike south-west and burn the country as far as Kilmartin Glassary, while Montrose would lead the men of Badenoch and Atholl and swoop down by Glen Shira on Inveraray itself. By this means they would ensure the maximum area of destruction. All Argyll lay at the point of their swords.

CHAPTER 13

The Battle of Inverlochy

The MacCailein Mor was at his castle of Inveraray when his scouts brought news that the Clanranald were plundering Breadalbane. Not comprehending that this was preliminary to an invasion of Argyll itself, he summoned his clansmen to muster at Inveraray at the end of December preparatory to mounting a punitive expedition in the New Year.

Suddenly came the startling intelligence that the MacDonalds were through the passes and their war-smoke had been sighted in Glenorchy. Glenure and Achloin were in flames, and more terrifying still, from the watch-tower on Duniquoich came word that Montrose himself was only a few miles away and coming fast.

The MacCailein Mor took to the sea. Sending instructions that the prisoners – Colkitto and Alasdair's two brothers – were to be conveyed hastily to Dumbarton, but without otherwise pausing to organise any kind of defence, Argyll boarded his galley and escaped down Loch Fyne to Roseneath, leaving his people to the mercy of their enemies, and Duncan MacIvor of Asknish, the hereditary Keeper of the castle, to hold out as best he could.

Montrose marched into Inveraray without encountering any resistance. According to tradition, the day was so cold that the edges of Loch Fyne had frozen over and seagulls were walking on the ice – which greatly startled the Athollmen who had never conceived that the sea itself could freeze. But their apprehensions were soon dispelled by the sight of the hated Campbell gallows going up in flames, and as the town itself was set ablaze, the Highlanders turned their attention to the prospect of plunder. Montrose saw no advantage in tying down his small force to a prolonged siege of the castle, which was too strong to be taken by assault, while the defenders for their part were unlikely to venture from the safety of its walls. The royalists leaguered on the top of Creagh Dhu, a steep hill behind the town – bleak upland, but ideally suited for herding a great *Creagh*, since on the boggy ground there was no shortage of water while the marsh grass and birch and fir trees guaranteed an abundance of provender and firewood. From there, the clansmen ranged out in small bands to pillage the Campbell lands around and drive in the sleek black cattle which represented the main source of wealth among the Highlands. It was later claimed that no cock crowed and no chimney smoked within twenty miles of Inveraray after they had passed.[43]

Loose in the west, the Clanranald were revenging themselves with feral savagery, cutting a swathe of destruction south as far as Kilmartin. All the lands and homesteads were burned along their route, and small groups of Campbell clansmen on their way to Inveraray to answer the MacCailein's summons were promptly put to death. Apart from the desolation in their wake, the clan later boasted of having killed 'eight hundred four score and fifteen men'[44], and herded a thousand cows to the camp at Inveraray.

To the north, Alasdair, most terrible of them all, earned his Campbell appellation – Alasdair MacColla, 'the Destroyer of Houses'. After committing more than a million merks worth of damage in Glenorchy itself, he led his Irishes on to Glenoe before wheeling in a great arc by Knapdale to ravage along the shores of Loch Awe. Yet along with the ruthless bloodshed and destruction, local traditions recall odd acts of mercy. In Glenoe, near the head of Loch Etive, the people had fled at his approach and he ordered his men to fire the empty dwellings. The Irishes had started with the house of the local chief, taking a live coal from the hearth to set the thatch ablaze, when Alasdair learned that the inhabitants were MacIntyres – a clan previously related to the MacDonalds but who had become vassals of the Campbells when Donald of Harlaw was still Lord of the Isles. Because they were distant kin, he promptly had the flames extinguished, and it is said that the coal was removed from the roof and preserved by the MacIntyres of that Ilk in memory of the event.

In south Knapdale, it was told how Alasdair, hungry after raiding along Loch Fyne, stopped at a cottage and asked for some food. An old widow who lived there gave him a cup of milk – which was all she had – and for this, word was passed down the marauding column that her house was to be spared. He also ordered his men not to pillage the village of the MacCorquodales of Loch Ballenoir, since the chief had held the land for the Crown and was his friend as well as the MacCailein's. But the inhabitants had fled from their clachan to the tower of Tromlee, and as the warban passed by, a defender on the walls shot and killed a member of the Irish rearguard. Alasdair's men turned about and burned the place.

Passing along Lochaweside he continued his work of destruction. The Irishes burned every home except for strongly fortified castles, slew or drove off all the cattle, and utterly spoiled all the grain and goods which they could not carry. In this manner they marched around the northern end of Loch Awe and by Glen Aray to Montrose's main leaguer above Inveraray.

The army regrouped during the last days of December 1644. The camp was now amply supplied with grain and meat, and the Gaels had amassed a prodigious quantity of plunder, arms, and goods. But although well armed and fed the army was now overladen – encumbered with booty and the vast herd of cattle – and thus slow-moving and vulnerable on the march. In the Lowlands Argyll had not been idle, and as he gathered the Covenant power in the south, the surviving Campbells were emerging from their hiding places among the smoking ruins of their homes, to muster for revenge. Providence, and exceptionally good weather conditions had so far ensured the success of the winter campaign, but to linger now would be dangerous, and by 14th January 1645, Montrose judged it time to leave.

The army marched to the head of Loch Awe, and then north by Brander to Loch Etive. Now the weather finally broke, and in the teeth of a south-westerly gale they kept along the southern shore to the Connel of Lorne from where they hoped to cross into Benderloch. Here the tide can be fierce, and they were obliged to camp along the shore until sufficient boats could be found. The proximity of Dunstaffnage Castle on their flank made this position precarious and uncomfortable, but fortunately boats were obtained through the agency of Campbell of Ardchattan, who was a MacDonald on his mother's side, in return for an assurance that his lands would be spared. Ardchattan procured four boats, one of which, when repaired could carry forty men at a time, and the others five each. By this means it took two days and nights to ferry the army across the narrows, although a number of cattle were swept away on the tide. During the first night in Benderloch a Covenant sloop which Argyll had sent to harass their crossing was wrecked on the beach, and the royalists were able to recover its armament of brass cannon.

Gathering a further 150 recruits from among the Appin Stewarts, Montrose now continued north to the River Cona which he crossed near its mouth. In a thunderstorm the army entered Glencoe by the foot of Meall Mor and the Field of Dogs at Achnacone, where they were joined by more of the MacIans who led them up the Devil's Staircase and over the high passes to Inverlochy at the entrance to the Great Glen. But they only stayed one day there, and it was not until they reached Kilcummin

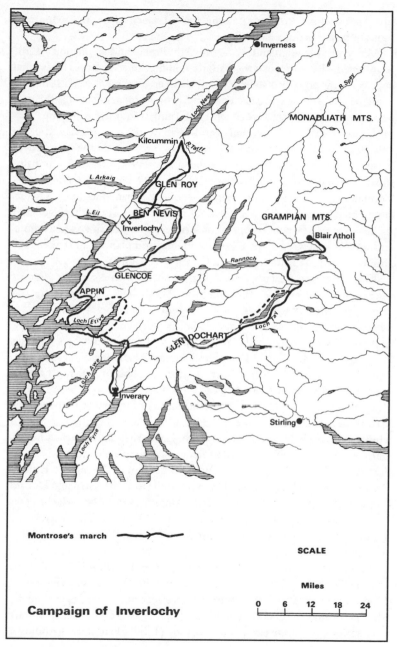

Inverness

MONADLIATH MTS.

R. Spey

Kilcummin

R. Tarff

L. Arkaig

GLEN ROY

L. Eil

BEN NEVIS

Inverlochy

GRAMPIAN MTS.

Blair Atholl

L. Rannoch

GLENCOE

APPIN

Loch Etive

L. Tay

GLEN DOCHART

Loch Awe

Inverary

Loch Fyne

Stirling

Montrose's march

SCALE

Miles

0   6   12   18   24

Campaign of Inverlochy

(the present Fort Augustus) at the foot of Loch Ness, that Montrose thought it safe to call a halt.

Many of the Highlanders – the Athollmen and a portion of the Clanranald – left to deposit their spoils at home, and Montrose found that once more his army had shrunk to a little over 1500 men. Against him he could now reckon on three Covenanting armies preparing to take the field – the main force of regular regiments emerging from their winter quarters in the south-east; the Campbells banding in devastated Argyll and probably already in pursuit; and the northern army with the garrison of Inverness blocking the Great Glen ahead. His latest intelligence put this third Covenant force in Inverness at around 5000 horse and foot – Lothian's and Lawers' regiments whom he had fought last year, augmented by the northern levies under the Earl of Seaforth. Given that the levies would be poor troops – conscripted peasants, drovers, servants, and the like – he judged the odds acceptable, and planned to strike north and bring them to battle at the head of the Great Glen.

First, however, he hoped to capitalise on the success of the winter's campaign, since news of the raid into Argyll had travelled fast, and although many clansmen had returned home, others might fill their place while a number of western chiefs who had previously hung back now came to Kilcummin to proffer their support. They included such names as Sir Lachlan MacLean of Duart, and Aeneas MacDonald of Glengarry, and Montrose conceived the value of a formal Band of Alliance to unite the Highlands against Argyll and the Covenanters. The resulting Kilcummin Bond, signed on 'the penult days of January 1645' contained fifty three signatures – some of them added later – including that of Montrose himself, his son Lord Graham, Lord Airlie and his son Thomas Ogilvie, Alasdair, John Moydartach, Glengarry, Keppoch, Duncan Stewart of Appin, MacLean of Duart, MacLean of Lochbuie, Donald Farquharson of Strathawin, Donald Robertson of Struan, Donald Cameron, Tutor of Lochiel, the MacPherson, the MacGregor, Drummond of Logiealmond, and others. The chiefs then returned home to call up their men, and Montrose prepared to march up the Great Glen and fight Seaforth.

Meanwhile in the Lowlands, the Covenant authorities had been provoked into considerable agitation and activity. Montrose's victories at Tippermuir and Aberdeen had had their effect upon morale, and 'many who had formerly been violent in the popular cause now began to talk moderately'[45]. Sixteen companies of foot (1100) men were withdrawn from England, and Lieutenant-General William Baillie of Letham was recalled from Leven's army to take command of the Covenant forces in Scotland.

After escaping from Inveraray, Argyll hurried to confer with Baillie at Dumbarton. The two men apparently disliked each other on sight. Although Argyll had resigned his commission and did not want the responsibility of military commander, he made it clear from the first that he still intended to direct the conduct of the war. Baillie was forced to hand over the new companies of infantry which Argyll required to support his clansmen in the west, and joined the main Covenant army in Perth.

Argyll next sent for his kinsman, Sir Duncan Campbell of Auchinbreck a veteran Highland soldier who had hitherto been employed in Ireland. Auchinbreck's estates had suffered extensively during Alasdair's depredations of the winter, and he hastily returned from Ireland to raise the full fighting strength of the Clan. On 18 January, the Committee of Estates in Edinburgh received a letter from Argyll in which he said that he had fallen from his horse and dislocated his shoulder – but that he intended to pursue the rebels into Lochaber and bring them to account. Despite their previous defeats, the Covenanting authorities were still confident that Montrose and his wild cateran army were no match for the forces now deployed against them. As one of the Covenant commissioners in London noted: 'If we get not the life of these worms chirted out of them, the reproach will stick on us forever'.[46]

Argyll knew that shortage of food would sooner or later force Montrose to leave Lochaber, and so he set out at once to follow the royalists' route north. The Campbells marched through Lorne and crossed Loch Leven by the ferry at Ballachulish. There is a story that they met a woman who had the sight, and boasted to her of the revenge they would take and what they would recount on their return. But she is said to have looked strangely at them and only answered that perhaps they might not come back that way. On 1st February, the Campbell army camped at Inverlochy, the strategic centre of the western Highlands. Montrose at Kilcummin was barely thirty miles ahead of them.

According to the Clan Donald tradition, it was Iain Lom MacVurich, the bard of Keppoch, who hurried over the mountains to warn Montrose of the danger at his back. 3000 Campbells at Inverlochy gave him cause to reconsider. Given a choice, Montrose guessed that Argyll would prefer not to fight, but rather hang on his track until the royalists were engaged against Seaforth at Inverness. Caught between two Covenant armies at either end of the Great Glen, the better strategy would be to turn about and attack Argyll, even though this meant facing odds of almost two to one. The problem would be in forcing a battle since the Campbells would have ample warning of any royalist advance along the valley. It would be necessary therefore to catch the MacCailein unawares.

Montrose called a hurried council of war to propose that they should attack the Campbells at Inverlochy and destroy the MacCailein Mor's reputation in the Highlands once and for all. To avoid the enemy scouts who would come probing up Glen Albin, Iain Lom would guide them by a circuitous route over the high plateau of Lairctuirard to the Spean. From there they might swoop down on Inverlochy to surprise the Campbells with their backs to the loch, and force an issue on the shore.

It was a plan of exceptional daring. No-one had heard of an army traversing that region, and such tracks as existed were known only to drovers and hunters of deer in the mountains. At this time of year the whole area was covered in snow. But the Highland chiefs were inspired by the prospect of a battle against their ancestral enemy, the Clan Diarmaid, and after some discussion as to the best route to follow, they voted unanimously to make the attempt.

Montrose ordered the army to break camp at once. The march which they were about to undertake was if anything even more daunting than the December campaign into Argyll. It would mean struggling for two days over high wilderness, exposed to the intense cold of Highland winter, without pause for shelter or rest, and without food except for what each man could carry or kill along the way. For Ogilvie's precious troop of horse the going would be truly terrible. And at the end they would have to fight an uneven battle against a fresh, and numerically superior enemy. But Montrose now believed that if they could surprise and engage Argyll at Inverlochy, the spirit and superb fighting qualities of the Irishes and Highlanders would bring victory against the odds.

Thus began what has been called the most incredible flanking march in the battle history of Scotland. They started early in the morning of Friday 31st January and it took them two days and a night. They climbed abruptly eastwards out of the Great Glen up the lower reaches of the River Tarff and thence onto the high bleak plateau that stretches towards the Pass of Corrieyarack and the remote headwaters of the Spey. At the narrow entrance to the Glen, a picked force of Highlanders remained to seal the pass behind them and prevent any word of their movements from reaching the Campbells in the valley. Somewhere above Cullachy, the main force waded the river and turned south across the moors parallel to the Great Glen until they struck the Calder Burn, and then climbed the steep hollow to its source. From there the route was probably over the shoulder of Cairn Dearg along the Burn of the Pass to the headstreams of the Turret and by Turret Bridge down into Glen Roy. It is said that they bivouacked briefly at Achvady. This was Keppoch country known to Iain Lom, but barely eighteen miles from Inverlochy, and they could expect Campbell patrols to be on the move.

On the second day, the army cautiously descended Glen Roy by the Parallel Roads. On the way they had warning of an enemy force plundering the area of Bohenie, and so kept high on the slopes of Bohenture Hill above the burning village, and hurriedly forded Spean above Corriechoille where the Cour joins the main river. Very close now, they shunned the open Dalach, striking up the shallow trough of the Cour and along the Altan Loin to the cover of Leanachan and the skirts of Ben Nevis. At 5 o'clock on the evening of Saturday 1st February, they finally halted at the base of Meall-an-t'suidhe, and through the gathering dusk, saw below them the watchfires of the Campbells around the old castle of Inverlochy.

Nothing could be done at once. The army was strung out along the march, and the rear contingents did not arrive until after 8 o'clock. The men were falling from fatigue. Even for the toughest hill-men the march had been an ordeal. 'The most part had not tasted bread these two days, marching over high mountains in deep snow, wading brooks and rivers up to their girdle.'[47] All were suffering from the extreme cold. The army could not fight without a rest.

Below them, in Inverlochy, word spread through the Campbell camp that a hostile band of Highlanders was somewhere on the slopes above them. Shortly before nightfall, some of Montrose's men clashed with a Campbell patrol and killed almost all of them, but the few who escaped had given the alarm. However, Campbell of Auchinbreck, as commander in the valley, had no means of telling the strength of the force on Ben Nevis, and merely sent out skirmishing parties to probe up the hill-sides and obtain further intelligence. Montrose for his part, was still anxious lest Argyll might try to evacuate his army under cover of darkness, and so ordered the freshest of his men to form a thin screen in front of his position to keep the enemy skirmishers confused. Small groups on each side were thus engaged throughout the night, and while the musket fire continued at desultory intervals, both camps were wakeful. But if the surprise was not complete, it was enough. The Campbells had not realised that Montrose's entire army was poised above them in the darkness, but the tired yet triumphant men who waited on the heights now knew that a bloody reckoning with their enemy was certain come the morning.

For the small royalist army it was still an awful pause. After the terrible march, the night was a long freezing vigil. The moon shone almost as clear as daylight, and they could count the camp-fires of the Campbells strung out along the shore and multiplied by reflection in the waters of the loch. They could watch too the movement in the camp where Auchinbreck's pickets stood to arms, and in the early hours of the morning, they saw the MacCailein Mor leave his clansmen and board his galley.

Argyll's detractors were subsequently quick to impute his action to personal cowardice. But it can be argued that he was still incapacitated by his disjointed shoulder and could hardly carry sword or pistol, while Auchinbreck was the most experienced Campbell commander and best qualified to order the clan in battle. Argyll's safety was important to the Covenant cause, and so his removal at this time, until the situation became clear, was a prudent precaution. Nevertheless, among Highlanders, for the chief to leave his clansmen on the eve of battle was likely to have a demoralising effect.

Dawn on Sunday 2nd February found the royalists gaunt and wolf-hungry. There was nothing to eat but *drammachs* – a little oatmeal and cold water mixed with the point of a dirk – for officers and men alike. Those who won and lived could feed thereafter. Some time before daybreak, the commanders began moving their men into position – except for Iain Lom, the Keppoch bard, who now walked apart from the rest, so that Alasdair is said to have called to him; 'Iain Lom, wilt thou leave us?' To which he answered; 'If I go with thee today and fall in battle, then who will sing thy praises and prowess tomorrow?' Whereupon he took his station on the heights to watch and record the fight. For this would be a battle in the antique Highland way – sword to sword between the clans in might – and the final Gaelic 'burial blent' which would resolve the issue between the Heather and the Gale. Inverlochy was historically a great battlefield of the Clan Donald, for it was on this same ground that Donald the Black had defeated the combined forces of Mar and Huntly in 1431. Under the eye of the hereditary Bard of Keppoch, win or die today, 1500 Gaels and a galaxy of chieftains would be remembered by their posterity as the heroes who fought Clan Campbell on the Feast Day of St Bridget 1645.

Montrose deployed his army in four divisions. The right wing under Alasdair was composed of the musketeers and pikemen of the first Irish regiment. O'Cahan led on the left, his regiment slightly forward of the main battle line and likely to be the first into action, since by attacking the Campbells' right, the royalists would hope to prevent the enemy from withdrawing to the south. The Highland contingents held the centre – the Clanranald with men from Glengarry, Keppoch, Glencoe, Appin, MacLean, Atholl, and Lochaber, drawn up in two fighting lines under their respective chieftains. To their rear, the third Irish regiment under Sir James MacDonnell formed the reserve. Montrose himself took position in the centre close to the Royal Standard with Thomas Ogilvie's troop of horse. The royalists had no cannon at this time.

It was Candlemas, the first day of spring, and the Catholics in the army knelt in their ranks while the Irish priests passed along the files granting absolution and blessing their arms with the sign of the Cross. Then gathering in the pickets who had been skirmishing through the night, the army moved down from the heights and halted on the lower slopes overlooking the flats of Inverlochy.

In their camp, the Campbells had concluded that the Highlanders on Ben Nevis were merely a force of caterans out raiding from Montrose's army. But as it grew light and the sun dispersed the morning mist, they began to realise that this was a more formidable enemy than they had at first supposed. Among the men massing on the hill they soon distinguished the famous green banner of the MacLeans, while amid the shouts of hatred and defiance that carried down into the valley, they could hear the fierce pibroch of Clan Cameron; 'Come you dogs and we shall give you flesh!' But only when a fanfare of trumpets saluted the raising of the Royal Standard did they finally understand that it was the King's Lieutenant and the royalist army who were advancing upon them.

The Campbells were taken by surprise. They had not thought to fight at Inverlochy. Yet they were no cowards and keen enough. They too had waited for such an hour. Their lands had been devastated, their cattle taken, homes burned, and crops destroyed. All winter the Clanranald had ravaged unopposed through the heartland of Argyll. But now the Campbells had gathered in strength. 3000 were camped at Inverlochy, and among them the prime swordsmen of the clan.

Campbell of Auchinbreck hastily began to put his army into battle order, and now had cause to regret the careless insecurity of the Campbell leaguer sprawled around the estuary. One contingent had camped on the further side of the Lochy in the angle between Loch Linnhe and Loch Eil, and because the River Lochy then flowed rapid and deep, they could not be brought across to join the main body before the battle began. Nevertheless, the bulk of the army was bivouacked on the eastern bank, and the force at his disposal still substantially outnumbered the royalist force above him.

The Campbell army was also drawn up in four divisions along a ridge of firm ground running roughly north-south and rising above the alluvial soil of the estuary. The Lowland troops were posted on the wings – about 500 men and two cannon in each contingent. These were the companies withdrawn from the Scottish army in England – regular troops from Stirlingshire, who had marched south with Leven and fought at Marston Moor. In the centre, the main battle-front massed on a prominent outcrop. Here were the prime Campbell fighting men commanded by the Lairds of Lochnell and Rarra, and the Provost of Kilmun, drawn up around the standard and supported by two culverin. Before them, on the level ground and slightly in advance of the main position, the rest of the Campbell clansmen armed with an assortment of guns, swords, and axes, formed a vanguard led by the chieftain Gillespie, son of Gillespie Og, Lord of the Bingingeadhs.

On the extreme left of the army, a pistol shot from Campbells' flank, stood the ancient castle of Inverlochy, once a stronghold of the old kings of Caledonia. Though ruinous, it was still a formidable defensive work, with a curtain wall thirty feet high and nine feet thick, and circular loop-holed towers at each of the corners. The whole quadrangle was surrounded by a ditch some forty feet across. Here, Auchinbreck stationed a further 50 musketeers from the Lowland companies, so that they could enfilade the royalist flank.

Auchinbreck could be satisfied with the position, but it was not ideal. Out of deference perhaps to the Lowland infantry, whose disciplined volleys were intended to stand off the royalist advance in conventional style, he had adopted a static and defensive posture. If Montrose's Highlanders charged the line – as they were likely to do – the Campbell clansmen would have to meet it standing. Moreover, the whole position around the ridge was somewhat confined, the slope to the rear of the centre outcrop was very steep, and the clansmen packed close with little space to fight in.

While the Campbell army was being hastily marshalled into line in front of them, Montrose's Highlanders could hardly be restrained from rushing down the slope. When Gillespie's vanguard began to advance onto the open ground below the ridge, the whole royalist battle-line began to edge forward in their impatience to charge, yelling their wild war shouts, and lashing at the turf in fury with their broadswords. In those critical moments Montrose appeared to hesitate, and Alasdair shouted furiously at him to order the attack. But the Highlanders would no longer wait for the command, and the royalist army suddenly burst like a torrent down the hillside in a broad screaming avalanche of steel.

O'Cahan's regiment set upon Gillespie's division, holding their fire until the muzzles of their firelocks were in the very faces of the enemy, and then storming through the smoke to smash a way through and in a solid wedge hurl themselves against the Lowland troops on the Covenant right. Simultaneously, Alasdair threw his Irish division at Auchinbreck's left, and behind him, the clansmens' charge tore into the disordered remnants of Gillespie's vanguard and drove them back against the Campbell centre.

On the wings, the Covenant regulars tried to maintain their front and fire in line, but the Irishes ran in low under the volley, and the Lowlanders had no time to reload before the attack was into them and the Gaels clubbed their way through the files with swinging swords and musket butts. In England, Leven's troops had never suffered this butchery at close quarters. Those behind watched the front rank spitted and tossed on the Irish spikes, and would stand no more. The flanks of Auchinbreck's army simply disintegrated under the terrible ferocity of the attack, and as the formations broke in disorder, the Irishes turned inwards to converge against the centre. On the Campbell's left, some 200 of the Lowland infantry tried to reach the safety of the castle, but Sir Thomas Ogilvie, who was following up the advance, guessed their intent, and led his troop in a charge that drove them back onto the shore where there was no hiding place. Tragically, Ogilvie himself was mortally wounded in the action, and was not there to see them make an end.

In the centre, the Campbells on the ridge were packed too tight to open their files and allow the fugitives through. The fleeing men were brought up short in confusion in front of their own cannon, and while they faltered, the Gaelic whirlwind engulfed them. Overborne by the whole weight of Montrose's army charging home, they were cut to pieces before the horrified eyes of the watching Campbells who could only brace themselves to meet the final assault. The impact buckled their line, but for a space the Campbell swordsmen held the ridge, and a savage hand to hand struggle developed around the centre. But they were outflanked now, and unsupported, and the weight of the attackers began to push them off the outcrop and down the steep slope behind. The issue was finally resolved when Alasdair led a great surge against the standard. When his wedge bit through the last resistance and the banner dipped and fell, the Campbells turned to flee. Behind them in the loch, the galley of Argyll spread its black sails like a bird of ill omen, and headed out to sea. The MacCailein Mor had left his stricken army to its fate.

Some tried to swim to the ship and were drowned. Others searched frantically for a ford across the Lochy. On the beach, few survived. Here and there, scattered groups bravely tried to make a stand, but were quickly over-run by the exulting MacDonalds. One party of Lowland officers succeeded in reaching the shelter of the castle and subsequently surrendered to Montrose in person. Most fled along the shore, hoping to escape by the way the had come and find refuge in Lochaber, and a running slaughter continued for fourteen miles as the clans chased after them. 1500 are said to have been killed, and only sheer exhaustion prevented Alasdair's men from pursuing them further.

It was told afterwards that the last man to give up the chase was a Highlander called Deors MacAlaster, who had killed nineteen men in the battle itself, and went after two more Campbells who were trying to escape up the hillside above Loch Eil. Seeing that he had far outdistanced his companions, these two turned round to kill him, but he despatched both of them before himself collapsing from exhaustion and loss of blood.

On the shore, Alasdair killed twenty men – nineteen, as he claimed, with single sweeps of his great broadsword. On the ridge, the Campbell gentry fought gallantly to the end, but according to one tradition, Campbell of Auchinbreck himself was captured and brought to Alasdair. Dragged before the furious MacDonald he possibly tried to appease his captor by reminding them that they were distant kin. But Alasdair was not in a merciful mood that day. Auchinbreck was hated for his cruelties in Ireland, and was reported to have been responsible for a party of Campbells who had recently seized Alasdair's old wet nurse at her home in the Isles, and brutally carved off her breasts because, they said, she had suckled such a monster. Alasdair curtly gave the Campbell general the option of being hanged or beheaded, and when Auchinbreck objected that this was 'two bads without a choice', the huge MacDonald split his skull from ear to ear and left his corpse anonymous among the pile of Campbell dead.

Another Highlander – an Atholl blacksmith named Robertson – had also killed nineteen Campbells in the fight. When the battle was over, the starving clansmen found food and utensils among the wreckage of the enemy camp, and sat around the cooking fires. Alasdair, however, had neglected to procure a bowl for himself, and sent a gillie to take one from the group near Robertson. The other Highlanders would have given up their breakfast rather than risk offending the terrible MacColla, but Robertson refused to give up his plate, remarking loudly: 'If he killed twenty men today, I killed nineteen; and if two more had come my way, I believe I would have beaten him.' On hearing of this, Alasdair came to search him out, but Robertson moved away since he did not want a fight. Alasdair, however, insisted on knowing his name, and when Robertson said modestly that he was only a poor tinker from Atholl, the MacDonald is said to have exclaimed: 'Would the Athollmen had all been tinkers this day' – and then to his companions: 'I thought I had done very well today in killing twenty Campbells, but there was a man with a black dirk (Deors MacAlaster) who killed one more, and what is even more humiliating, here is an Atholl tinker who brought down only one less.'

And while the Highlanders ate, or looted through the Campbell camp, the bard Iain Lom of Keppoch came down from his place on the mountainside, his head full of battle-song which he would write of Alasdair of the cleaving blades, and the victory of Clan Donald over their ancestral enemy on St Bridget's Day at Inverlochy.

> Heard ye not! heard ye not! how that whirlwind the Gael –
> To Lochaber swept down from Loch Ness to Loch Eil, –
> And the Campbells to meet them in battle array
> Like the billow came on, – and were broke like its spray!
> Long, long shall our war-song exult in that day.
>
> 'Twas the Sabbath that rose, 'twas the Feast of St Bride,
> When the rush of the clans shook Ben Nevis' side;
> I, the bard of their battles, ascended the height
> Where dark Inverlochy o'ershadowed the fight,
> And I saw the Clan Donald resistless in might.

Through the land of my fathers the Campbells have come,
The flames of their foray enveloped my home;
Broad Keppoch in ruin is left to deplore,
And my country is waste from the hill to the shore, –
Be it so! By St Mary there's comfort in store!

Though the braes of Lochaber a desert be made,
And Glen Roy may be lost to the plough and the spade,
Though the bones of my kindred, unhonoured, unurned,
Mark the desolate path where the Campbells have burned, –
Be it so! From that foray they never returned.!

Fallen race of Diarmed! disloyal, untrue,
No harp in the Highlands will sorrow for you;
But the birds of Loch Eil are wheeling on high,
And the Badenoch wolves hear the Camerons' cry, –
'Come feast ye! come feast where the false-hearted lie!'

CHAPTER 14

The Retreat from Dundee

The day after the battle of Inverlochy, Montrose sent a dispatch to the King. He believed that he had won a significant victory and hoped that news of it would revive royalist spirits in both countries. There had been disturbing rumours that Charles was considering negotiations with the Scottish Covenanters, and after reporting the course of the Highland campaign, he urged the King to make no concessions: –

'The more your Majesty grants the more will be asked, and I have too much reason to know that they will not rest satisfied with less than making your Majesty a king of straw.

... And give me leave... to assure your Majesty that, through God's blessing, I am in the fairest hopes of reducing this kingdom to your Majesty's obedience. And if the measures which I have concerted with your other loyal subjects fail me not, which they hardly can, I doubt not before the end of the summer, I shall be able to come to your Majesty's assistance with a brave army, which, backed with the justice of your Majesty's cause, will make the Rebels in England as well as in Scotland, feel the just rewards of rebellion. Only give me leave, after I have reduced this country to your Majesty's obedience, and conquered from Dan to Beersheba, to say... as David's general did to his master, 'Come thou thyself lest this country be called by my name'...'[48]

Alasdair, however, while exulting in the victory, may have been less sanguine as to its significance. The Campbells had been badly mauled, but they were not defeated as a clan. Sixteen Campbell lairds had fallen in battle, but doubtless they left 'sixteen wives at home... with sixteen Campbells in their wombs.'[49] The MacDonalds' vengeance was by no means complete while the MacCailein Mor himself had escaped the slaughter and was even now summoning the Covenanting power.

Argyll reached Edinburgh on 11th February, and appeared before Parliament with 'his left arm tied up in a scarf as if he had been at bones breaking.'[50] His account of Inverlochy was less than full, but the House did not wish to dwell upon the disaster, and contented themselves with approving the Campbell's conduct, while declaring Montrose and Alasdair, and the other principal royalists, forfeited for treason.

By now, the attrition of war had caused a general mood of despondency to settle over a large proportion of the Scottish people. Initially, the Covenanters had been pleased to contemplate a civil war fought south of the border across English land and with English money, but now that they were forced to maintain a second front against Montrose, the burden fell upon the Scots themselves, and the true cost of supporting a campaign on their own soil was brought home to them.

Moreover, the diplomacy of the Scottish Commissioners in London was proving increasingly ineffective. The English were less concerned with the fetish which the Scots made out of their National Covenant, than with the military practicality of bringing a Scottish army south as the nucleus of a new force to be used against the royalists in the west. With an army to back them, the Scots had been listened to – but the depletion of his forces because of regiments drafted north to contain the 'rebels', and the possibility that the King might try to link up with Montrose, was keeping Leven close to the Cumberland border. The influence of the Scottish Commissioners declined as the English grew more dissatisfied and impatient at their ally's failure to deliver.

Declarations of brotherly conformity could not conceal the growing rift between the Scots and the Independents, whose insistence on lay predominance in religious affairs brought them into sharp conflict with Presbyterian ideals, and who were now aiming at nothing less than the exclusion of the King from any future form of government. Although by January 1645, the split between Presbyterians and Independents was open and possibly irreparable – the first yet hoping to be reconciled with the King, the second seeing in such a reconciliation 'the abandonment of everything worth fighting for at all' – the Presbyterians (now the Peace Party) still had enough support to secure the agreement of Parliament to the opening of negotiations with the King at Uxbridge on 31st January. The Scots were the prime movers in this, their last chance to bring about a Presbyterian settlement, and when the negotiations inevitably failed, their influence in England went into ultimate decline. By contrast, the star of Cromwell – the 'darling of the Sectaries' – was now in the ascendant, and in time to come he would punish the Scots for their presumption.

Meanwhile, as the true facts of Inverlochy became widely known, the Kirk extremists began clamouring for the execution of royalist prisoners in Covenant hands. The Scottish Parliament, however, while commending the brethren for their 'great zeal and piety', prudently demurred. They had just received Montrose's cartel, dispatched after Inverlochy, offering an exchange of prisoners, and with so many prominent Campbells captured, they dared not risk the possibility that the King's Lieutenant might retaliate in kind.

They therefore suggested that any executions of captured royalists should be deferred until Montrose 'could be brought lower'. In the event, Colkitto and his two sons were probably released some two months after Inverlochy, and a number of other royalists were freed upon payment of fines and sureties intended to relieve the Covenanters' dwindling war-chest. Nevertheless, the lot of those prisoners who were still confined became increasingly grim. These included Lord Ogilvie, the Earl of Crawford, several of the Grahams including Montrose's natural brother, and Dr Wishart, his subsequent biographer. The Napiers, suspect from the first as close friends of Montrose, were put under house arrest at their lodgings at Holyrood upon a massive surety of £1,000 sterling, and although they might have escaped execution for the time being, their lives were by no means safe. Plague was creeping through Edinburgh.

The Covenant authorities had by now fully woken up to the fact that Montrose's army was not the 'pack of naked runagates' that they had first supposed. Priority was given to mounting a major campaign in the north. In Lieutenant-General Baillie and his subordinate, Sir John Hurry, they appointed battle commanders of considerable experience. Parliament proposed to raise a new army of 10,000 foot and 600 horse, while a further 1500 infantry were withdrawn from Ireland and another 1400 veterans from Leven's army south of the border.

While these measures were being put in hand, Montrose had resumed his march. The western clansmen were now joining in greater numbers – old Lochiel with a force of Camerons, MacLeans, MacNeills, MacQuarries, a steady stream of MacDonalds, and other Highlanders 'all dressed alike'. He knew that the victory at Inverlochy was itself not sufficient to break the power of the Covenanting authority. The decisive battles would be fought in the Lowlands, and could not be attempted without a substantial force of cavalry. This meant that there was no alternative but to try the Gordon lands once more.

He therefore marched north up the Great Glen to Inverness. The town was strongly fortified, and garrisoned by two regular Covenant regiments, and the royalists had not the time nor the men to waste on a siege.

137

Montrose continued into Moray in the hope of seizing Elgin where the Earl of Seaforth and the other local Covenanting barons were gathering to concert measures for defence. But they hurriedly dispersed at his approach, and a number rode in to make their peace with the King's Lieutenant. The Earl of Seaforth and the Laird of Grant (whose wife was Huntly's niece) even signed the Kilcummin Bond. But they were at best doubtful allies, and Montrose was content to let them return to their own lands – where they promptly resumed their Covenant affiliations.

The royalists reached Elgin on 19th February, and proclamations were sent throughout Moray summoning all men between the ages of sixteen and sixty to enlist under the King's banner on pain of fire and sword. 'This bred great fear', and a number of recruits were accordingly forthcoming. Against those who disobeyed, Montrose carried out his threat with the utmost rigour. The lands of prime Covenanters were systematically pillaged and their property destroyed. These depredations were conducted in a comparatively disciplined manner, and any unauthorised looting was punishable by death. It was a calculated cruelty and a stern application of the lessons of 1644.

At Elgin, Nathaniel Gordon rejoined the army, this time bringing with him Lord George Gordon himself and his youngest brother, Lord Lewis, together with 200 well mounted troopers. This was undoubtedly the greatest recruiting success so far. Lord Gordon was an experienced soldier, having fought in Alsace and Lorraine, and his influence among the clan second only to that of Huntly himself. Lord Lewis was gallant enough, as had been demonstrated at the Battle of Aberdeen, but he was somewhat volatile, and at times, perverse. (The second of the Gordon brothers, Viscount Aboyne, was still cooped up at Carlisle.)

Montrose and Huntly's heir 'supped joyfully together', and during the next week the Gordons, having watched Argyll spoil their lands all the previous summer, went raiding to pay off old scores in kind. By 4th March, however, it was clear that not much was to be gained from the gentry of Moray, but a great deal in Banff and Aberdeenshire where Lord Gordon's influence would assure them of more substantial reinforcements, and so the royalists crossed the Spey and camped at Gordon Castle in the Bog of Gight.

There, personal tragedy overtook Montrose. His eldest son, John, Lord Graham, now only fourteen years of age, fell sick of a fever and died within a few days. He was buried in the kirkyard of Bellie, just beyond the castle grounds near the east bank of the Spey, and the worn memorial, grass grown now, is still there today. The boy had joined his father immediately after Tippermuir, and had marched with the army into Argyll and through the grim Lochaber passes to the fight at Inverlochy. The long winter campaign had overtaxed his strength, and his death was a tragic instance of promise unfulfilled. But Montrose, with the weight of the war upon him, had no time to indulge in private sorrow. The army marched again almost immediately.

News of their approach caused panic in Aberdeen, and the burgesses, who were in terror of the Irishes, sent a delegation to Montrose at Turriff to ask for mercy. The King's general had no desire to witness a repetition of the ghastly events of the previous year, and returned an assurance that the Gaelic troops would not come within eight miles of the town, while he and his officers would seek entertainment at their own expense. The army marched south through Inverurie and camped at Kintore where they were joined by a body of militia and 500 foot and 160 horse whom Lord Gordon had recruited from among his father's tenants.

But the comparative success of recent weeks had caused the royalists to grow careless, and on 9th March, they paid dearly for it. Nathaniel Gordon had ridden into Aberdeen with 100 troopers to receive the keys of the town. He released a number of prominent royalist prisoners who had been confined in the Tolbooth, and then raided the Covenant arsenal at Torry, where he surprised the guard and carried off a large quantity of pikes and muskets. Three days later he returned to Aberdeen with Donald Farquharson of Strathawin and a number of other cavaliers – apparently with no other reason than to enjoy themselves. They posted no guards at the gates, but dispersed through the town, to eat and drink, and take their ease. Covenant spies quickly sent word to Sir John Hurry, who with General Baillie and the main Covenant army, was camped at North Water Brig.

Hurry was an opportunist in more ways than one. He was a soldier of fortune who had won distinction abroad before first joining the Parliamentary army in England and then subsequently defecting to Prince Rupert. Charles I had knighted him for bearing the intelligence that occasioned the battle at Chalgrove Field where Hampden was killed. In July 1644 he had been captured by Fairfax's men in Lancashire, and in true mercenary style had been induced to switch his allegiance again and take service with the Covenanting Committee of Estates. (He was to change his coat once more before the war was out, and the consequence would be fatal.)

Hurry came from Pitfichie near Monymusk, and therefore knew the country well. Hastily assembling 160 troopers of Balcarres's Horse, he dashed at Aberdeen, arriving before the undefended gates on the evening of 15th March. The Covenant dragoons burst into the town and galloped through the streets, cutting down any royalist whom they caught in the open. Among the dead was Donald Farquharson of Strathawin, who had been one of the best of the Highland captains. Hurry rode next to Old Montrose where he seized Montrose's second son (and now his heir), the twelve-year old James, Lord Graham, and carried him off to be imprisoned in Edinburgh Castle.

At Kintore, the old Earl of Airlie was also taken ill, and was carried to Lethintie, where his daughter was the chatelaine. When his condition did not improve, Montrose detached a strong escort to convey him to Huntly Castle until he should recover.

The royalists now marched southwards, crossing the Dee and continuing by Elsick Mounth to Stonehaven, where they devastated the lands around Dunnottar Castle. Moving through Fettercairn and Arbuthnott, they encountered little opposition. At Halkerton Wood a detachment of Covenant cavalry were severely mauled by the Irish musketeers when they tried to ambush part of the column, and the army marched unmolested to Brechin, where they plundered the Castle, and burned part of the town.

Montrose was now able to obtain clearer intelligence of the main Covenant army. The appointment of General Baillie with Sir John Hurry as second in command, portended a more professional and enterprising approach to the conduct of the war. The Covenant army had been reinforced by Lothian's and Loudoun's regiments, and by the 1400 troops recalled from Ireland, bringing the numbers up to something over 3000 foot and 700 horse – for the most part veterans. Against them, Montrose had some 3000 foot and 300 horse, and despite his inferiority in cavalry, he felt under pressure to move south since he had recently received a letter from the King in which Charles spoke of coming north to the borders, and promising to send 500 cavaliers to support the Scottish royalists. But before he could cross the Forth and break through to the Lowlands, Montrose would have to bring Baillie to battle and defeat him.

The Covenant general calculated as much, and decided to hold the river crossings. Shadowed by Baillie, the royalists moved south, keeping close to the safety of the Grampians where the enemy cavalry could not catch them at a disadvantage. The two forces confronted each other briefly across the River Tay, but Montrose dared not risk a crossing under fire, and with Baillie still hovering on his flank, withdrew to Inverquharity Castle. In the last days of March the armies again faced each other at the River Isla, but having stood-to all night, again neither would attempt a frontal assault across the river. Montrose chaffed at the delay, and even sent Baillie a challenge – offering to withdraw two miles and allow the Covenanters passage of the ford if he would engage to fight immediately afterwards. But Baillie was in no hurry, and replied that he would fight at his own pleasure and not another man's command.

After two days of this frustration, Montrose decided to try to elude Baillie altogether and decamped to Dunkeld, while the Covenanters, keeping always to the south of him, moved off in the direction of Perth. The King's Lieutenant now faced a dilemma. In the north, the various Covenanting clans were banding together for a retaliatory foray against Huntly's people, and he was compelled to grant leave of absence to many of the Gordons who wished to return and protect their lands. The Highlanders, as ever, would not submit to the restraint of remaining continuously with the army, and wearying of the constant marching, a number had gone home. The royalist army was soon reduced to a bare 2000 men, and as the number of desertions mounted, it became clear that the descent on the Lowlands would have to be postponed. The alternative strategy was to seek a decisive battle in the north and secure the Gordon lands from future Covenant reprisals. Only then would the Gordon cavalry be willing to campaign far from home.

At the same time, however, he did not want to give the Covenanters the satisfaction of forcing the royalists to withdraw without having accomplished anything, and he now looked around for something to do which might redeem the campaign. On 3rd April he learned that Baillie had crossed the Tay to seize the fords of Forth against his likely approach, and thus reckoning that the enemy was now marching away from him, he decided to make a surprise attack on Dundee, which Baillie's movement had left unprotected. Success here would be calculated to raise the spirits of the army since Dundee was strong for the Covenant and one of the richest cities in Scotland. What Montrose did not know was that the information of his scouts had been incorrect. Only a part of the Covenant army had actually crossed the Tay. The main force was still at Perth.

Unaware of the danger, the royalists detached their wounded, the women, and the less well armed, with orders to escort the baggage to Brechin where the army would regroup. Then, with a picked force of 300

Irishes, 300 Gordon foot, and 150 horse, Montrose left Dunkeld at about mid-night and set out for Dundee. They arrived in front of the town the following morning (4th April) and formally demanded its surrender in the King's name. When the city authorities arrested the herald and returned no reply, Montrose set up his headquarters on Dundee Law from where he could overlook the siege, and ordered his men to assault the walls.

At that time, the street plan of Dundee resembled a parallelogram, with a church and market place at the centre of the town approached by four main streets – two from the east and two from the west. In the north-west corner, within the walls, a battery of artillery sited on the bastion of Corbie Hill commanded the entire town and its defence works. Other cannon were positioned to fire along the streets. The encircling walls had been built by the French troops of Mary of Lorraine, and were consequently strong and well designed, with eight main portes, each mounting heavy ordnance. But there was one weak spot, at the point closest to Corbie Hill, where the wall was under repair and municipal incompetence had delayed the works. In 1645 there was no regular garrison, and the ramparts were manned by militia and townspeople summoned to defend the walls.

The royalists invested the perimeter at three different points, but the main assault was directed at the weak section of the wall. Overcoming the spirited but unprofessional resistance of the town militia, the Irishes did not take long to force an entry, and then promptly stormed Corbie Hill to swing the cannon around to sweep the west and nethergate portes. Bombarded from the rear, the defenders were driven back into the streets, and elsewhere in the town the strongpoints were quickly over-run. From Corbie Hill, a hundred yard dash and some sharp fighting brought the Irishes into the open market place where they were joined by the other royalist contingents who fought their way inward to seize the centre of the town.

The Church of St Mary and a number of houses were quickly set ablaze, but in general, the victorious royalists were intent on plunder before anything else, and set out to loot the town before burning it. Although sporadic fighting continued in the winds and alleys, more and more broke off the action to begin the spoil, and before long, the bulk of the army were squabbling over the vast quantities of booty. The looters quickly found their way to the citizens' wine cellars, and a large proportion of the royalist force were soon riotously drunk.

The process of pillage and outrage in varying degrees had continued well into the afternoon when suddenly scouts came galloping in with the news that the entire Covenant army, preceded by a large force of cavalry was barely two miles away, and Hurry's troopers would be on them in less than half an hour.

Something close to panic gripped the royalist officers as Montrose called an urgent Council of War. Opinions were divided, and few thought that the situation could be saved. The troops were scattered throughout the town, many of them drunk and out of control. They could not be dragged off their prey in time, and aside from the encumbering plunder, they had already marched twenty miles and fought a battle, and it was a clear thirty miles more over open country before they could reach the hills and safety. Some urged Montrose to abandon the men in the town. Only a portion of the royalist army had been engaged and their loss would not be disastrous. But his own survival was crucial to the success of the royal cause. Others argued for one final charge against the enemy and an honourable death in battle.

But Montrose would agree to neither course. He was not prepared to desert his men, while to charge headlong into Hurry's dragoons would be a foolish act of despair. Shouting to his officers to follow, he spurred down the hill into Dundee and started to whip in his drunken, scattered army.

Irregulars indulging their privilege of plunder and debauch in a captured town could not in theory be called off. But it was done. Drummers frantically beat the instant recall. Officers and sergeants moved eastwards through the streets, dragging their dazed and bewildered troops out of the houses and driving them towards the Seagate and East portes which were furthers from the enemy's approach. Drunk or sober, laden with spoil, some wounded, reluctant, and many in panic, Montrose somehow got his men out of that death trap, and the last royalists staggered through the seaward gate just as Baillie burst into the west porte of Dundee.

If they could march and keep marching, the royalists still had a chance. Even drunk, Highlanders could outdistance heavy infantry. The danger was Hurry's cavalry, but it was by now around 6 o'clock in the evening, and would soon be dark. 400 of those in worse condition were set marching straight away with instructions to keep in column, closely followed by 200 who were sober enough to fight if need be. Montrose himself commanded a rearguard composed of cavalry riding in open order and interspersed with light musketeers hanging to their stirrup leathers. In this manner, the force set off eastwards along the coast away from the town.

In Dundee, Baillie quickly ascertained the size of the royalist force and the direction of their escape, but for some reason he chose to wait until his infantry arrived before ordering the pursuit. The Covenant army divided into two. Hurry was to take his division of cavalry and attack the royalists' flank and rear, while Baillie himself with the bulk of the force, circled inland parallel to the fugitives' presumed line of march to cut off their retreat towards the hills. The Covenant general confidently expected to trap Montrose against the sea and destroy him in morning, and to encourage the pursuit, he offered 20,000 gold pieces for the King's Lieutenant's head.

Hurry's troopers quickly overtook the royalist rearguard but were repulsed with loss. This check discouraged them even as it raised the spirits of Montrose's men who gained in confidence as each attack was successfully beaten off. During the recriminations that followed, Baillie would complain that Hurry had deliberately neglected to press home his attacks out of a desire to deprive him of the credit that would have been his due. The two Covenant commanders disliked each other intensely, and the lack of co-ordination between them at this time was at least partly responsible for their failure. However the blame truly lay, in the event, Hurry lost his chance to destroy the royalist rearguard and was forced to break off the running fight at nightfall.

During the early part of the night, the royalists continued along the coast by Carnoustie, and at about midnight arrived at Eliot Water near Arbroath. Montrose guessed correctly that somewhere to his left, Baillie's main army would be marching to block his route towards the Grampians, and now adopted one of those daring stratagems that marked his genius as a soldier. Halting the column, he doubled back on his tracks as far as Panbride, where he found the small road west to Carmylie and thence by Guthrie and Melgund to Careston Castle, having actually passed around Baillie's army during the small hours of the morning.

Careston Castle could offer only temporary refuge, but the troops would march no further. In thirty hours they had covered over sixty miles, stormed a town, drunk themselves almost incapable, and skirmished throughout the night. Many were virtually unconscious on their feet, and now they collapsed in heaps around the castle lawns and slept like dead men.

Here a messenger from Brechin found them, with the news that the remainder of the army had had timely warning of Baillie's approach and were already moving towards the security of the hills. Montrose thus had the relief of knowing that a part of the army at least was safe. Dawn however, brought Baillie to Forfar, and when he discovered that his prey had eluded him, the Covenant cavalry immediately began to sweep the area in search of the royalists. It did not take long for Hurry's patrols to discover their whereabouts, and the look-outs shortly brought urgent intelligence to Montrose that a large force of enemy cavalry with infantry in support was advancing towards Careston. The castle was barely three miles from the hills and safety, but it seemed as if those three miles could still be their destruction. The exhausted men would not awake. The officers finally resorted to pricking them with the points of their swords before they would stir, but eventually the column was reformed and the retreat began again. Once more, the beleaguered rearguard fought doggedly mile on mile to hold off Hurry's cavalry as the battered little army stumbled on towards the mountains – until incredibly, they got to safety. And when Baillie saw the royalists slipping away into the upper reaches of the Esk, he called off his forces and prepared to answer for his failure.

Covenant propaganda recorded a great victory, even claiming that Alasdair and O'Cahan had been killed together with 400 of their Irishes, and that the royalists had lost all their baggage and ammunition. But within the high command there was recrimination and dispute. Baillie was particularly incensed at Sir John Hurry's part in the affair, believing that his cavalry commander had deliberately misdirected the pursuit – 'yet he was exonerated there, and I charged with their escape'.[51]

In Glenesk, Alasdair and O'Cahan were very much alive, and although some royalists had fallen prisoner at Dundee, few men had been lost during that desperate retreat. Montrose had been extremely lucky to escape, and his vulnerability to bad intelligence in Covenant held country was a stark lesson to be remembered. But the army was unbeaten, and when rested, would be ready to fight again. The royalists camped on the edge of the Highlands where the exhausted soldiers could sleep in safety, within the shelter of their inviolable hills.

CHAPTER 15

The Battle of Auldearn

In Glenesk, while his army rested, Montrose paused to reconsider the campaign. The threat of fresh Covenant depredations in the north was drawing the Gordon contingent home again (it is possible that Lord Lewis Gordon left at this time). With something less than 2000 men, the royalists were too weak to risk a set-piece battle against the main Covenant forces, and any descent on the Lowlands was not practicable without substantial cavalry reinforcements.

The army split up for a time. Lord George Gordon led his contingent north again to raise recruits in Banff and Aberdeenshire against the Covenanting lairds who were preparing to attack the Gordon lands, and to fortify the strongholds at Huntly, Auchindoun, and the Bog of Gight. Alasdair took his Irishes and some Highlanders into the Braes of Mar and through Glen Tanar to create a diversion in that region, while Black Pate Inchbrakie returned to Atholl to call up the Stewarts and Robertsons, and other Badenoch men who had returned home after Inverlochy. Montrose himself retained a small force of 500 foot and 50 horse, and moved in the direction of Strathearn in the hope of linking up with the Viscount Aboyne, who according to rumour, had broken out of Carlisle and was riding north to join the army. Passing by Dunkeld, in mid-April he was at Crieff, camped near the castle of Inchbrakie and uncomfortably close to Baillie's army then occupying Perth some seventeen miles away. According to a tradition of the Graham family, during an incident that took place at this time, Montrose only escaped from a Covenant patrol by hiding in a large yew tree which stood in the grounds of Inchbrakie Castle.

When Baillie learned of the royalists' proximity, he hastily assembled his regiments and marched all night in the hope of surprising them unawares. But the look-outs gave the alarm, and while the small force of cavalry fought a series of rearguard actions to cover the retreat, the royalists withdrew towards Strathearn until they could occupy the narrow pass into the hills, and the Covenant general called off the pursuit.

Montrose now continued along the southern shore of Loch Earn, pillaging the house and lands of Kilpont's murderer, Stewart of Ardvoirlich, and then by Lochearnhead, Balquhidder and Strathyre into the Trossachs, recruiting among the outlawed Clan MacGregor. On 19th April, the small band of fugitives from Carlisle successfully found them by Loch Katrine – Aboyne with a badly dislocated shoulder injured during their flight – and on the same day, passing through Mentieth, they were also joined by Montrose's nephew, the Master of Napier, who had escaped from Holyrood. But there was no word of the promised cavalry reinforcements from England – and Montrose wrote disconsolately to the King, that without such support or the 'very nerves of war', his task was next to impossible. 'Howsoever, though you have not assisted me, I will yet still do my best to bar all assistance coming against you... for so long as it pleases God I am alive and free...'[52] He was understandably growing discouraged. The victory at Inverlochy seemed to have achieved little or nothing. Unsupported, and still trying to raise a sizeable army, he could only fight to contain the Covenant forces in Scotland.

The letter to the King miscarried, since the courier was caught and hanged. From the papers found on his person, the Covenanters were able to deduce that the King's position in England was critical, and they were made alive to the danger that Charles might attempt to come north to join Montrose and thus shift the seat of the war to Scotland. In retrospect, some civil war historians have maintained that had the King marched north, his presence would have removed the principal difficulties which then beset Montrose and so turned the balance. Huntly's opposition might have ceased had the King been in Scotland to command in person, and the entire Gordon clan would have rallied to the standard. In potentially royalist areas, the influence of the Covenant, dependent as it was on terror, might have been broken. A proportion of Leven's army, discontented because they had not received the pay promised them by the English Parliament, might have changed sides. Montrose and Rupert in concert could have matched any generals in the country.

All this might have been. But the King did not receive Montrose's request, and he hesitated for lack of news and clear advice. The Covenanters, with this intelligence in their hands, at once took measures to prevent any junction of the royalist armies in the Lowlands. South of the border, the disposition of Leven's forces was rearranged so that when Charles did eventually move slowly north, he found the way barred against him. In Scotland, the Estates ordered a new levy of 8800 infantry and 485 cavalry from the counties south of the Tay, and recalled a further

1000 veterans from Ireland. Baillie kept his main force at Perth with instructions to block the passes to the capital and the southern shires and contain Montrose within the Highland line until the fresh troops arrived. In the meanwhile, Sir John Hurry was sent north with two regular regiments of foot (Lothian's and Loudoun's) and a regiment of horse (Hackett's) to join the two regiments at Inverness (Lawers' and Buchanan's), and raise troops among the northern Covenanters. Baillie and Hurry would then concert to bring Montrose between them.

Lord George Gordon, in Aberdeenshire, advised Montrose of Hurry's northern progress. The King's Lieutenant could not risk the Gordons being defeated, and so decided to march to their assistance. That the Covenanters should have divided their forces in fact suited his strategy. Combined, he could not have matched Baillie and Hurry together on the battlefield, but separated, he might hope to engage and defeat each in turn.

Alasdair made a diversionary raid into Angus which drew Baillie eastwards and gave Montrose his chance to slip through Balquhidder to Loch Tay and thence by the familiar road along Loch Tummel to reach Atholl without being intercepted. Gathering up Black Pate Inchbrakie and the Badenoch men, he continued north with characteristic speed through Clova and over Capel Mounth to Glen Muick and along Deeside to Aboyne. Alasdair and his Irishes came in from Glen Tanar, and Lord George Gordon with his levies from Auchindoun. The royalists, with 2500 foot and 250 horse, now matched Hurry's northern force, and having obtained fresh supplies and ammunition by a daring raid on some Covenant ships in Aberdeen harbour, Montrose marched to Strathbogie on 2nd May.

Sir John Hurry had believed the King's Lieutenant to be still south of the Grampians, and at the startling news of a superior royalist army on his heels, he hastily crossed the River Spey into Moray. The royalist advanced patrols came into contact with the Covenant rearguard on 4th May, and a running fight developed along the road to Inverness. Hurry was an experienced commander, however, and while his forward units kept safely ahead, a series of rearguard actions drew Montrose further into Moray and away from the hills and the friendly Gordon country. For three days he was content to retreat along the coast by Elgin and Forres towards Nairn – always in contact, but not stopping to give battle. On 8th May, he linked up with the two regular regiments from Inverness, and thus reinforced, turned around to strike.

Campaign of Dundee and Auldearn

Montrose's march before taking Dundee ————

Montrose's march after taking Dundee - - - - - -

SCALE

Miles

0   6   12   18   24

Montrose had pressed Hurry almost to Inverness itself, but realising that the Covenant army now out-matched his own, he withdrew some fourteen miles to the village of Auldearn, east of Nairn where he camped somewhat 'commodiously'. The royalist army had been reduced during the previous few days by the departure of the Athollmen who had heard that Baillie's forces were plundering their lands. Now deep in hostile territory, precise intelligence was difficult to obtain, and thinking perhaps that Hurry would pause at Inverness to organise his regiments, Montrose did not expect Hurry to attack. The night was wild and wet, and the royalist scouts, in unfamiliar country did not go far from the camp. Only a freak of the wind gave them warning of the enemy's approach.

The Covenanters had marched all night, by Culloden Moor and across the River Nairn – hoping to surprise the royalists at daybreak. They might have succeeded but for the fact that it had been raining continuously during the march, and near Nairn the infantry were ordered to clear their muskets in case the powder in the barrels had been soaked and spoiled. Rather than go through the laborious process of drawing the charges, the troops fired their weapons into the air, thinking that by pointing their muskets towards the sea, on such a wild night the sound would not carry as far as Auldearn. But by some chance of the wind, one of Nathaniel Gordon's advance outposts heard the volley and gave the alarm. The royalists thus had almost an hour in which to prepare.

It seems certain that Montrose was taken by surprise, and now suddenly found himself in a dangerous situation. Because the royalists were widely dispersed when the alarm was given, only 600 men were immediately available to mount a defence, and the units furthest from the village could not be placed in battle order before Hurry arrived. (On the morning of Auldearn the royalist army probably mustered about 2000 men all told.)

Having already passed through Auldearn some two days previously and finding it adequate as a place to camp, Montrose probably had made some study of the ground. At that time, the village consisted of a number of cottages built along a ridge running roughly south from the church along the line of the present Boath road. At its northern end the ridge merged into a steep circular mound called the Castle Hill (the present site of Boath Dovecote). The steep side of the ridge faced west – almost at right angles to Hurry's line of approach – and on this slope, below the cottages, the gardens and enclosures of the villagers fenced in by a series of dry stone walls, formed a natural system of defence works. To the west, the ground over which the Covenanters would advance was at first comparatively flat, though covered by bushes and rough undergrowth, and then sank gradually away into a marsh. This boggy ground was caused by a burn that flowed from near the Castle Hill before curving back into a ravine which thus protected the southern end of the ridge where it continued behind the village. At the southern edge of the hamlet, east behind the ridge, the ground sloped gently back into a large hollow, masked from anyone looking eastwards from the direction of Inverness. Thus while the burn and marsh-land effectively constricted the line of approach and prevented any outflanking movement, the steep slope of the ridge, broken by the walled enclosures, might constitute a tenable defensive position. The whole situation could be overlooked by a command post in the church tower to the rear of Castle Hill.

The 600 men immediately available within Auldearn were sent to take station on the slope of Castle Hill among the dykes and enclosures at the northern end of the ridge. They were probably deployed in two divisions – with Nathaniel Gordon commanding the extreme right with Alasdair immediately to his left. There is a tradition that at this critical moment Alasdair and Lord George Gordon decided, as a gesture of mutual friendship and respect, to exchange their troops – a bargain which left Alasdair with only 50 of his veteran MacDonalds and some 300 untrained Gordon levies. It is more likely, however, that this represents the proportion of Gordons and MacDonalds available at the time, and that the rest of the Highlanders, with the Irishes, were still being mustered to the east of Auldearn. Because the Gordons were showing signs of nervousness, Alasdair was obliged to draw up his command with 25 of his veteran swordsmen in the front rank to give a lead to the levies behind, and the remaining 25 at the rear to drive them on or stop them from running away when the fight began.

On the high ground near the church behind Castle Hill, Montrose placed the great yellow standard of the King in the hope that this would draw the main Covenant attack. Alasdair was ordered to hold his position at all costs. Among the enclosures in the centre of the ridge, Montrose deployed a thin screen of musketeers with a large number of battle standards and orders to move about and maintain a brisk fire that would give the impression of a large concentration of men. Considered therefore in terms of a conventional battle line, while Nathaniel Gordon and Alasdair held the right, the centre was almost non-existent, and 'left to the imagination of the enemy'. The left wing itself had not yet reached the field.

While Alasdair's men and the Royal Standard conspicuous behind them gave the appearance of an army drawn up in a strong defensive position, the rest of the royalist force were hurrying into Auldearn to be marshalled in the hollow behind the ridge and out of sight of the enemy. Montrose himself took command of the infantry – about 1000 Irishes and Gordons, in a single formation, while the 250 cavalry troopers were divided into two companies under Lord George Gordon and Viscount Aboyne, drawn up on the extreme left of the position south-west of the village. With the main force still converging on Auldearn, there was no time to organise a reserve. Mounted couriers stationed on the ridge kept the two halves of the army in communication.

On the logical assumption that the Royal Standard must mark Montrose's command post and the main royalist position, Hurry would hopefully direct his assault against Alasdair's men on the ridge. While the Covenanters were heavily engaged on that front, the rest of the royalist army would have time to form up behind the hill and at the critical moment advance to fill the vacant left and centre of the line. The cavalry on the extreme left would burst over the southern, lower end of the ridge to wheel right and attack the exposed flank of the enemy. But the crucial factor would be Alasdair's ability to hold on against extreme odds until the rest of the army could enter the fight.

Approaching from the west-south-west, at Kinnudie Sir John Hurry drew up his army in order of battle. Looking across the flat ground towards Auldearn, he could distinguish the Royal Standard near the northern end of the ridge, and as anticipated, took it to mark the core of the royalists' defence and thus his objective. He decided on an immediate frontal assault.

As the Covenanters started to advance, they began almost at once to experience difficulty on account of the boggy ground. The heavy rain had swollen the burn and filled the marsh, and even on the higher ground, thick mud made the going slow. Constricted by the bog, Hurry could not extend his battle line to take full advantage of his superior numbers and the Covenant army was forced to advance on a narrow front – probably with Lawers' regiment of Campbells forming the vanguard supported by the other four regular regiments, roughly in echelon two abreast. The northern levies were on the left of this formation and slightly withdrawn. On the right flank, Hurry posted a detachment of horse under a certain Major Drummond, while to the rear, the main cavalry division under his personal command formed the reserve. Although the nature of the

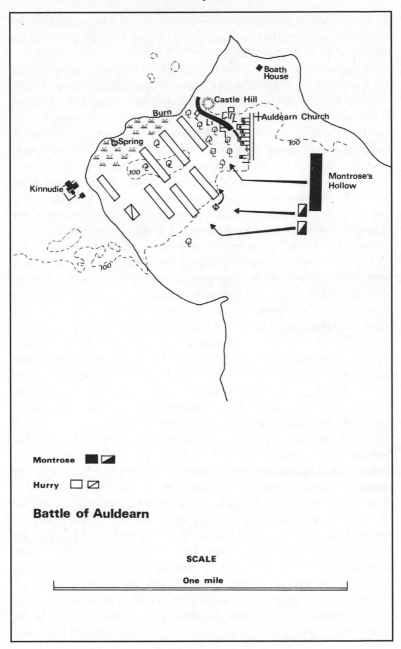

Boath House

Castle Hill

Burn

LI

Auldearn Church

Spring

100

Montrose's Hollow

100

Kinnudie

100

Montrose

Hurry

Battle of Auldearn

SCALE

One mile

ground prevented any full deployment to overlap what he presumed to be Montrose's position, the Covenant general counted on the weight of his attack to drive a wedge into the royalist defence.

At the foot of the ridge, Lawers's Campbells inclined slightly to their left and began to assault the perimeter of Alasdair's position. Under covering fire from the musketeers, the Covenanters launched a series of attacks across the broken ground, but although these were pushed home with considerable spirit and determination, the dykes and dry stone walls broke up the advancing formations and prevented Lawers's men from concentrating their full weight against a single critical point. As one wave of attackers tired another moved forward to take their place, and fierce hand to hand fighting continued along the slope and around the enclosures. But after two prolonged assaults had been beaten off with loss, the Covenanters at length withdrew to the foot of the ridge to reform.

Then Alasdair left the safety of his position. He had been given the battle's anvil – to withstand the repeated blows that Hurry would deliver against the standard, and hold out at any cost until Montrose could come to his assistance. But as a Highland fighting man, the defensive posture possibly made him impatient and uneasy – and especially when the enemy regiment in front of him was composed of Campbells. Stung perhaps by the taunts of the Covenanters or forced to take the initiative because of the unsteadiness of the Gordon Levies, he left the enclosures and started down the hill – not in a wild Highland charge, but walking backwards with his face towards his own men calling them on to follow. Their counter attack halted the Covenanters for a moment, but Lawers's Campbells were accounted one of the finest regiments in the Scottish army, and would not flinch from a claymore. They absorbed the impact of Alasdair's attack, but then the pikemen started forward again, and the solid weight of their formation relentlessly drove the royalists back. The situation suddenly became extremely desperate, and Alasdair shouted to his men to get back to the enclosures before they were surrounded and cut off. The gave ground before the long pikes, moving backwards step by step under a hail of arrows from the Covenant archers, while the few MacDonalds covered their retreat. Last of all was Alasdair, '... and covering himself with a huge targe, single handed he withstood the thickest of the enemy. Some of the pikemen by whom he was hard pressed again and again pierced his targe with the points of their weapons which he mowed off by[53] threes and fours with his broadsword.' In the hand to hand fighting among the dykes, the great sword finally broke, but his brother-in-law, Davidson of Ardnacross, threw him another, and the desperate melée continued around the enclosure as Alasdair and his MacDonalds held the entrance until the rest could get through.

The Gaels put up an heroic defence. One of the Highlanders called Ranald MacDonald, son of Donald, son of Angus Mackinnon of Mull, was cornered against the wrong side of the wall by a body of Covenant pikemen. He carried a targe on his left arm while he held them off with a hand gun and tried to edge his way to the enclosure entrance. An archer who had been firing at the Gordons saw him, and changing his aim, shot the retreating MacDonald through the mouth – the arrow skewering his tongue and coming out a fist's breadth through his cheek. Ranald paid no attention to the archer, however, but coolly fired his gun into the face of the nearest pikeman, and stretching out his targe to ward off the spears of the others, reached for his broadsword. But the weapon was stuck – perhaps clotted with blood – and would not move from its sheath. He tugged at it again, but the cross-hilt whirled loose in his hand, and he was forced to lower his shield arm to grip the scabbard while he drew the blade. In this brief moment he took the points of five pikes in his chest and chin, but kept his feet and slicing through the shafts with his freed broadsword, continued moving sideways with his back against the wall. Fortunately for him, the pikemen broke off their attack to go after easier prey – except for one man who kept after the wounded MacDonald and continued to thrust at him with his long spear. Ranald fought him off with sword and targe until the doorway was behind him. Then he sprang back, turned, and ducked quickly through the entrance – and when the pikeman followed, Alasdair, on the other side, decapitated him with one downward stroke of his sword so that the body fell across the doorway and the head bounced off Ranald's shins into the garden. Someone cut the arrow out of the MacDonald's cheek, and it was discovered – to his own surprise – that he could still speak.[54]

But with the Gordon levies close to panic, 50 Highlanders could not hold out indefinitely against 500. The Covenanters began to sense victory. Lawers's men again stormed the enclosure and it seemed certain that the royalists must soon be over-run. 17 of Alasdair's swordsmen were lying dead or disabled around the doorway, and many of the others were wounded and could not fight on much longer.

One of the mounted couriers saw the desperate situation on the ridge, and galloping down into the hollow, whispered to Montrose that Alasdair seemed done for. From their position in the depression the rest of the army could not see what was happening on the further side of the hill, but rumours of Alasdair's plight would have panicked the Gordon levies. There could be no hesitation now, and Montrose called to Lord George Gordon, sitting his horse in front of the royalist cavalry: '… What are we waiting for? Our friend Alasdair on the right has routed the enemy… shall we look on idly and let him carry off the honours of the day?'[55]

The Gordons needed no urging. They were intent on avenging the death of Donald Farguharson at Aberdeen and more recently the[56] murder of the young Gordon laird of Rhynie who had been killed by Covenant troopers when he lay helplessly wounded at Strudders, and shouting these names, they drew their swords and followed their chieftain. The squadrons galloped over the southern end of the ridge, and bursting suddenly into view, wheeled right to charge into the broad flank of the Covenant regiments which Hurry's formation had exposed to their attack. Without checking to fire their carbines, the cavalry smashed into the Covenant files at full gallop. The Covenant horse offered no resistance. Drummond's detachment saw them coming, but in their panic, or on a wrong command, instead of wheeling to meet them, turned inwards and rode down their own infantry. The Gordons cut their way through the confusion, broke the right hand regiments, and turned to attack again. Covenant formations, outflanked or caught in the rear, scattered in front of the charging horsemen and tried to flee across the muddy grounds with the Gordons after them in full cry.

Montrose meanwhile, led his infantry out of the hollow and over the ridge to join the battle in the centre. Sweeping away the remnants of the battalions in their path, they converged on Alasdair's besieged enclosure, and the great MacDonald saw them coming and called on his tired men for one final effort. To face the new danger from their right, the Covenanters began to disengage, and once more the royalists broke out of their dykes and attacked down the slope. At the foot of the ridge Alasdair and Montrose combined to close relentlessly around Lawers's men. The Covenant vanguard was now isolated, but the Campbells would not run. A bloody attrition followed until the regiment was finally annihilated almost where it stood.[57]

Most of the Covenant cavalry escaped – due largely to a misunderstanding among the royalists. Aboyne's squadron, who were brandishing some captured enemy standards, were mistaken for the enemy and attacked by their own men, and although the error was quickly realised the delay was long enough to allow Hurry's dragoons to get clear. The

Covenant infantry were less fortunate, and the Gordons took few prisoners and gave little quarter. The pursuit lasted fourteen miles, and the mass graves uncovered later indicated the extent to which Hurry's force was scattered. Covenant casualties were afterwards put at about 3000 killed. The dead included Sir Mungo Campbell of Lawers himself, and a number of senior officers (some of whom are buried in Auldearn churchyard). Losses among the northern levies were catastrophic. Of the Frasers, 'besides what fell unmarried, there were eighty seven widows in the Lordship of Lovat.'[58] The MacLennans, who guarded the *Caber Feidh* – Seaforth's banner – were wiped out, and it is said that eighteen of their widows married MacRaes and the two tribes amalgamated. The Covenanters lost sixteen colours and all their baggage. Hurry blamed the luckless cavalry commander Major Drummond for the terrible defeat – and he was court martialled and executed by firing squad shortly after the battle. The broken army withdrew to Inverness.

Montrose did not pursue, having no wish to be drawn into a protracted siege. Royalist casualties in the battle have been variously estimated – the most likely figure being some 22 officers and 200 private soldiers killed outright. There were a large number of wounded, mainly from Alasdair's division, and those whose hurts were serious were next day carried to Gordon Castle in the Bog of Gight.

Among the music of the Graham family is a piece called the Blar Aultearn in celebration of this victory. Although he had been taken largely by surprise and forced to improvise a defence with few troops and on unreconnoitred ground, Auldearn is sometimes seen in tactical terms as the most brilliant of Montrose's battles. His use of the available terrain was marvellously conceived, the timing cool and judged to a fine moment. On this first occasion when he had a sizeable force of Gordon horse to command, he directed the charge as Rupert might have done, and demonstrated an ability to deploy cavalry as a tactical arm. His detractors had sometimes argued that his victories were obtained over poor and undisciplined troops – second line regiments with no experience and little training – but at Auldearn this was clearly not the case. Apart from the northern levies who took no part in the actual battle, and excluding also Seaforth's MacKenzies, the Covenant army included four regular front line regiments, and Lawers' Campbells were held to be among the best that Scotland could show. Sir John Hurry was a commander of considerable experience, and the royalists were outnumbered by almost two to one.

It remained to be seen what advantage would accrue from the battle. One half of the Covenant army in Scotland had been decisively beaten, but on the day Auldearn was fought, Baillie's main forces crossed the Grampians. It could not be a matter yet of riding south tomorrow.

CHAPTER 16

The Battle of Alford

Shortly after Auldearn, Alasdair learned that his father and two brothers had been released a few days before the battle. Negotiations had been continuing for several months and eventually an exchange of prisoners had been arranged at Duart Castle in Mull on 1st May 1645. Argyll's agent at Dunstaffnage had released old Colkitto with his sons Gillespie and Angus, and also Gillespie's son, Coll, in return for Alasdair's prisoners at Mingary and a number of prominent Campbells captured at Inverlochy. The commander of Mingary had exceeded his instructions in releasing James Hamilton the minister of Dumfries, whom Montrose had intended to exchange for his own brother Harry Graham, but as Alasdair's officer, he could hardly be blamed for having acted in the MacDonald's interest.

In the meanwhile, the condition of royalist prisoners in Edinburgh was continuing to cause concern. Predictably, the treatment meted out to the Napier family was especially severe and the Master of Napier's escape was promptly and heavily visited upon his near relations. Lord Napier and Sir George Stirling of Keir were arrested and imprisoned in Edinburgh Castle and their situation became even more precarious when Napier's elder brother, John Napier of Easter Torrie was caught carrying messages from Montrose to the King. Lady Elizabeth Erskine (the Mistress of Napier) and Lilias Napier were also confined in Edinburgh – as also was Montrose's son, James Lord Graham. In a letter of 27th May to Robertson of Inver who commanded the royalist garrison at Blair and was also involved in negotiating a exchange of prisoners, Montrose ordered that the Covenanters should be left in no doubt that if they thought to execute Napier in 'ane seeming legal way... I will use the like severity against some of their prisoners'. The threat had the desired effect and on 13th June, the Estates released John Napier of Easter Torrie into the custody of Sir Archibald Campbell. Similar arrangements were in hand for further exchanges – the Earl of Kinghorn for Harry Graham, Murray of Gask for Dr Wishart, and others on a man for man basis.

However, these negotiations appear to have progressed more slowly, and Montrose was constantly pressing Inver for news. James Lord Graham refused to be exchanged lest he should cost his father the benefit of an important prisoner in return. Montrose's third son, Robert was allowed to remain in the custody of his mother, who was possibly staying with her father, the Earl of Southesk, at Kinnaird Castle, and took no part in Montrose's affairs.

Too many men had been wounded at Auldearn for Montrose to consider fighting another battle immediately, and the army spent three days at Elgin where surgeons and medicines were readily available. Aboyne (who may have been hurt in the fight) left on temporary sick leave, and as usual, a number of Highlanders also returned home. On 14th May, Montrose moved to Gordon Castle in the Bog of Gight, and from here the Gordon cavalry patrols carried out a series of punitive raids against the local Covenanters. Alasdair took a force of Highlanders and Irishes into Easter Ross and 'raised flames of fire in the land of Lovat'. It seems that after Auldearn, the Earl of Seaforth again made hasty submissions to the King's Lieutenant, but the MacKenzies and the Frasers were made to suffer for their association with the Covenanters. Alasdair's men swept through their lands 'like fiends and foes... with spullying and rapin up and down the country, killing sheep, cows and oxen, to the shame of their profession in a civil country.'[59] The Frasers came to terms, and having punished them severely, Alasdair rejoined Montrose.

The Covenant army under Baillie meanwhile, after making 'an unnecessary voyage into Atholl' at the insistence of the Committee, had crossed over Cairn O'Mounth on the day of Auldearn and camped at Birse in the district known as Cromar. On 19th May, Baillie reached Coklaroquhy Wood, about two miles west of Strathbogie, where he was joined by Sir John Hurry who had slipped through the cordon of royalist patrols disguised as one of Lord George Gordon's men, together with 100 troopers who had survived the Battle of Auldearn.

News that the Covenanters were threatening Huntly Castle reached Montrose at Birkenbog, and he hurried to arrive there before them and began constructing earthworks as if he intended to make a stand. In fact, he was reluctant to fight at this time, but hoped that if Baillie could be engaged and drawn away from Strathbogie, it would then be possible to outmanoeuvre him in Strathspey. Baillie's own account of the action reflected the Covenanters' frustration in trying to come to grips with the fast moving Highlanders and Gaelic Irish who could literally disappear in the night:

'At our approach the rebels drew into places of advantage about the yards and dykes, and I stood embattled before them from four o'clock at night until the morrow, judging them to have been about our own strength. Upon the morrow, as soon as it was day, we found they were gone towards Balveny. We marched after them, and came off in a fight about Glenlivet, some few miles west of Balveny: but that night they outmarched us, and quartered some six miles from us. On the next day early, we found they were dislodged, but could find nobody to inform us of their march; yet by the lying of the grass and heather, we conjectured they were marching to the wood of Abernethy upon Spey. Thither I marched, and found them in the entry of Badenoch, a very strait country, where, both for inaccessible rocks, woods, and the interposition of the river, it was impossible for us to come at them.'[60]

The two armies confronted each other for several days, but while the royalists could obtain supplies from Badenoch and the friendly country to their rear, the Covenanters began to run short of food and fodder, and Baillie was forced to withdraw to Inverness. Having replenished his commissariat, he crossed the Spey and marched into Aberdeenshire and camped in the Garioch.

This gave Montrose an opportunity to stage a quick raid into Angus where he hoped to surprise and destroy the new Covenant regiments that were being mustered and trained at Newtyle of Angus, under the Earl of Crawford-Lindsay (Lindsay of the Byres). He knew well enough that he would have to settle with Baillie's veterans before marching south in earnest, but his intention was to snatch a cheap victory over the raw levies as a means of boosting the royalists' morale. He therefore struck south by Rothiemurchus and the track through Glen Dee into the Braes of Mar and then by Glen Clova and Auchtertyre. Lindsay's levies, barely seven miles off and unaware of their approach, would have been at his mercy had not the entire Gordon contingent (with the exception of Lord George Gordon and Nathaniel Gordon) chosen this critical moment to leave the army and ride home. Wishart, in his biography of Montrose (written two years later) imputed their desertion to secret orders from Huntly to Aboyne (who was still on sick leave at the Bog of Gight), but it is as likely that they were not willing to campaign away from home at a time when Baillie was clearly shaping to attack Strathbogie and their lands in

Aberdeenshire. Montrose might still have attacked Lindsay with the Irishes alone, but as the enemy had by now had wind of his coming and had withdrawn to a strong position, he decided that it was no longer worth the risk, and the Covenanters thus 'escaped a scouring'. The royalists withdrew into Strathardle.

Recruitment again became the most urgent priority. Lord Gordon was furious over the apparent 'desertion' of his followers, and taking Nathaniel Gordon with him, rode north to the Bog to call them back. Montrose also sent Alasdair to the western Highlands again to seek help from John Moydartach of the Clanranald – and possibly so that he could see old Colkitto and his brothers and celebrate their release. The Irish regiments remained with the army, as did a band of MacDonald clansmen under Glengarry. But there were signs that Montrose was becoming concerned about the strength of the Highland support since he now began issuing specific promises of rewards when the war was won. On 7th June he formally promised Patrick Roy MacGregor that he and his clan would be restored to all their ancestral lands in Glen Lyon, Rannoch, and Glenorchy, and further promises to the MacGregors at the end of July might indicate some reluctance among that clan to continue with the campaign.

The army camped among the ruins of Corgarff Castle at the head of Strathdon from where they could either retreat into the safety of the hills or descend on Aberdeenshire. Aboyne eventually returned, but fell sick again almost immediately, and under the pretence of requiring an escort to Strathbogie, took away another troop of horse whom Lord Gordon afterwards had great difficulty in persuading back to the standard. Gordon jealousies, stirred by the absent Huntly, continued to hinder progress of recruiting, and a fortnight passed while the levies were induced to return to the army. It was a slow, wearisome business, but Montrose could only wait, hoping for news of Alasdair and Highland reinforcements, but desperate for the Gordon cavalry without whom he could not face Baillie in the field.

The Covenant general, however, had troubles of his own, being faced with mutiny by his veteran regiments and bombarded with instructions from the Committee of War in Edinburgh – composed of such strategists as Argyll, Burleigh, Elcho, and others, whose memory of their own defeats did not deter them from trying to dictate the conduct of the campaign. He was ordered to transfer 1200 of his best infantry and 100 cavalry to Crawford-Lindsay in exchange for 400 raw recruits, and while

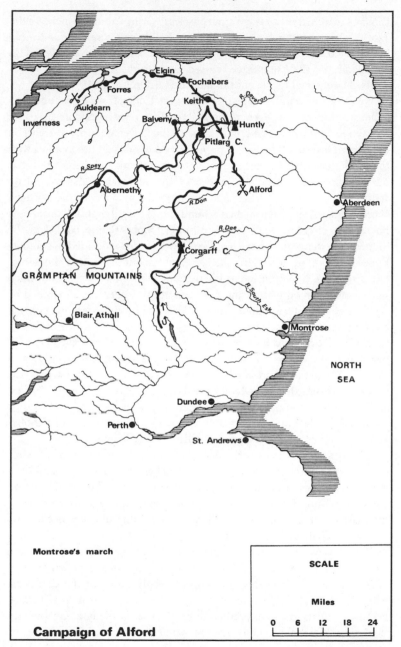

Montrose's march

SCALE

Miles

0   6   12   18   24

Campaign of Alford

Lindsay marched off to wage a purposeless war in Atholl – where he did a lot of damage but achieved little else – Baillie was commanded to lead his depleted force against Montrose. He would willingly have resigned his command, but the Committee refused his request, and somewhat reluctantly, he returned north and threatened Gordon Castle.

News of his march reached Montrose at Corgarff on 25th June, and feeling confident that even without Alasdair's reinforcements he could face Baillie in the open, he caught up with the Covenant army at Keith on the River Deveron. The Covenant infantry were drawn up on a hill with the cavalry occupying a narrow pass in front of them, and the position was too strong to risk a frontal attack since the enemy had also moved up artillery to sweep the defile. Having probed for a weak spot with no success, the royalists skirmished around the gap until nightfall, but made no serious attempt to force the position. Since Baillie could not be induced to offer battle on the open ground, Montrose decided to simulate retreat in the hope of enticing the Covenanters out of the area altogether. On 28th June, he withdrew to Pitlaig, and the following day continued south – as if contemplating another descent on Angus – and marched by the Suie Road to Drumninor Castle. There, he received intelligence that Baillie had left Keith and was advancing after him through Strathbogie. In fact, Baillie had just heard of Alasdair's absence – whose name inspired terror among the Covenant levies – and thus reassured, was in hot pursuit to catch Montrose before the MacDonald could return. On 1st July, the royalists crossed the River Don by a ford known as the Boat of Forbes, and halted on Gallows Hill near the hamlet of Alford – which at that time consisted of a few buildings including a Kirk, a smithy, and an alehouse about two miles west of the present village of that name.

The Boat of Forbes was the main ford on the upper Don which then flowed broad and deep through long stretches of undrained marshland. The Covenanters would almost certainly cross the river at this point, where, emerging from the ford, the Suie Road ran due south to traverse the marsh over a short causeway before continuing in a straight line up the side of Gallows Hill at its steepest point.

The royalists initially took position slightly behind the crest, and facing north astride the road. To their immediate front, the northern face of the hill overlooking the ford sloped steeply down to the causeway, while on the right, the gradient was less steep ad the ground fell away, north-eastward, in a long gradual descent towards the bog. On the left, the Leochel Burn flowed down to the main river through a marshy ravine which effectively prevented any flank attack from that quarter. To the rear of the position, the steep crest of the hill concealed a shallow plateau that subsided gently towards the Leochel marsh along the line of the Suie Road.

Early on the morning of 2nd July 1645, the royalist scouts north of the river brought word that the Covenanters were marching towards Forbes. At daybreak, the army stood to arms while Montrose himself rode out with a cavalry patrol to reconnoitre for any smaller fords in the vicinity which the enemy might attempt to use. However, fresh reports made it clear that Baillie was heading directly for Alford, and leaving the patrol to shadow the Covenanters' approach, he returned to make his final dispositions for battle.

Montrose now conceived the idea that the Covenant general would not wish to attempt a frontal assault up the steep northern face of Gallows Hill, but after crossing the ford might try to outflank the position by turning left along the edge of the marsh to circle the crest from the east in the hope of cutting the Suie Road at the royalists' rear. He therefore realigned the army to face north-east, looking down the gradual slope towards the bog, with the left flank resting on Gallows Hill and the Leochel Burn to his rear. He withdrew the formations slightly behind the crest so that their strength and disposition would not be visible to the Covenanters as they approached the ford.

An accurate assessment of the numbers engaged at Alford is virtually impossible, but Montrose probably had about 2500 infantry, including the Irishes under their regimental commanders, and 250 cavalry. The royalist army was drawn up in four main divisions. On the left, Viscount Aboyne led 100 Gordon horse with a small force of Irishes under O'Cahan in support. Lord Gordon led a similar formation of cavalry on the right with another body of light musketeers under Nathaniel Gordon. The centre was composed of Gordons and Irishes, a detachment of the Clanranald, Farquharsons, MacPhersons from Badenoch, Athollmen, and 200 clansmen from Strathavon, drawn up in files six deep, and commanded in Alasdair's absence by Angus MacDonald of Glengarry. The Master of Napier led the reserve which was concealed in a slight depression some distance behind the main battle line.

As he approached the Boat of Forbes, Baillie still believed that the royalists were some miles ahead of him and in full retreat. From the ford, he could not see Montrose's army drawn up behind the crest, and such detachments as were visible on Gallows Hill he took to be a rearguard posted to cover the withdrawal. To engage them on the steep slope was clearly not to his advantage while any circling movement to the right would bog down in the marshes bordering the Leochel Burn. A flank march around the eastern slopes of the hill seemed preferable, and any doubts that he may have had were brushed aside by the attendant committee and Sir David Lindsay of Balcarres who commanded the forward cavalry detachments.

With Balcarres's horse leading, the Covenanters crossed the river, and traversing the causeway, began to deploy to their left along the edge of the marsh – very much as Montrose had anticipated. Balcarres was already committed to this movement before Baillie realised that he had fallen into a trap, and that his manoeuvre was taking him across the front of the entire royalist army which now had him pinned against the bog. Given a choice, he would have withdrawn, but the forward cavalry squadrons had already advanced onto the slight ridge that formed the glacis of Montrose's position and could not be extricated. If the royalists were determined to fight, a battle was unavoidable.

The Covenanters halted irresolutely on the fringe of the marsh. Baillie's force was slightly inferior to Montrose in infantry, but his two regiments of horse (Hackett's and Balcarres's) amounting to 600 troopers, gave him the advantage in cavalry. Seeing that he would be forced to fight, Baillie made what hasty dispositions he could – largely determined by his army's existing order of march. Balcarres's squadrons, whose advance had brought them closest to the enemy position, were already ranged against Lord Gordon and the royalist right. He now deployed Hackett's regiment at the other end of the line to confront Aboyne's division. In the centre the Covenant foot took up a defensive position, drawn up three deep among a series of dykes and small enclosures along the edge of the boggy ground.

For a while, neither army seemed willing to take the initiative. Baillie would not storm the hill, and Montrose was reluctant to abandon his advantageous position on the higher ground to assault the defence works by the marsh. However, the Covenanters had been driving with them a quantity of cattle lifted in Strathbogie, and the sight of these stolen beasts herded behind Balcarres's division so infuriated the Gordons on the royalist right that finally they could be restrained no longer, and they charged down the slope. Balcarres, confident in superior discipline and numbers, led out his front two squadrons to meet them, and the two forces crashed together at a gallop and became locked in a tight melée

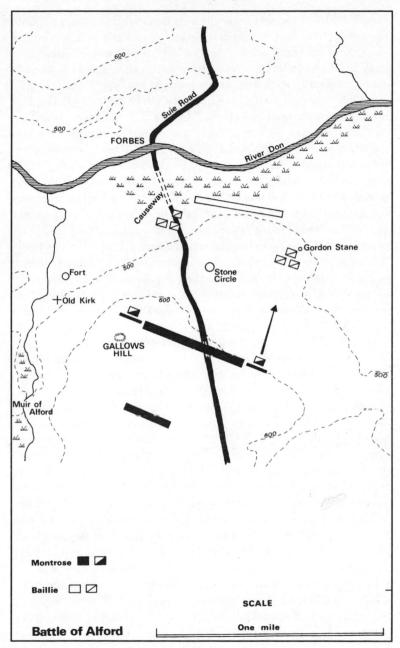

600

500

Suie Road

FORBES

River Don

Causeway

Gordon Stane

Fort

500

Stone
Circle

Old Kirk

600

GALLOWS
HILL

500

Muir of
Alford

600

Montrose

Baillie

SCALE

One mile

Battle of Alford

along the edge of the ridge over the area now called the Feight Faulds. The fight swayed back and forth with neither side able to make ground, while the thick press of men behind prevented those in front from breaking off or attempting to manoeuvre. In this close quarter battle individual antagonists with little or no room to swing a sword, grappled together – '... seizing each other's heads with their left hands and striking one another on the head with pistols.' The royalist musketeers in support could not fire into the struggling mass for fear of hitting their own horsemen, and a Clanranald man, Alaster son of Ranald, recalled afterwards that he had stood for a time with his sword point resting in the earth 'not knowing on whom he could strike a blow' because in the press he could not distinguish friend from foe. Balcarres himself had his helmet struck off in the first onset, but he called to his men to come on again, and the Gordons could make no swordway. Baillie, watching the battle in the balance, ordered the reserve squadrons to charge the royalist flank, but in the confusion the command was misunderstood and they drove in behind their fellows and were in turn sucked into the murderous scrimmage. Yet it seemed that by weight of numbers the Covenanters might 'wring back the victory', and seeing the Gordons checked, Montrose ordered a general attack on the Covenant centre.

On the right, the situation was finally resolved by Nathaniel Gordon, who cut his way out of the fight to call up the Irishes – shouting at them to throw away their muskets and hamstring the enemies' horses with their swords and dirks. The Irishes dropped their useless matchlocks and ran in among the Covenant horse, slashing at legs and girths, and dragging the troopers out of the saddles to kill them on the ground. Beasts and men started to panic, and confused by this method of attack, Balcarres's men suddenly broke. The Gordons cut their way through the confusion and turned inwards to charge the flank of Baillie's centre which was by now embattled against Montrose. From the rear, the Master of Napier flung his reserve into the attack and even the 'peddies' – the boys left to guard the baggage train – jumped on mules and rode into the fight. Although their cavalry were in full flight to the east, the Covenant foot fought on doggedly until nearly 1600 had been killed, but when the royalist reserve came streaming down the slope, the survivors threw away their weapons and tried desperately to escape. The royalists pursued them to the Howe of Alford and beyond. At Tough, four miles to the east of the battlefield itself, the Blaudy Faulds recall the last stand of some who could run no further.

But the victory was turned to ashes. Lord Gordon had sworn that he would take General Baillie himself, and when the enemy broke and ran, he had gone seeking the Covenant commander among the fugitives. At the very moment, it was said, that he was reaching out for Baillie's belt to drag him from the saddle, a musket ball struck him in the back. The wound was mortal, and as the news spread that he had fallen, Gordons and Irishes alike broke off the pursuit to gather around his corpse.

'Conquest and plunder were forgotten as they crowded round his lifeless body, kissing his face and hands, weeping over his wounds, praising the beauty of his person even in death, and extolling a nature as noble and generous as his birth and fortune. They even cursed a victory that was bought so dearly.'[61]

In their grief, the royalists had more the appearance of a beaten army than victors on the battlefield. This had been the best of the Gordons, the one great hope of the north. Loyal where his father Huntly was jealous; true where his brother Aboyne was fickle; he had won the dearest friendship of Montrose and the respect of the fighting Alasdair. How much they had lost by his death, subsequent events would surely show.

At Alford a monolith was left to mark the place where he fell, and called the Gordon Stane, it stood as a memorial for three hundred years until, in more recent times the area was surrounded by corrugated iron and turned into a rubbish dump. In Aberdeen Cathedral where the royalists carried him for burial, no inscription signifies his tomb.

CHAPTER 17

The Battle of Kilsyth

The war allowed no time to dwell upon misfortune. In England, the Battle of Naseby had been fought and lost, and although the full implications of Parliament's victory were not yet apparent, it was clear enough that if he was to intervene effectively on the King's behalf, Montrose could not delay his march south much longer. After Alford, some of the Highlanders again returned home to deposit their spoil, but with another fight in prospect, many could be expected to return. Black Pate Inchbrakie was in Atholl mustering the men of Badenoch. In the west, Alasdair was gathering the western clans. Viscount Aboyne was sent north to recruit cavalry in Buchan, but made slow work of it, and when he returned with only a small following, Montrose sent him back with orders to do better.

The perverse influence of Huntly was still apparent, and he was reluctant to let his clan ride south. Aboyne himself was brave enough, but he was closer to his father, prone to fits of jealousy, and lacked the constancy of his late brother. Recruiting proceeded with maddening slowness. The time called for a supreme effort, but clearly it would take several weeks to muster sufficient men – and particularly cavalry – for the invasion of the Lowlands.

There was now little to keep them north of the Grampians, and Montrose crossed the River Dee and marched into Angus. Inchbrakie arrived with the Athollmen, and Alasdair returned with a warband of 1500 Gaels. Once again the loyal clans of the western Highlands had answered the call in strength. Donald, son of John Moydartach, led 500 fighting men of the Clanranald. Lachlan MacLean of Duart with MacLean of Lochbuie and MacLean of Treshnish brought 700 swordsmen from Mull – new to war, but old enemies of Clan Campbell – and marching with them tribe by tribe came MacPhersons from Badenoch, Camerons and MacSorleys from Lochaber, Appin Stewarts, and Farquharsons from Braemar, MacNabs from Glen Dochart, and MacGregors from Rannoch and Glen Lyon. Glengarry and his MacDonalds were still with the army after Alford.

Montrose now had some 4400 foot, but only 100 horse. Nevertheless, the Highland contingents would not thrive on idleness and Montrose moved south to Methven Wood to harass the Covenanting Parliament which was currently meeting at Perth. The town was defended by 400 cavalry under Sir John Hurry, who eventually discovered the royalists' deficiency in horse and by advancing out of Perth, forced Montrose to withdraw to Dunkeld. Hurry's men occupied the camp at Methven, and somewhere close by, rode down a band of Irish women and camp followers who had straggled behind the main column, and butchered them with great brutality. The ferocity of Irish depredations in the ensuing weeks was largely inspired by revenge for this massacre. Baillie, the Covenant Commander in Chief, remained content meanwhile, to keep his main forces between Montrose and Stirling, since he also was awaiting reinforcements.

During this time, Montrose had repeatedly sent messengers to Viscount Aboyne urging him to hasten south with the northern cavalry, and finally the Gordon arrived with 200 troopers and 120 mounted musketeers – fewer than the King's Lieutenant had a right to expect, but clearly all that he was going to get. However, at Dunkeld the old Earl of Airlie, with his son Sir David Ogilvie and young Ogilvie of Innerquharity returned to the army with 80 well equipped cavaliers. Montrose could now muster 4400 foot and 500 horse – the largest force that he had so far commanded – and he resolved to take the initiative and threaten the main Covenant leaguer north of Stirling.

At the news of his approach, Baillie withdrew his outposts from the Bridge of Earn and hastily constructed a series of earthworks along his threatened quarter, since he was unwilling to fight until his own fresh levies arrived. Nor could Montrose risk a frontal assault against a strong defensive position, and thus had to concede a temporary stand-off. However, he now obtained more detailed intelligence of the Covenanters' intentions which determined his next move in the campaign.

Fresh orders had been issued to the Lowland Covenanters and the Scottish Parliament had called for an additional levy of 10,000 foot and 500 horse. After the Battle of Alford, Baillie had offered to resign his commission, but the Parliament had pressed him to retain command – albeit with a new war committee which included Argyll, Burleigh, and Tullibardine. Baillie, still discontented, had blamed Hurry for failing to catch Montrose at Methven, and resigned again – only to have his resignation refused once more. He was currently awaiting reinforcement by three new regiments of Fifeshire levies and 1200 Campbell Highlanders. In the west, the Earls of Cassilis and Eglinton were raising another Covenant army with Glencairn, while Lanerick had gathered 1000 foot and 50 horse among the Hamilton tenants of Clydesdale and was preparing to march east and join the main force under Baillie.

Montrose could safely ignore Cassilis and Eglinton since they were too distant to be able to affect the immediate issue. It was vital, however, to prevent any junction between Lanerick and Baillie. The expected Fifeshire levies were of lesser importance, because they would be raw recruits, reluctant to march far beyond the boundaries of their own county – and indeed the need to wait for their arrival was keeping Baillie close to the Fife border and thus away from Lanerick.

Montrose feinted east as if to smash the Fifeshire levies while they were mustering, and on 10th August he marched to Kinross on Loch Leven, forcing Baillie to follow. The Covenant general had no sooner joined up with the Fifeshire regiments, however, when he heard that the royalists were turning his southern flank. From Kinross Montrose had wheeled west along the south side of the Ochil Hills to Dollar, where the MacLeans burned Castle Campbell (known as Castle Gloom) in revenge for ancient wrongs. Baillie now saw the issue clear enough, and set out in pursuit, but his troops could not match the speed of Montrose's Highlanders, and his march was delayed by Argyll and the committee who insisted on burning Castle Menstrie[62] and the Graham house at Airth[63] in reprisal for the destruction of Castle Gloom. As they approached the River Forth near Stirling, the Fifeshire men began to grumble and threaten mutiny, but the ministers were set to work among them, and with tales that Lanerick was advancing to their aid, they were persuaded to march for one more day.

Montrose, keeping a day's march ahead, avoided Stirling by fording the river at the Falls of Frew, and passing over the old battlefield of Bannockburn, crossed the River Carron at Denny and reached Kilsyth on the Garrel on 14th August. The royalists camped near old Colzium Castle about a mile northeast of the village. Baillie, taking the easier route, crossed the Forth at Stirling, and marching also by Denny, halted the same night at Hollanbush, about four miles off.

Baillie's intention, in all probability, was now to wait for Lanerick. He pointed out to Argyll and the committee the difficulties of marching directly on Kilsyth since the only road would bring them out immediately below Montrose's position. But Argyll wanted to get closer to the royal-

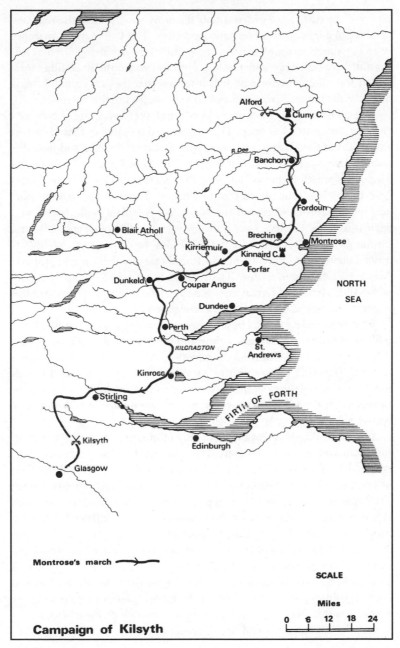

Alford
Cluny C.
R. Dee
Banchory
Fordoun
Blair Atholl
Brechin
Kirriemuir
Montrose
Kinnaird C.
Forfar
Dunkeld
Coupar Angus
NORTH
Dundee
SEA
Perth
KILGRASTON
St.
Andrews
Kinross
FIRTH OF FORTH
Stirling
Kilsyth
Edinburgh
Glasgow

Montrose's march ⟶

SCALE

Miles

0   6   12   18   24

Campaign of Kilsyth

ists, and the committee ordered that the army should leave the road and advance in a more direct line across country. The Covenanters marched over the rough braes of the Campsie Hills to Auchinclogh, where the ground became boggy and further progress was difficult. Baillie again halted the column because he still intended that the army should dig in and wait for Lanerick who was now barely twelve miles distant.

This, however, did not suit Argyll and the committee whose one thought was to attack at once. They convinced themselves that Montrose was finally at their mercy away from the shelter of the hills and forced to fight at their dictation. To the north, the River Forth barred him from the Highlands which hitherto had been his sanctuary. The Covenant army held the high ground above him to the east. Lanerick was behind him, and in the open Lowlands to the south his irregulars could not survive against superior cavalry. Since their own army of 6000 foot and 800 horse outnumbered the royalist force in the meadow below, they saw no need to await Lanerick's reinforcement and feared that any delay might still give Montrose a chance to escape. Their desire to prevent this and to seal off all possible avenues of retreat inspired the battle plan which these military experts now forced upon their reluctant general.

The projected battlefield in some way resembled a huge amphi-theatre with the royalists in the arena below and the Covenanters on the eastern ridge above them. To prevent Montrose from trying to break out north towards Menteith, the committee proposed that the army should circle northwards along the ridge and take possession of the high ground on the royalists' left flank. Once this was done, the enemy would be hemmed in on two sides and the trap sealed shut.

In vain Baillie argued against the folly of initiating a battle when reinforcements were only hours away. He explained the dangers of a flanking march directly across the enemy's front, and pointed out the difficulties of executing such a manouevre with heavily armed infantry over rough and broke terrain. To reach the high ground to the north, the Covenant regiments would have to cross the Banton Burn which flowed through a deep-sided ravine that was almost impassable to cavalry and a formidable obstacle for foot-soldiers to cross without losing their formation and exposing themselves to the Highlander's attack. Montrose might well anticipate the manouevre, and compared with the risks involved, it was even arguable whether possession of the hill in question would yield the advantages that Argyll and the committee so confidently predicted.

But the committee would brook no contradiction, and Baillie's arguments were swept aside. That the foremost of them – Argyll, Burleigh, Elcho, Tullibardine – had been individually or collectively beaten by Montrose did nothing to shake their confidence in the scheme. Balcarres alone – the most competent soldier among them – sided with the general. At this point Baillie lost his temper. He angrily confronted Argyll with his accumulated grievances over the previous months. The Covenanting committee had by-passed his authority whenever it suited them. Prisoners had been exchanged without his knowledge; fire raised without his consent. Now he washed his hands of the whole affair. Henceforth he would do only as the committee explicitly demanded, and if they wanted the direction of the battle they could also bear the responsibility for what happened. The committee ordered him to begin the flanking movement.[64]

The Covenant army was drawn up in line of march. The division of the extreme right – which now became the vanguard – was to be guided by a certain Major Haldane who had reconnoitred the position, to take station among some enclosures on the side of the northern hill which was their main objective. On their left (to follow behind them) were Balcarres's cavalry, then Lauderdale's regiment, Hume's redcoats, Argyll's, Cassilis's, Glencairn's, Lindsay's, and the three regiments of Fifeshire levies. Baillie's instruction was that the army should turn right into column, keeping the appropriate distance between divisions until the movement was completed. The regiments would then face left into line again towards the enemy. Success depended on their keeping behind the crest of the ridge and thus out of sight of the royalists. It also depended on the regiments keeping formation, but Baillie later recalled that as he galloped along the column he discovered at the outset that numbers of musketeers were already straying from their units.

When the army had been set in motion, Baillie rode over the brae to view the royalist dispositions in the meadow below, and from the ridge noticed that a band of Highlanders was moving up the glen. Returning from this reconnaissance, the Covenant general saw to his horror that instead of keeping behind the crest as ordered, Haldane had left the line of march and was leading a company of musketeers against some cottages at the head of the glen. A galloper sent to call off the attack was ignored, and even as Baillie watched, the Highlanders counter-attacked.

Hurrying back towards the main body, Baillie now discovered that the foot regiments had apparently misunderstood their orders, and instead of moving in column of march, had only inclined to the right before advancing over the ridge on the direction of the enemy. Lauderdale's regiment was out on its own, and Hume's, Argyll's, Cassilis's, and Glencairn's had occupied a large enclosure on the slope from which they could no longer be withdrawn. Thus the Covenant army was already fragmented and in confusion before the battle had properly begun. Baillie was still frantically trying to bring up Lindsay's regiment to plug the gap on Lauderdale's left when the royalists charged.

Montrose had selected his position at Kilsyth with a view to keeping his options open. If Baillie had chosen to try to join up with Lanerick, one or other of them would have had to pass along the low road through the village and so been exposed to attack from the high meadow above. If, however, the Covenant general decided to occupy the eastern ridge (as in the event he did) then Montrose was content to hold the lower ground since the enemy cavalry would be unable to attack down the rough and broken hillside and the marsh-meadow at the bottom was unsuitable for horse. Regular infantry descending the steep slope would lose discipline and formation, while an uphill charge was nothing to Highlanders – and it was Montrose's intention to attack should an opportunity present itself. This would be the decisive battle that he had been seeking – with Scotland as the prize – and when he had asked his officers whether they wanted to retreat or fight, the chiefs' fierce answer assured him of the spirit of the Highland men.

Early on the morning of 15 August, it became clear that the Covenanters did not intend to wait for Lanerick, and the royalists stood-to in expectation of battle. It promised to be a scorching summer's day and the Highlanders discarded plaids to fight only in their yellow shirts which they knotted between their legs for ease of movement. Remembering the confusion at Auldearn and Alford, Montrose also ordered the cavalry to wear their shirts outside their buff coats so that they would be easily distinguished from the enemy. He then made his dispositions for the battle.

At the head of the glen, some way in front of the royalist position, were a number of cottages with gardens surrounded by dry stone walls. They constituted a natural strongpoint between the two armies which any commander would want to hold, and MacLean of Treshnish with 100 of Alasdair's advance guard were sent to occupy them. (These were the Highlanders whom Baillie saw moving up the glen.) Behind, and within sight of the cottages, the royalist vanguard was composed of the main Gaelic division under Alasdair with the MacLeans and the Clanranald drawn up separately under Lachlan of Duart and the young Moydartach.

To their rear, the cavalry and the other infantry detachments were still being marshalled into line when Haldane's musketeers attacked the cottages. After Lord Gordon's death at Alford, Montrose was unwilling to risk Huntly's new heir in the forefront of the battle, and so Aboyne was ordered to remain among the reserve with only a small escort of Gordons.

When the Covenanters attacked the cottages, Treshnish drove them off and then promptly counter-attacked. Haldane's undisciplined action uncovered the movement of the Covenant column – and Montrose's initial reaction was probably one of sheer surprise that a general of Baillie's calibre should have attempted such a dangerous manoeuvre across the royalists' front. Before he could make any formal move to exploit the situation, however, the main body of MacLeans, animated by Treshnish's success and without waiting for orders, started to charge up the ravine of the burn towards the enclosure where the four regiments of the Covenant centre were taking their position. Not to be outdone, the Clanranald also broke from their station to race them to the ridge, and the wave of Highlanders – MacLeans, MacDonalds, MacGregors, in a mass – swept up the slope and hurled themselves against the enemy's perimeter. The Covenant musketeers with time only for a single volley, fired too soon, and the Gaels ran in low under their shot to cut them down before they could reload. Screaming half-naked caterans rushed the enclosure, leaping the walls with their heads down and targes high to begin a dreadful killing at close quarters. Helpless musketeers, their weapons useless, were quickly butchered as the Covenant defence was hacked apart and the Gaels boiled around the position and on to attack those behind. When they saw the forward companies over-run and resistance disintegrating under the swords and axes of the Highlanders, veterans and levies alike broke ranks and started to run back to the ridge. Within minutes the enclosures were taken and the Covenant regiments in flight – looking desperately for flank support to check the Gaels who came howling at their heels.

Baillie hurriedly threw Lindsay's regiment and 200 fresh cuirassiers into the widening gap, and a wild fight developed across the centre of the ridge. The impetus of their charge carried the Highlanders to the crest itself, but here they found themselves facing the rest of the Covenant army and were suddenly isolated and exposed. Battle hot, they charged on, but were checked by the fresh Covenant formations and soon in danger of being overwhelmed themselves by weight of numbers. From the meadow below Montrose could see their peril, but a critical development on the royalist left was forcing him to direct his immediate attention towards his flank.

A part at least of Baillie's vanguard had succeeded in crossing the ravine of the burn, and rounding the head of the glen, had reached a point roughly identifiable with the site of the present farm of Wester Auchinrivoch. Their objective was clearly the northern ridge, and quickly realising the danger, Montrose sent 200 Gordon horse to seize the position before they could reach it. However, probably because a large part of the leading Covenant division had followed Baillie's orders in keeping behind the shelter of the crest, he had gravely under-estimated their numbers. The Gordons reached the slope to find themselves engaged by a vastly superior force of infantry backed by Balcarres's regiment of lancers. They were soon surrounded, and if not supported at once, it seemed certain that they would be shortly annihilated.

From his position among the reserve, Viscount Aboyne saw his Gordons cut off and in an apparently hopeless situation, and disregarding Montrose's orders not to risk himself, he led his small bodyguard in a gallant but foolhardy attempt to rescue his clansmen. On reaching the hill, his way was blocked by a solid phalanx of Covenant pikes, but he wheeled left and led his troop at full gallop into the exposed flank of a body of enemy musketeers. The charge momentarily relieved the hard-pressed Gordons, but Aboyne's small escort were too few to tip the scale and they too were quickly swallowed up in the struggle and encircled by Balcarres's horsemen.

Montrose saw the issue suddenly in the balance, and urgently ordered the royalist horse to advance and support Aboyne. But at this critical moment, the cavalry baulked and would not move, even though they must have seen that the battle might be lost through their default. He galloped desperately to where old Airlie and Ogilvie of Baldovie sat their horses in front of the family troop, and appealed to them to save the day.

The Ogilvies did not hesitate when Airlie called the charge and the 80 cavaliers drew swords and wheeled for Slaughter Howe. The old Earl drove full gallop into the side of Balcarres's squadrons, and the Covenant lancers reeled beneath the impact and began to fall back. This gallant action put heart into the rest of the royalist cavalry who now followed Nathaniel Gordon's order to attack, and they drove the Covenanters off the hill. Catching the rising impulse of the moment, Montrose now called for a general assault on the eastern ridge where Alasdair and the western clansmen were still holding their own in the desperate struggle around

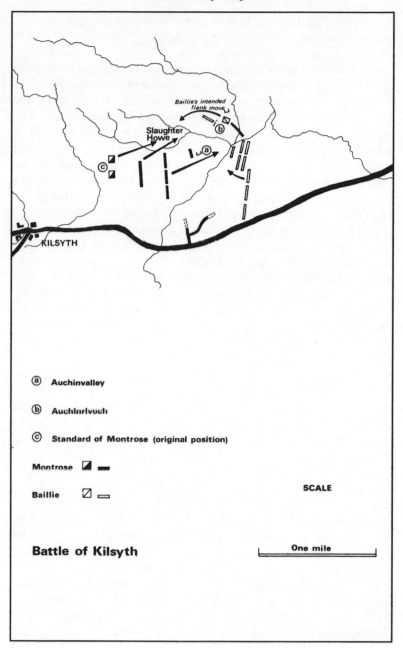

the Covenant centre. The Irish regiments and the rest of the infantry needed no urging, and reaching the crest, they joined the Highlanders and began to fight across the battle's anvil.

When Baillie saw his vanguard breaking up, he galloped back across the burn to call up his reserves. But the Fifeshire levies at the rear of the column had watched their centre smashed and the cavalry scatter, and were already starting to leave the field. Rallying together a few of their remaining officers, Baillie made a vain attempt to check the rout, but all along the ridge the Covenant regiments were falling back as the royalist advance swept over the crest. The cavalry as so often before, left the wretched foot-soldiers to shift for themselves and rode for Denny. The committee also fled in several directions, and finally, seeing that all was lost, Baillie too left the field and galloped for his life.

The Covenant infantry on the battlefield had no chance of safety, and were massacred as they tried vainly to escape. Weighed down by their equipment and tired by the long march of the early morning, they could not outdistance the Highlanders' terrible pursuit. The Gaels ran them down over eighteen English miles, and as usual, the killing during the aftermath far exceeded the slaughter of the battle. But the carnage after Kilsyth was more unsparing and extreme than anything hitherto. The Highlanders cut down every living thing in their path, and the names later given to the hills and hollows of the area – Slaughter Howe, The Bullet, Kill the Many Butts – recall the several massacres where isolated Covenant units were brought to bay and slaughtered without mercy. In the confusion of the rout, many innocent peasants were killed together with the fleeing enemy, and whole families were later buried in common graves. Airlie spared a man who clutched at his saddle-bow and then saw him promptly stabbed by a soldier of his own troop. Only a few officers who surrendered to Montrose in person were lucky to be spared. Although they had taken no part in the battle itself, and were the first to leave the field, the Fifeshire levies were virtually annihilated in the pursuit. In Kirkaldy alone it was recorded that 200 women were made widows on that day. Entire companies who had marched away to join the army were simply never heard of again, and for generations afterwards the battle was remembered with horror by the Covenanting communities of Fife. Total casualties in Baillie's army were computed at the time to have been in the region of 6000 killed – the majority of them infantry. Baillie himself, the committee, and most of the cavalry got away.

Montrose rested his army for two days at Kilsyth while the royalist wounded were attended to, before marching to Glasgow. In the meanwhile, Lanerick had disbanded the Hamilton levies on news of the defeat, and had fled to join Argyll who had taken refuge at Berwick. Alasdair and a Highland division were sent to put down the Covenanting force in the west, but met with no resistance. Cassilis and Glencairn fled to Ireland, and Eglinton's recruits dispersed when they heard that the Gaels were coming. Alasdair marched triumphantly through Ayrshire.

Commissioners from Glasgow came to plead for the citizens, and when Montrose made a formal entry into the town he was given a dutiful reception by the populace. Accepting a tribute of £500 to placate his army, he spared the city and forbade looting, withdrawing his main leaguer to Bothwell Brig six miles away and allowing the burghers a token garrison of their own. Now the main towns and shires also sent commissioners to tender their submission to the King and plead for favour. The nobility, so conspicuously absent hitherto, rode in to proffer their loyalty, and would-be royalists till now afraid to declare for Charles I, waverers, and even erstwhile enemies hurriedly flocked to Bothwell to recognize the new power in the land. Kilsyth had changed the face of affairs throughout Scotland.

Montrose's most immediate concern, however, was to procure the release of royalist prisoners still in Covenant hands. Lord Napier, Sir George Stirling of Keir, and the ladies of the Napier family were liberated from Linlithgow. The city of Edinburgh surrendered and 150 royalists were released from the Tolbooth, including the Earl of Crawford, the Master of Ogilvie, Gordon of Drum, and Dr Wishart – all of them gaunt and in pitiful condition. The city was so stricken by the plague that many of the gaolers were dead or fled, and the prisoners, abandoned to the pestilence in foetid and infested cells, had only survived on food brought in by devoted friends outside. Wishart bore the marks of the rats' teeth on his body to the grave. But Edinburgh Castle remained in Covenant hands and the royalists held within its walls, including Montrose's son, Lord Graham, could not be freed as yet.

There was news too from England, Sir Robert Spottiswoode arrived with a letter from the King in which Charles stated that he was sending 1500 horse to rendezvous with Montrose on the border. Spottiswoode also brought the King's Commission appointing Montrose Captain-General and Deputy Governor of Scotland, and under this power he summoned a new Scottish Parliament to meet at Glasgow on 20th October. He also used the authority inherent in this new Royal

Commission to reward the foremost of his officers, and after a brief parade during which he formally thanked his soldiers for their outstanding valour and achievement, Montrose knighted Alasdair in front of the army.

For Montrose, these days after Kilsyth were a brief moment of glory. A bare twelve months previously he had crossed the border as a fugitive in disguise with two followers. He had found a vagabond army wandering in the hills, and with this small and improbable nucleus, he had set out to conquer a country. In one year, with a force of poorly armed irregulars, lacking material help or support of any kind, and against a background of faithless friends and dubious allies, broken promises and personal sorrow, he had fought and been victorious in six pitched battles. Five times he had watched his army melt away, and each time he had built another army to fight and win again. The power of the Covenant in Scotland had been broken, its armies decimated, and its leaders driven into hiding and exile. Courage and sheer ability had achieved the seemingly impossible. And so he had kept the first part of his promise to the King. 'From Dan to Beersheba' he had mastered Scotland. Now he would honour the rest of his pledge. The road to the borders was open. Beyond was one more army of the Covenant – the last one – and the most formidable of all – to be brought to battle and destroyed. But 'though it should rain Leslies from heaven' the King's new Captain-General would be riding south tomorrow.

And it was a delusion – for Kilsyth had indeed changed many things. Before, the clansmen had always returned home to deposit their spoil – but now it was something more than that. Highlanders have beaten Lowlanders in battle, but they have never been able to consolidate the conquest. It was difficult to attach the clans permanently to a cause – that was never the way in the Highlands – and in a later century not even Bonnie Prince Charlie could prevent his men from returning home with their loot. But if booty was the rightful reward of victory, after Kilsyth there was little booty to speak of, and certainly not the spoil of Glasgow on which they had set their hopes. For Montrose's own role had changed. In contrast to the destructive war that he had hitherto waged against the Covenanters and their property, the very consequence of victory now obliged him to build and consolidate a civil authority corresponding to the one that he had won in battle. The people on whom he had encouraged the Gaels to prey, as the King's Representative in Scotland he now had to protect against pillage by his own men.

In this he gave offence, for the Gaels had difficulty in appreciating the fine distinction. Discontented, the Highlanders began to drift away. Disillusioned by Montrose's 'failure' in denying them the sack of Glasgow, they felt slighted that the man they had come to follow as a chieftain of their own, now consorted with the Lowlanders whom they despised and had so recently defeated in battle. The invasion of England did not attract. The constitutional struggle between a distant King and an English Parliament did not concern them, and they had a more pressing feud of their own.

The Athollmen and the MacLeans asked leave to return and rebuild their homes which had been burned during the punitive raids of the Covenanters, with vague promises to rejoin the army when this was done. It was a fair excuse and they would not be persuaded. It was September already and winter came early in the Highlands. Provisions must be got in, and they would be on their way.

But worst of all, Alasdair also departed from the army at this time. He had learned that his father and kinsmen had retired to the island of Rathlin pursued by the Campbell Laird of Ardkinglas under orders from Argyll. Old Colkitto had a mind to revive the MacDonald claim to Kintyre and was beckoning him to the family quarrel. Alasdair would have been no true Highlander had he preferred the King's war to that of his own blood and kindred. On 3rd September 1645, he left the camp at Bothwell with 500 MacDonalds and most of the Irishes of his lifeguard. Montrose protested in vain that his desertion would be the ruin of them both. Alasdair marched to an older battle-cry and the longer feud against MacCailein Mor. Colkitto and the tribal pibroch called him, and he left the King's cause for that other quarrel of his own and the ancient struggle between the Heather and the Gale.

PART V
RETRIBUTION

CHAPTER 18

Philiphaugh

In the short space of a week while the army lay at Bothwell, Montrose lost 2000 men – on furlough, through desertion, or upon other excuse. Yet this did not cause him to alter his plans – perhaps because he was under strong pressure from the King to march south at once and probably felt himself committed beyond recall. However, it was also the opinion of some of his friends that after the Battle of Kilsyth he grew dangerously overconfident.

Experience had clearly demonstrated that an army of Highlanders would not have been able to hold down Scotland, and the clansmen had proved unwilling to contemplate an extended campaign into England. Montrose possibly counted on the victory to conjure an army of Lowland royalists from the border regions – lairds who had been cowed and passive until now, but from weariness of Argyll's tyranny might be induced to declare for the King and join the Royal Standard.

A small nucleus of disciplined infantry remained, since Manus O'Cahan and his regiment of Irishes to their honour and credit, had elected to stay with the army and did not leave with Alasdair. Douglas and Ogilvie were sent to recruit in Annandale and Nithsdale with orders to combine with the Earls of Traquair, Home, and Roxburgh (whose support the King had guaranteed) and then rejoin the main royalist force when it marched south. Douglas initially succeeded in mustering a substantial number of local levies, but as the first flush of enthusiasm waned he had difficulty keeping then with the colours. The truth of it was that Douglas was no longer the name it had been once, and the old moss troopers had vanished as a breed. Notorious borderers such as Kinmont Willie and the Carleton brothers were dead and gone, the days of reiving and Hot Trod with them, and their descendants had grown soft on peace and porridge. Douglas's recruits were mainly herdsmen and shepherd boys who had never fired a shot in anger.

Montrose broke camp at Bothwell on 4th September and began the march south. Next day at Calderhouse there occurred the most serious defection yet. Since Kilsyth the cancer of jealousy had eaten at the heart of Aboyne. From his father Huntly he had inherited that uneasy ambition of the Gordons, and he felt slighted by the reception given to the Lowland gentry who had made their peace with the King's Lieutenant after what seemed the decisive battle had been won. It had angered him that a pamphlet written by Sir William Rollo largely ignoring his contribution to the cause had not been repudiated by Montrose and he suspected that the Grahams had even connived at belittling the role that he and his dead brother had played in the Highland campaigns. He felt personally wronged when Crawford was given command of the cavalry in preference to himself, and he resented the reappearance of Lord Ogilvie, who since his release from prison, seemed to threaten his own favoured place in the counsels of the General. There were fears upon which Argyll's creatures, easily penetrating the open leaguer, could play with great effect, and Ogilvie's attempts to befriend Aboyne and allay this envy met with no response. Aboyne claimed that he had received letters from his father, now returned from exile, summoning him back to Huntly, and despite Montrose's protests, he left and took all the northern levies with him. Of his clan, only Nathaniel Gordon remained with the army.

The royalists were now reduced to 700 foot and 200 mounted gentlemen, but apparently hopeful still of substantial reinforcement from the border lairds, Montrose continued south by Edinburgh to Cranstoun. On 6th September he received intelligence that David Leslie[65] (later Lord Newark) was at Berwick with a strong force hurriedly withdrawn from the Scottish army in England. An intercepted letter also revealed that Argyll had ordered Tullibardine to muster all available Covenant troops and block the route north.

Lord Erskine and others now urged Montrose to turn back and withdraw again beyond the Highland Line before it was too late. But he still felt bound to carry the war into England, and possibly counting on Douglas's levies and the support promised by the border Earls, he persisted in his southward march and continued down Gala Water. Douglas and Ogilvie rejoined the army with a body of horse from Nithsdale, but they were mainly bonnet lairds and their followers were deserting daily in large numbers. Traquair met them at Galashiels, outwardly friendly and enthusiastic, and sent his son Lord Linton as a pledge for his loyalty with a well equipped troop of horse. Thus reinforced, on 8th or 9th September, Montrose moved on to Kelso where he had agreed to rendezvous with the Earls of Home and Roxburgh – only to find that they had been captured by the Covenanters (and probably by their own contrivance – a measure of caution which enabled them to preserve their apparent fidelity to the King while simultaneously ingratiating themselves with Argyll).

Montrose's state of mind on receipt of this news can only be guessed at. To retreat once more behind the Highland Line would have meant abandoning everything that he had won at Kilsyth, and to begin recruiting again among the western clans would have involved an intolerable delay – and time was against him. He may still have hoped for help from England – often promised but never delivered – and he may, even now, have under-estimated the strength of the Covenanting forces that were closing in around him.

At Jedburgh, not one single recruit could be induced to join the colours, and Montrose at last abandoned the march south to turn west again towards the Tweed in the hope of drawing men from the Douglas tenantry in Annandale. Evening of 12th September 1645 found him at Philiphaugh near the village of Selkirk.

The royalists leaguered at the further end of a level meadow about a quarter of a mile wide along the northern bank of Ettrick Water, a short way below its junction with the Yarrow. Strategically, the place seemed defensible enough, since here the 'haugh' formed a recess in the hills, protected to the south and east by the Ettrick stream itself, to the north by high ground, and to the west by the Yarrow and a steep wooded slope known as the Harehead-shaw. The army camped with the left wing resting on the edge of Harehead Wood, while on the level plain below, the Irishes dug a line of shallow trenches to protect the right, which faced up the narrow expanse of Philiphaugh itself. Behind them, the strait passes of the Ettrick and the Yarrow afforded a line of retreat. The cavalry were billeted across the stream in the village of Selkirk itself, which was built on a height about a mile from the camp.

Montrose also established his headquarters in Selkirk, and prepared to pass the night in writing despatches to the King. By now he had probably reached the bitter conclusion that the advance into England would have to be abandoned, and he faced the difficult and distressing task of finding words to tell Charles that unless he received cavalry support – and urgently – he would be forced to retreat again to the Highlands. For the first time in the entire campaign he neglected to set the watch or brief the scouts in person, but left all camp duties to his officers. They were in hostile country and David Leslie could not be far off, and he therefore intended to march early in the morning. Reveille was set for dawn.

In fact, Leslie was much closer than the royalists knew. He had been with Leven at the siege of Hereford when news of Kilsyth caused him to ride north with every mounted man he could muster. Collecting reinforcements from the Covenant garrisons at Newcastle and Berwick (together with the inevitable committee including Argyll, Lanerick, and Lindsay) he crossed the Tweed on 6th September with an army grown to 5000 horse and 1000 foot. A flying column raced to Kelso where they captured Home and Roxburgh, while the main force took the coast road north to circle round Montrose and cut him off from the Highlands.

On 11th September, when Montrose was at Jedburgh, Leslie held a Council of War at Gladsmuir in Lothian where he received a letter (it is generally presumed from Traquair) informing him of Montrose's whereabouts and his weakness in numbers. Leslie promptly turned in is tracks and hurried south down Gala Water. On 12th September he forded the Tweed and by nightfall was at Sunderland Hall, barely four miles from the royalist camp at Philiphaugh.

Montrose wrote his despatch unaware of the danger. During the night there were confusing rumours of an enemy force in the vicinity. Around midnight a cavalry outpost near Sunderland was suddenly attacked, but the incident was attributed to a drunken brawl and the general was not informed. In the early morning, scouts sent to reconnoitre the surrounding countryside reported that there were no enemy within ten miles. Yet the patrols were made up of Traquair's men and their loyalty was questionable. A dense autumn mist filled the valleys and visibility was reduced to a few yards. The army awoke and began to cook breakfast. It was discovered that Traquair's son, Lord Linton, had left the camp sometime during the night. By strange irony, 13th September was the anniversary of the Battle of Aberdeen. In Paris, Queen Henrietta Maria is said to have been singing a *Te Deum* for the victory that heaven had vouchsafed her husband's cause at Kilsyth.

Shortly before first light, Leslie closed for the kill. He split his army into two. The main force, led by himself, advanced up the left bank of the Ettrick under cover of the dense mist, while 2000 dragoons, guided by a local Covenanter, crossed the water and circled round the royalist camp to seal the trap. Half an hour before dawn, Leslie launched his attack.

Montrose was at breakfast when his scoutmaster burst in with the news that the entire Covenant army was less than half a mile away and coming fast. Simultaneously, a ragged fusilade of shots announced that the royalist pickets were being driven in. Rushing out into the street,

Montrose threw himself onto the nearest horse and galloped furiously down the hill towards the camp, his officers following as best they could, but even as he reached the stream Leslie's bugles were sounding the charge and the Covenant squadrons broke onto the meadow between him and his army.

On Philiphaugh there was complete confusion. Most of the royalist cavalry were still in Selkirk and separated from their horses which had been turned loose to graze in the field below the village. Consequently, many of them never reached the scene of action. The Douglas levies fled at the first shot, and making for the woods, most got safe away. But with their flight, the Irishes were doomed. Leslie's cavalry were the cream of the Scottish army, and the heavy cuirassiers charged with the advantages of numbers and surprise. O'Cahan's disciplined Irish counter-attacked and momentarily checked the advance, but they were overwhelmed by odds of almost ten to one and driven back into their trenches. Here and there a few isolated groups fought their way out and reached the woods, but the fate of the rest was sealed by the arrival of the second force of 2000 dragoons at their rear.

To the right of the shattered royalist line, Montrose rallied 150 cavaliers and rode recklessly into the path of Leslie's squadrons. They took the brunt of the Covenanters' charge, checked it, and tried hopelessly to cut a way through to the beleaguered Irish. Montrose led like a man demented – seeing in his disintegrating army the ruin of everything he had striven for and with no apparent thought but to die on the field. His small band was soon reduced to only 50 men, but they continued to charge the enemy and all of them would no doubt have been killed or taken if Douglas and the other surviving officers had not finally prevailed upon him to escape while it was still possible. Insistently they pleaded that Philiphaugh need not be the end – so long as the King's general was yet alive and free. But if he was killed, the royalist cause would go down forever.

The fifty separated. Montrose went one way; Douglas and Airlie another; and the two parties broke out of the melée and fled towards the north-west. On 19th September they regrouped at Buchanty and reached the safety of the Highland fringe.

But at Philiphaugh, Manus O'Cahan and 500 of the Irishes were left to die. Surrounded, and with no chance of rescue, the Irishes defended their breastworks for an hour until over half their number were dead, and finally, on being offered quarter, the surviving officers surrendered to

Leslie. According to Covenant reports, 1000 of the 'rebels' were killed at Philiphaugh, but not more than 500 of these could have been soldiers under arms. Some 200 camp followers, cooks, and peddies were slaughtered. The rest were women and children who had followed the Irishes, and incited by stories of the Gaels' brutality, it was now the turn of the Covenant troops to show what they could do. According to the gruesome account of the contemporary Gordon historian:

> 'With the whole baggage and stuff which was exceeding rich, there remained now but boys, cooks and a rabble of rascals, and women with their children in their arms; all those without commiseration were cut to pieces; whereof there were 300 women, that being natives of Ireland, were the married wives of the Irishes. There were many big with child, yet none of them were spared, but all were cut in pieces with such savagery and inhuman cruelty... For they ripped up the bellies of the women with their swords, till the fruit of their womb... some in the embryo, some perfectly formed, some "crouling" for life, and some ready for birth, fell down upon the ground, weltering in the blood of their mangled mothers.'[66]

Eighty more women and children who somehow escaped the initial massacre were rounded up by local people and taken to Linlithgow where they were thrown from the bridge into the River Avon. Those who survived the fifty foot drop and tried to reach the bank were spitted or pushed back into the deep water by lines of pikemen until all of them were drowned. The countryfolk around Selkirk murdered dozens more.

The surviving Irish soldiers were taken to Newark Castle and placed under guard until their fate should be decided. David Leslie was a professional soldier and unaccustomed to butchering his prisoners in cold blood, but the Kirk triumphant was set upon a tour of vengeance, and the ministers were 'rouping like ravens'. Any quarter, they argued, had been offered to certain officers alone and did not include the ordinary soldiers. Clemency would be an offence against the Almighty – for had not Samuel so rebuked Saul for sparing the kine of the Amalekites? And they pointed at the waiting captives and howled for blood. The Irishes were stood in rows and shot, and their bodies thrown into a mass grave which was thereafter given the name of 'Slain Man's lee'. Manus O'Cahan and Thomas Lachlan, as officers of rank, were taken to Edinburgh and hanged from the south wall of the castle.

A number of prominent royalists had also been taken prisoner at

Philiphaugh, including the Earl of Hartfell, Drummond Earl of Perth and his son, Sir Robert Spottiswoode, Sir William Rollo, Sir Philip Nisbit, Andrew Guthry, William Murray (Tullibardine's brother), Lord Ogilvie, Ogilvie of Innerquharity and Sir John Hay of Barro – all of whom surrendered upon promise of quarter.

Few of them would escape. Hay of Barro, a Senator of the College of Justice, bribed Lanerick with the rents of his estates in Galloway and survived to die a pauper. Young Drummond also lived to become the third Earl of Perth. Lord Ogilvie made an unique escape from the bottle dungeon at St Andrews on the eve of execution by changing clothes with his sister – and because Argyll suspected the connivance of the Hamilton faction, he arranged a pardon for Hartfell on whose death they had counted.

But there was no hope for the others since the Kirk would not be denied its revenge. Synods and presbyteries throughout the country petitioned Parliament in a tone of ferocious superstition. A previous reluctance to shed the blood of the wicked had brought the sword and the plague upon them. Let the Estates remember the sea of blood that lay before Jehovah's throne, crying out for vengeance against these butchers of innocent souls. If the promise of quarter were sustained, the sacred oath of the covenant would be broken. Through war and pestilence, God had shown his anger unto them, and only blood could propitiate that terrible deity. It was the voice of the Kirk in full cry.

Rollo, Nisbit, and Innerquharity were taken to Glasgow, where they were tried and condemned by a committee of Parliament. Rollo and Nisbit were hanged at the Market Cross on 28th October, and young Innerquharity was executed the following day. Resourceful to the last, Nathaniel Gordon dealt for an exchange with Loudoun's son who was a prisoner at Blair, but even the Chancellor could not avert Argyll's justice. Nathaniel Gordon was beheaded together with Andrew Guthry on 26th January 1646. William Murray was executed three days later when Tullibardine's pleas for mercy failed.

Sir Robert Spottiswoode was also beheaded, even though he ranked as a civilian and had never actually borne arms against the Covenant. While in prison awaiting death, he was visited by the young Cameron of Lochiel who was at that time a ward of Argyll, and the conversation determined the Highlander's future as a royalist. Immediately afterwards, Lochiel dissociated himself from Argyll, and in due course he would be one of the first Jacobites and lead the western clans to fight under Claverhouse at

Killiekrankie. Spottiswoode also wrote a last letter to Montrose, his friend for many years, 'to recommend the care of my orphans to you', urging him not to lose heart but continue 'by fair and gentle carriage to gain the people's affection to their prince rather than imitate the barbarous inhumanity of your adversaries.'[67] But the extremist ministers sent to torment his final hours reported that Spottiswoode had died as he had lived – 'full of malice against the cause and Covenant'.

For Montrose, Philiphaugh was not the end, but there would be no more victories. A large proportion of his army had survived the defeat. They regrouped, and began once more to campaign along the fringes of the Highlands, but they were powerless to prevent the execution of the prisoners captured at Philiphaugh, and never strong enough to face the Covenant army in open battle. Further negotiations with Huntly failed, and although the Gordons were still in arms, they rode no more beneath the Royal Standard. There was no help from Alasdair, and the best of the Irish lay under Slain Man's Lee.

On 5th May 1646, Charles I gave himself up to the Scottish army before Newark, and the terms of his surrender included the provision that Montrose should disband his army. The King was in no position to bargain, and his Lieutenant, however he might have wished to fight on, could not in honour wilfully sacrifice his followers in a cause that was clearly lost. In the last week in July the little army paraded at Rattray near Blairgowrie, and in a scene charged with emotion, Montrose thanked them for their gallantry and fortitude, and tried to explain that 'their present submission was as essential to the King's cause as their past achievements.'[68]

For general and soldiers it was a long farewell. Montrose himself was not included in the amnesty, but allowed one month in which to leave the country. For the next three years he lived in exile, frustrated by the intrigues of the Queen's court in France and powerless to assist his royal master. Cardinal Mazarin offered him the baton of a Marshall of France, but Montrose distrusted the Frenchman's motive, and travelling to Geneva and Prague, he accepted instead the appointment of Marshall of the Holy Roman Empire with a commission to raise a force for Charles along the Flanders border.

On 30th January 1649 he was in Brussels when the dreadful news arrived that King Charles I had been publicly executed in London. The King's death, and above all the manner of it, was a terrible shock from which Montrose never recovered. He became a sombre figure with a bitter and brooding sense of destiny that drove him ultimately upon his own destruction. He served the second Charles, and early in 1650 led a last ill-fated expedition against the Covenanters. The small invasion force landed in Orkney and subsequently crossed to Caithness. But it was a forlorn hope, conducted in an atmosphere of pre-ordained disaster. While waiting at Carbisdale for promised reinforcements and a royalist uprising that never materialised, the army was surprised and cut to pieces by a force of Covenant cavalry. Montrose himself escaped the battlefield, but at Ardvreck Castle in Assynt, he was captured by the MacLeods and delivered to his enemies. The Covenanters led him south in triumph to Edinburgh and the vengeance of Argyll. After a brief trial in front of Parliament he was condemned to be hanged and quartered, and died on the gallows on 21st May 1650.

For Montrose, the dream had been true while it and he had lasted, and a fragile gleam of honour faded also with their passing. Charles II made accommodation with the Presbyterians at Breda – since for a cynical young man who must bargain for his throne, the crown was worth a Covenant or two. But their alliance was uneasy and short-lived. The Scottish armies were destroyed at Dunbar and Worcester, and the country made to endure an ignominious yet not intolerable servitude in which the Presbyterians' pretensions submitted to the reality of the Cromwellian occupation.

The old Lord Napier had died shortly after Philiphaugh. The Marquis of Huntly, upon whose foolish jealousy the northern cause had foundered, had been executed early in 1649. Viscount Aboyne had died of an ague in France a few months previously. In England, the Duke of Hamilton had been executed some weeks after the King whom he had so pusillanimously betrayed.

A number of Kirk extremists were executed following the Restoration, including the fanatical James Guthrie who had clamoured for the death of Montrose's friends. In 1663, Johnstone of Wariston, who had been the original architect of the National Covenant, was found hiding in Rouen and brought back to Edinburgh to be hanged. But the chief victim of the Restoration would be Argyll himself, who was beheaded on 27th May 1661. The bitter cup was to pass among them all, and they went each to his individual calvary.

CHAPTER 19

Dunaverty and Dunyveg

The campaign in the west for which Alasdair had left Montrose was largely determined by family interest since its ultimate objective was the repossession of the old Clan Donald territories of Islay and Kintyre. The authority of the Campbells had been seriously weakened by their defeat at Inverlochy, but in the intervening months they had been re-establishing their control over the heartland of Argyll. Alasdair's intention was therefore to thwart this recovery and destroy the power of that hated clan for all time. In this, he hoped to obtain the assistance of the many vassal clans – the Lamonts, MacAllisters, MacLachlans, MacDougalls, and MacNeills – who now saw an opportunity to throw off the Campbell yoke.

He left Montrose's camp at Bothwell Brig on 3rd September 1645, and bypassing the strong Covenant fortress at Dumbarton, obtained boats from the Lamonts to cross from Roseneath into Cowal. During the weeks that followed, Alasdair and Archibald Lamont marched their warband through Cowal, Argyll, Lorne, and Kintyre, gathering in the other clans until their force amounted to some 2000 men. In the north and west meanwhile, the Camerons, with the Clanranald, the MacIans of Glencoe, and the MacDonalds of Glengarry went raiding through Glen Dochart and Glen Lochy, and as far as Glen Falloch at the head of Loch Lomond. The MacLeans of Mull joined the rising, and sometime during December the main Highland forces joined up in Lorne, when Alasdair and Sir Lachlan MacLean of Duart signed what the Covenanters called 'a most cruel, horrid, and bloody band' for 'the rooting out of the name of Campbell'.

By the end of 1645, the Campbell presence in Argyll was limited to a number of scattered garrisons. In the countryside, Alasdair met little organised resistance, and when bands of Campbells did gather to fight – as at Lagganmore in Glen Euchar – they were overwhelmed and killed. The population were cowed by the MacDonalds' atrocities, and a large proportion of the fighting force of Clan Campbell were still with the Scottish armies in Ireland and the borders. Even after Philiphaugh, the Covenanters still feared that Alasdair and Montrose might again unite for an attack on the Lowlands, and would spare no troops to campaign in the west. In February 1646, a Highland regiment of Campbells under the Laird of Ardkinglas who had recaptured Castle Dochart from the MacNabs, were severely beaten at Callander by the Athollmen under Black Pate of Inchbrakie. The Marquis of Argyll crossed to Ireland to request the return of his clansmen.

But although many of the vassal clans had been willing to rebel, in Alasdair's own words, 'lime and stone' remained loyal to the MacCailein Mor. The Campbell garrisons refused to surrender, and despite the lack of reinforcement and a shortage of supplies, none of the major strongholds fell. Alasdair had no artillery, and the wild clansmen whom he led preferred a war of skirmish, raid, and movement to the rigours of prolonged siege. Apart from fortresses such as Dunstaffnage (the Campbells' headquarters) which were virtually impregnable, Alasdair failed to take the other castles – Kilberry, Duntroon, Craignish – in the vicinity. One of his brothers was killed in an unsuccessful assault on Skipness. Nevertheless, in the early months of 1646, he largely controlled Kintyre, and in the meanwhile a force of MacDonalds cleared the Campbells out of Islay and reoccupied their ancestral stronghold of Dunyveg. Possibly out of dynastic considerations, at this time Alasdair married the daughter of MacAllister of Loup (an offshoot of Clan Donald) by whom he had two sons in the twenty months that followed.

The dynastic aspect of the campaign was confirmed when in May 1646, the Marquis of Antrim arrived in Kintyre, styling himself 'General of the Highlands and Islands' and bringing the long awaited reinforcements of Irish troops. He was given the welcome accorded to a chieftain of Clan Donald in the words of a praise song to celebrate his coming:

'Welcome to Scotland to the Marquis and his army, as they march with martial strains to the lands of their ancestors, the royal people who were lordly.

MacDonalds of Islay were they, and Kings of the Isles of heroes. May sovereignty over land and sea be to the royal company of the banners...

Every deceiver will get what he deserves, and every traitor will be laid low. We will not have a yoke to bear, and offenders will not have their will. The people of the wry-mouths (the Campbells) will be trampled under our heels, and Clan Donald will be on top, as was usual for that people.'[69]

Antrim set up his headquarters at Lochead. His intention was presumably to take possession of the old Clan Donald lands in Kintyre that Charles I had promised him at the beginning of the Troubles (1638). It was probably also agreed that Alasdair should have Islay.

But any attempt to revive the ancient glories of Clan Donald was doomed to be short-lived. A few days after Antrim's arrival came the news that Charles I had surrendered to the Scottish army before Newark, and on 19th May, the King ordered all royalist forces in Scotland to disband. In the north of Scotland, the Marquis of Huntly promptly obeyed. Montrose would do so two months later. Almost simultaneously a large force of Campbells landed in Cowal and attacked the Lamont strongholds of Toward and Ascog. Their chief, Sir James Lamont of that Ilk, surrendered on promise of quarter, but the castles were plundered and burned, and 100 of the clan together with their leaders were murdered in the kirkyard at Dunoon. The Lamonts were thus subdued and the Campbells regained control of Cowal.

The King's order to disband – dutifully relayed by the Covenant authorities – placed Antrim and Alasdair in a difficult position, since if they could no longer present themselves as fighting in the royal cause it would prove harder to retain the support of the other clans – who were now beginning to waver, since with the cessation of hostilities in Scotland it seemed likely that the Campbells would triumph in the end. In their anxiety to restore peace, the Covenanters were free with their offers of pardon, and there were signs that the MacLeans of Lochbuie and Duart, the MacMillans, and many of the MacNeills were ready to negotiate. Both Antrim and Alasdair wrote to the King complaining that their service had deserved some better reward and referring to previous promises and guarantees that he had given. Antrim returned to Ireland at the end of the year taking a number of his followers with him.

His departure left Alasdair dangerously isolated. During the winter there were rumours that Seaforth and the MacKenzies, MacDonald of Sleat, Glengarry, MacLean of Duart, and the MacNab had all sued for pardons. In January 1647 the main Scottish forces in England were withdrawn and the Covenanters now had sufficient resources to deploy against the remaining pockets of royalist resistance. Aware that the forces of retribution would gather against him in the spring, Alasdair wrote to David Leslie (the victor of Philiphaugh) offering to leave the Highlands if he and his followers were permitted safe passage to Spain. On 4th March 1647, however, an Act of Parliament expressly ruled that he was not to be pardoned or granted terms, and the MacCailein Mor was reported to have remarked that the only alternatives open to the MacDonald was whether to be longer or shorter than he was (that is: to be hanged or beheaded) – which was the choice that Alasdair had given Auchinbreck after the Battle of Inverlochy.

Alasdair therefore remained defiant, giving out that he fought neither for the King nor against the Covenant, but to recover his ancestral lands and revenge himself upon his enemies. In Kintyre he commanded some 1500 clansmen and Irishes, and during the first months of 1647, his lieutenants, Archibald Mor MacDonald of Sanda and Duncan MacDougall, laid waste the districts of Kilmartin and Kilberry at the northern end of the peninsula, while MacDonald of Largie burned the burgh of Inveraray. Alasdair himself remained at Tarbert and Lochead, in communication with the MacLeans of Mull, and the MacDonalds of Sleat and the Clanranald. Rumours that he was expecting further reinforcements from Ireland prompted the Covenanters to attack as soon as sufficient forces could be assembled. On 24th May, David Leslie invaded Kintyre with an army of nearly 3000 men.

Access to Kintyre depended on control of the narrow passes at the neck of the peninsula, which 100 resolute men might have defended against 1000. But for some reason – perhaps because Leslie caught him unawares, or because he was already in the process of evacuating his followers to Gigha – Alasdair had not posted any detachments to hold them. The Covenant cavalry swept through Tarbert and along the shore of the West Loch onto the flat sandy level of Rhumahaorine Point, where they attacked and scattered a force of about 1200 clansmen who had been hurrying north to meet them. However, Leslie could not follow up his victory, having far outstripped his slower-moving infantry, and the MacDonalds escaped during the night.

Alasdair now divided his force into two, taking the greater part across to Gigha and thence to Islay, but leaving some 400 men under Archibald Og of Sanda (possibly because there was no room in the boats) to hold the Castle of Dunaverty at the southern tip of Kintyre. On 25th May, Leslie found the Castle of Lochead abandoned and the MacDonalds gone. The Covenanters continued their march south and on 31st May laid siege to Dunaverty.

The castle was small and short of supplies, but its greatest weakness lay in that it depended for water on two ponds which were outside the walls and defended only by an earthwork and a ditch. In this situation, the

400 MacDonalds stood little chance, and an account of what happened was later given by Sir James Turner who was at that time Leslie's Adjutant and afterwards a witness at Argyll's trial.

'We besieged Dunaverty which held out well enough, till we stormed a trench they had at the foot of the hill whereby they commanded two strips of water. This we did take in the assault. Forty of them were put to the sword. We lost five or six with Argyll's major. After this, inexorable thirst made them desire a parley. I was ordered to speak with them; neither could the Lord Lieutenant be moved to grant other conditions than that they should yield on discretion or mercy: and it seemed strange to me to hear the Lord Lieutenant's nice distinction that they should yield themselves to the Kingdom's mercy and not to his. At length they did so; and after they were come out of the castle they were put to the sword, every mother's son, except one young man Mackinnel whose life I begged to be sent to France with a hundred country fellows whom we had smoked out of a cave as they do foxes, who were given to Captain Campbell, the Chancellor's brother.'[70]

In ordering the massacres, Leslie acted under pressure from his chaplain, one John Nevoy. In fact he hesitated for two days before allowing the prisoners to be slaughtered, and in the end may rather have given way to the demands of his soldiers. Some months previously, after the fight at Glen Euchar, the MacDonalds had filled a barn at Lagganmore with men, women and children before setting it alight, and the Campbells were hot for revenge. Archibald Og MacDonald of Sanda was sentenced to be hanged, but being a very tall man, the gibbet was too short and he was shot instead. The dead at Dunaverty also included Alasdair's father in law, Hector MacAllister of Loup and two of his sons.

On 24th June, Leslie crossed to Islay where he discovered that Alasdair had departed for Ireland some sixteen days previously, leaving a garrison of 200 men under his father Colkitto to hold the castle of Dunyveg. At first the garrison refused to surrender and Leslie prepared to assault the walls. However, before the attack began, Colkitto emerged to propose terms of surrender – which the Covenanters rejected, but Colkitto continued to communicate with the Covenant camp. On 29th June he again came out to speak with the Captain of Dunstaffnage whom he knew well from his earlier period of captivity. Perhaps not realising the grim and bloodthirsty turn that the war had taken, the old chieftain surprisingly did not ask for guarantees of safe conduct, and when on 1st

July, he again left the castle, the Covenanters took him prisoner together with his escort.

Thereafter, the garrison resisted strenuously, but after three days hard fighting the MacDonalds capitulated, and on 4th July, articles of surrender were signed by Argyll and Leslie with Alasdair's brother Ranald MacColla, Donald O'Neill, and Donald Gorm MacDonnell. The garrison agreed to leave without arms or baggage and upon oath never to bear arms in Scotland again. The Irishes among them, together with three surviving officers were to go to Ireland or France. In all some 176 fighting men were spared, but Ranald MacColla and Donald O'Neill were executed for crimes which had been conveniently omitted from the terms of the amnesty.

Alasdair's bastard brother Angus MacColla continued to hold out among the ruins of Finlaggan, refusing to surrender even when Leslie threatened to hang Colkitto in sight of the castle. (He said it was no more than his father deserved.) But he too was eventually forced to submit and was probably hanged shortly afterwards. Donald Gorm, who had fought in Montrose's wars, was also executed. There was talk of sending Colkitto to Edinburgh for trial, but in October 1647, Argyll in his capacity of Justice General sentenced him to be hanged from the mast of his own galley beneath the walls of Dunstaffnage Castle. The MacCailein Mor had reason to feel satisfied that winter. MacDonald pretensions in Kintyre had been effectively crushed, while the family of Colonsay (saving Alasdair himself) was virtually exterminated.

CHAPTER 20

The Departure of Alasdair

Alasdair's subsequent career in Ireland was short and violent. After leaving Islay he sailed to Dundrum in the south of County Down, and abandoning his ships, occupied the confederate Irish stronghold at Charlemont. He had with him at this time about 800 men – the remnants of the original force of Irish Gaels who had landed in Ardnamurchan in July 1644 – together with the young Archibald of Sanda (son of the MacDonald captain executed at Dunaverty) and Angus MacDonald of Glengarry.

If indeed it had been his intention, he quickly discovered that there was no hope of obtaining Irish reinforcements to continue the campaign in the Western Isles. The Catholics of the Confederation were perilously divided among themselves, while the Protestant armies under Murrough O'Brien, Lord Inchiquin, were carrying all before them. Alasdair's force was divided into two – Glengarry taking 400 men to join the Catholic army in Leinster, while he himself was appointed Lieutenant General of the army of Munster under Lord Taaffe, and Governor of Clonmell.

On 8th August 1647, the army of Leinster was defeated by the English at Dungan Hill, and 300 of the Irishes who had fought in Montrose's war were butchered during the aftermath. In the same month, Inchiquin outmanoeuvred Lord Taaffe and invaded County Tipperary to devastate the countryside around Cashel. In November of the year, the Protestant forces concentrated at Mallow in County Cork as if to make a push into eastern Ireland and Lord Taaffe with Alasdair marched to bar their way at Cnoc na n'Dos (Knockanuss).

Taaffe had an advantage in numbers with 1200 horse and 7000 foot against Inchiquin's 1200 horse and 4000 foot, and was therefore keen to give battle. He took up a strong position, and because of the terrain, divided his army into two unequal divisions without a centre. Taaffe himself commanded the larger left hand division of 4000 men while Alasdair led the remainder on the right. Each division was supported by two regiments of cavalry.

Opposing them, Inchiquin deployed his cannon and the bulk of his force facing Alasdair's position, and by making a series of feints against the Irish right, gave the impression that his main attack would be directed at that quarter. This caused Taaffe to begin transferring troops from his main division to that of Alasdair, but even while this manoeuvre was in progress, Inchiquin was seen to be switching his own divisions to assault the Irish left. Taaffe gave a general order to attack, but his men were confused and began to fall back before concentrated volleys of the enemy musketeers. The withdrawal became a rout and the Irish left was driven from the field.

On the right, however, Alasdair led a wild Gaelic charge that over-ran the Protestants' cannon and smashed into the massed regiments of Inchiquin's infantry. The Irishes attacked in their usual style, firing at close range and then storming into the enemy ranks with swords and clubbed muskets. The left hand division plundered the Protestant baggage train.

But even as he regrouped his men, Alasdair realised that Taaffe himself had been routed, and the enemy cavalry were turning back to encircle his own division. His Irishes were soon surrounded, and although they fought fiercely on, their numbers dwindled steadily under the relentless attrition of the Protestants' attack. Eventually, when all was hopeless, the survivors surrendered on hope of quarter. Most of the common soldiers were killed where they stood. Alasdair was taken prisoner to the Protestant camp at Cnoc na n'Dos, and Inchiquin's captains murdered him there.

Epilogue

Alasdair MacColla lies buried at Clonmeen among the O'Callaghans. One of the greatest fighting men of the Clan Donald, his name and his deeds became part of the popular tradition of the Western Highlands and the Isles. It was appropriate therefore that Ian Lom's Lament for the hero of Inverlochy should seem to echo to the old ambitions of his tribe – and an ancient quarrel not forgotten.

> "When Alasdair crosses over to us with conflict in his train, nine thousand stout warriors will be ferried across the sea; may as many again be with him who would not betray him in his trust in them, of the men with the fair locks and the red shield bosses...
>
> Clan Donald famed for galleys and tall swift ships, though you stand as you do at this present crisis, the blood spilt must be paid for, it was not the sea that took it from us.
>
> God the Creator is strong;
>
> > there is a tryst with victory."[71]

Footnotes

1 *The Book of Clanranald*
2 Father MacBreck's Account: *Memoirs of Scottish Catholics,* Forbes-Leith p287: *Britane's Distemper*, Patrick Gordon p63
3 *History of the MacDonalds*, Hugh MacDonald of Sleat
4 1598, *Record of the Privy Council,* V
5 Ibid
6 *Acts*, Vol IV, 1598, 175–6
7 1598, *Record of the Privy Council,* V
8 1605, Ibid VII
9 See Chapter 10
10 Sir R. Gordon's *History of Sutherland* p186ff: *Historie of James the Sext*, (Bannatyne)
11 The galleon was later blown up and sank in Tobermory Harbour – for which MacLean later received an official pardon.
12 See Chapter 2
13 *Record of the Privy Council*, 11 Aug & 26 Oct 1614: Corres. between the Bishop and Lord Binning – *Denmylne MS*, Nat. Lib. Sc
14 *Britane's Distemper*, Patrick Gordon p56/7
15 Clarendon, *State Papers* II p55
16 *Scots Affairs*, Gordon of Rothiemay, II p171/2; Guthry's *Memoirs* p41; Baillie's *Letters and Journals*, I p485
17 *History of the British Army*, Sir John Fortescue
18 *Montrose*, John Buchan p42
19 Heylin's *Life of Laud*, and *Commentary on L'Estrange* (1719)
20 *History of the Kirk of Scotland*, II, Cook
21 Buchan, *Montrose*, p72
22 Baillie, *Letters and Journals* I p67/8
23 Burnet, *Lives of the Dukes of Hamilton*, p57
24 Gordon, *Scots Affairs* II p238
25 Spalding, *History of the Troubles* I p119–22
26 Father MacBreck's Account; *Memoirs of Scottish Catholics* p 274
27 *Ormonde Papers* I p4

28 Hill, *The Macdonnells of Antrim*, p114 note
29 News from His Majesty's Army in Scotland... to the Lord Lieutenant in Ireland... by an Irish Officer in Alexander Macdonnels forces: *Ormonde Papers*
30 Spalding: Covenant casualties – 1300–1500 dead, 800 prisoner
    Wishart: 2000 dead
    Gordon: 2000 dead, 1000 prisoner
31 A True Relation of the Happy Success of His Majesty's Forces in Scotland under the conduct of the Lord James Marquis of Montrose, His Excellence against the Rebels there, p9
32 Account given to Sir Walter Scott by Robert Stewart of Ardvoirlich in 1830 and quoted in the Introduction to *A Legend of Montrose*
33 See Chapter 3
34 *Acts. Parlt. Scot.* VI Pt. 1, p359
35 The Master of Ogilvie was a prisoner (Chapter 8)
36 *Britane's Distemper* p82
37 A True Relation... etc. Wishart confirmed that the man recovered and did indeed become a cavalry trooper. (*Deeds of Montrose*)
38 Spalding, p161
39 Frank, *Northern Memoirs* p226
40 Wishart, *Deeds of Montrose* p70
41 Baillie, *Letters and Journals*, II p262
42 *Book of Clanranald*
43 *Memoirs of Scottish Catholics* I, p303–8
44 *Book of Clanranald*
45 Bishop Guthry, *Memoirs*, p134
46 Baillie, III, p234
47 *Britane's Distemper*, p100
48 Welwood's *Memoirs* (1699) quoted in Napier, *Memorials of Montrose* p179ff
49 Matheson, *Traditions* TGSG v35
50 Guthry *Memoirs* p141
51 Baillie, II, p264 (General Baillie's Vindication)
52 Letters published in *Mercurius Aulicus* 10 May 1645
53 Wishart
54 *Book of Clanranald*
55 Wishart
56 Rynie had been wounded on 5 May during the pursuit of Hurry
57 Either the whole regiment was not present or there were survivors,

since elements are recorded as having been at Alford. (*Acts. Parlt. Scot.* VI, i, p469)

58   *History of the Family of Frazer* p348 (MS Nat. Lib. Scot.)

59   Ibid: Sir James Frazer's History

60   Baillie, II, p417/8

61   Wishart, p111

62   Belonging to the Earl of Stirling who was the King's Secretary

63   Belonging to Graham of Braco

64   Baillie's Vindication

65   Son of Leslie of Pitcairlie and not related to the Earl of Leven then commanding the main Scottish army in England

66   *Britane's Distemper* p160; Guthry, p203, Wishart, XVI

67   Napier, *Memorials*, II, p254

68   Wishart, p84/5

69   Macdonald, *The Macdonald Collection*, p46/7, with trans. by MacLean: quoted from D. Stevenson, *Alasdair MacColla and the Highland Problem in the Seventeenth Century*, p225/6

70   Sir James Turner, *Memoirs of His Own Life and Times*, p46

71   A.M. MacKenzie, *Orain Ian Luim: Songs of John MacDonald, Bard of Keppoch* p28–31, and given in Stevenson, op. cit. p257

Select Bibliography

Adams, F., *Clans, Septs, and Regiments of the Scottish Highlands* (Edinburgh/London 1908)

Baillie, The Rev. Robert, *Letters and Journals* (Bannatyne Club)

Balfour, Sir James, *Historical Works* (Edinburgh 1824)

Buchan, John, *Montrose* (Nelson 1928)

Burnet, Bishop Gilbert, *Lives of the Dukes of Hamilton*
A history of His Own Times

Chambers R. *History of the Rebellions in Scotland under the Marquis of Montrose* (Constable 1828)

Claredson, Edward Hyde, Earl of, *The History of the Rebellion and Civil Wars* Clarendon State Papers

Forbes, Leith, W., *Memoirs of the Scottish Catholics*
(Father Macbreck's account) (London 1909)

Gardiner, S.R., *History of the Great Civil War* (4 vols. London 1893–4)

Gordon, James of Rothiemay, *A History of Scots Affairs* (Spalding Club)

Gordon, Patrick of Ruthven, *A Short Abridgement of Britane's Distemper* (Spalding Club)

Gordon, Sir Robert of Gordonstoun, *History of Sutherland*

Historie of King James the Sixth (Bannatyne Club)

Grant, I.F., *The Lordship of the Isles* (Edinburgh 1935)

— *In the Tracks of Montrose* (MacLehose 1931)

Grant, James, *Memoirs of Montrose* (Routledge 1858)

Gregory, D., *History of the Western Highlands and Isles to 1625* (Reprinted 1975)

Grimble, I., *Clans and Chiefs* (Blond-Briggs 1980)

Guthry, Henry, Bishop of Dunkeld, *Memoirs*

Gwynne, J., *Military Memoirs of the Great Civil War* (Ed. Sir Walter Scot 1822)

Heylyn, P., *Cyprianus Anglicus – or the History of the Life and Death of Wm. Laud* (1719)

Hill, G., *The Macdonnells of Antrim*

Hill, J.M., *Celtic Warfare 1595–1763* (John Donald 1986)

Johnston, Archibald of Wariston, *Diary 1634–9* (SHS)

Johnston, T.B., *Historical Geography of the Clans of Scotland, with a Narrative of the Highland Campaigns.* (Edinburgh/London 1899)

Lane, Jane, *The Reign of King Covenant* (Robert Hale 1956)

Macdonald, A & A., *Clan Donald* (Inverness 1896, 1904)

Macdonald, Donald J., *Clan Donald* (Macdonald Publishers 1978)

Macdonald of Sleat, H., *History of the Macdonalds* Highland Papers (S.H.S. 1914)

Macvurich, Iain Lom, *Book of Clanranald;* trans. by A. Cameron in *Reliquaie Celticae* (Inverness 1892)

Mathew, D., *Scotland under Charles 1.* (Eyre & Spottiswoode 1955)

Moncrieffe, Sir Iain of that Ilk, *The Highland Clans* (Barrie & Rockcliff 1967)

Morris, Mowbray, *Montrose* (Macmillan 1892)

Napier, Mark, *Life and Times of Montrose: Montrose and the Covenanters: Memoirs of Montrose.*

Memorials of Montrose (Maitland Club)

Napier, Priscilla, *A Difficult Country* (Michael Joseph 1974)

Prebble, J., *The Lion in the North* (London 1971)

Ramsay, A.A.W., *The Arrow of Glen Lyon* (Murray 1930)

Spalding, John, *Memoirs of the Troubles in Scotland and England* (Spalding Club)

Spottiswoode, Archbishop, *History of the Church of Scotland*

Stevenson, David, *Alasdair MacColla and the Highland Problem in the 17th Century* (John Donald 1980)

— *The Scottish Revolution 1637–1644* (David and Charles 1973)

Terry, C.S., *The Army of the Covenant 1643–1647* (S.H.S. 1917)

Turner, Sir James, *Memoirs of his own Life and Times*

Wedgewood, C.V., *Montrose* (Collins 1952)

Wilcock, J., *The Great Marquess* (Oliphant, Anderson & Ferrier 1903)

Williams, Ronald, *Montrose – Cavalier in Mourning* (Barrie & Jenkins 1975)

Williams, Ronald, *Lords of the Isles* (Chatto & Windus 1984 and House of Lochar 1997)

Wishart, George, *Res Montisros (1647) Montrose Redivivus (1652) Deeds of Montrose ed. by Murdoch and Simpson (1893)*

Index